T5-BZU-757

# THE DAY CAMP PROGRAM BOOK

# The Day Camp Program Book

# AN ACTIVITY MANUAL FOR COUNSELORS

## *by*  VIRGINIA W. MUSSELMAN

Association Press, New York

THE DAY CAMP PROGRAM BOOK

**DEDICATION**

in token payment
for patience and understanding
this book is dedicated to

# JEAN ROSBOROUGH

with affection and appreciation

# PREFACE

This book is written definitely as an activity book for day camp counselors. Just as Grace Mitchell's *Fundamentals of Day Camping,* published in 1961, filled a big gap in professional literature dealing with the organization and administration of day camps, this book should fill a gap in professional literature dealing specifically with program activity content geared to day camping.

The field of camping has its own literature, some of it very fine. The areas of nature, of crafts, of drama, of games, music, dance, and storytelling, all have excellent resource material. A day camp leader can dip into many very helpful books, taking a game here, a craft there, a bit of philosophy from one, a theme from another—*if* he has the time, *if* he can find the books locally, *if* he can afford to buy them, and, most important of all, *if* he knows what to look for.

However, unless he has been trained specifically in camping and other aspects of recreation, the average leader is likely to need guidance in his selection of those activities which will be the most meaningful to the child.

Max Eastman, in his *The Enjoyment of Laughter* (Simon and Schuster, Inc., 1957) gives, as the natural principle of education, the following very wise comment: "To one interested in furnishing the mind, the monotonous thing is to drop in one fact after another until it fills up from the bottom like a barrel of potatoes. To fit new ideas into a growing scheme of knowledge—to learn more where much is already known—is an exciting occupation."

The object of this book is to help the day camp leader or counselor "learn more where much is already known." If it makes of day camping "an exciting occupation," then the counselor will find that other books, other resources, can be used to enlarge and to strengthen his existing skills. As interest grows, so does knowledge.

VIRGINIA W. MUSSELMAN

# ACKNOWLEDGMENTS

No activity book can be the work of one person alone. Each builds on the foundations of others. The author of this book is deeply appreciative of leaders in the camping field like Maude Dryden, Cap'n Bill Vinal, Reynold Carlson, Grace Mitchell, John Ledlie, Catherine Hammett, Stanley Michaels, Emily Welch, Julian Smith, and many, many others. The expansion of the camping and day camping fields has been due largely to the efforts of such leaders.

Specific appreciation is expressed to the American Camping Association for permission to use its "Day Camp Standards"; to the New York City Department of Health for its "Health and Safety Check List for Day Camps"; to the Boy Scouts of America and to the Whitlock Division of the Plymouth Cordage Company for their sketches and directions for knots and lashings; to the Park and Recreation Department of Sunnyvale, California, for ideas for special themes; and to the National Recreation Association for ideas taken from its annual *Playground Summer Notebook*.

The author's personal thanks go also to Joseph Prendergast, Executive Director of the National Recreation Association for his permission to undertake this book, and to Amy Redman and Thelma Thompson who freed her of much office responsibility by taking it on their own shoulders.

# CONTENTS

Section IV   Composite Programs

Section V  In Conclusion

SECTION I

# Basics for Counselors

Now I see the secret of the making of
the best persons;
It is to grow in the open air and to
eat and sleep with the earth.

—WALT WHITMAN
*Song of the Open Road*

CHAPTER 1:

# FACTS, FIGURES—
# AND PHILOSOPHY

What is day camping? It is one in a series of different kinds of outdoor experiences that should lead eventually into enjoyment of, appreciation for, familiarity with, and survival in the world of nature.

It is one of the steps by which a child climbs from dependency upon a push-button civilization to the ability to use and enjoy the natural world wisely.

Interest in the world around him starts early in childhood. Parents, teachers, and leaders can fan this interest by opening door after door of novel experiences into a wider and wider world full of new, exciting, and interesting things to see, hear, touch, taste, try, learn, and do.

Even before the child can walk, his horizons begin to widen. The trips in the family car, the rides on the supermarket carts start early in our mobile America.

The neighborhood exploration of his small world expands, as he grows, into trips to the nearby park, the tot corner of the playground, the beach, the zoo—all full of new sights, sounds, smells—and questions. A natural step farther leads to the museum, the planetarium, and the public library.

Throughout his childhood the fortunate child reads and is read to. The adults around him encourage his interest in birds, animals, trees, flowers, rocks, shells, fish, and stars. He goes on rambles, short hikes, picnics, and boating trips. Unfortunately, not many youngsters are given such opportunities and experiences. These are areas, however, in which the day camp, with its trained counselors, can provide the less fortunate child with what the home environment may have lacked. In fact, a major strength of day camping is just such home-day camp relationship.

15

A logical next step is day camping—not as a substitute for camping, because it's not—but as a natural lead-up to the time when he is ready to make the transition from home bedroom to camp tent or tepee, with all that is involved in that transition.

When he has learned the elementary camp skills, has developed sufficient self-assurance and independence, his day camp experience should be supplemented with "overnights," exciting rewards for personal achievement. From the overnight to the weekend camping experience is a short step.

Again, if the child is fortunate, he may have an opportunity to take part in school camping, or "outdoor education," as it is called. His class, with its teacher, will work hard in preparing for it, and the culmination will be a school-away-from-school, combining instruction and play into a deeply meaningful experience.

The final steps lead the youngster into his first experiences in resident camping, perhaps from there into family or young-adult group camping via the family car. Hopefully, they may lead him, too, into using his camping skills and interests in working as a camp counselor or specialist in a camp or day camp during his college years.

His early experiences, in those formative years, may in fact influence his choice of a career, and will certainly result in avocational interests that will last his lifetime. It is upon the development of such interests and skills that the future of many of our national resources may well depend.

### Day Camping Comes of Age

Day camps, like playgrounds and many other youth services, started originally from a simple philosophy of "taking children off the city streets." It was a definite stepchild of resident camping, designed for those who could not afford to go away to resident camps, and for those who needed supervised care during the working hours of employed mothers. It started, in fact, as a sort of hybrid, or compromise, between resident camping, a "different" playground program, and child care.

This fact, first regarded as a major weakness, became the

strength of the day camp movement. Leaders in the camping field and leaders in public and private youth-serving agencies kept a wary eye on this young upstart, smacking it down once in a while, giving it encouragement at other times.

The depression years of the 1930's toughened day camping into a young giant, made it flexible, gave it self-identity. Federal support of many programs, through WPA, permitted many work projects that served as experimental laboratories. Boards of Education, private youth-serving agencies and public recreation and park departments all took advantage of WPA funds and leadership. The results were rapidly increased leadership training programs, increased sponsorship, and a great deal of useful, printed material in the form of manuals, now long since out of print.

The continuing good health of the day camp movement was due very largely to the philosophy and trained techniques of outstanding leaders. Maude Dryden, "Godmother of the day camp movement," developed an amazing program in New York City, working through the WPA, the Board of Education, and many private agencies. Her *Day Camp Manual,* published by the National Recreation Association, became the national guide for the movement for many years. It is now out of print.

Mabel Jobe, in Washington, D. C., developed day camp programs in the city parks, sponsored by the public recreation department there, and her *Handbook of Day Camping*, published in 1949 by Association Press, had a tremendous influence on the day camp programs. It, too, is out of print.

William M. Grimshaw organized and directed the Springfield College day camp for a number of years and contributed many studies and articles to the early movement.

Reynold ("Rey") Carlson, now professor in the recreation curriculum of the University of Indiana, worked as a district representative on the staff of the National Recreation Association from 1936 to 1947, thus providing a continuity of service which, with his sound camp philosophy, has meant much to the field of day camping as well as to resident and school camping. He was chairman of the first committee set up in 1945 by the

American Camping Association to define the term "day camping," and to formulate standards. His continued interest in and support of the day camp movement is a great asset.

These, plus many other dedicated leaders from public and private agencies, have been responsible for the conceptual changes regarding day camping; for its acceptance as a definite area in the general field of camping and outdoor education, psychologically important in its own right, with its own objectives, standards, literature, and leaders.

Their broad, early philosophy has also been a crucial factor in keeping the day camp movement from becoming formalized or static. Mrs. Dryden's comment, back in 1940, is still typical:

"Day camping is such a flexible plan that a variation of it can be suited to almost any condition, always being based on its principal function, that of leading back to simple, leavening pleasures of the woods and streams, and blue skies."

This flexibility has given day camping an "open end" quality that lends itself to use by a wide variety of agencies and departments both public and private, on a wide variety of sites, and under wide variations in schedules, numbers and ages served, fees, and other variables. It has also led to an increasing number of privately organized, commercially operated day camps—so much so that various city health departments have had to formulate specific regulations governing their operation.

There are no complete figures on the number of day camps now in operation under various types of sponsorship. Proof of the steadily increasing acceptance of day camping as an area of recreation can be found, however, in some of the conservative figures compiled by the National Recreation Association and those compiled by the American Camping Association, the former reporting on day camps conducted by public recreation agencies on a city and county level, the latter on day camps that have membership in the ACA, including many sponsored by private youth-serving agencies, and many operated for profit.

In the *Recreation and Parks Yearbook* of the NRA, compiled every five years, 747 day camps were reported by 285 cities in 1950. Only 173 of those cities reported an attendance in only

389 camps, but this figure for youngsters served was 638,116 campers. In 1955, 327 cities reported a total of 971 camps, and 157 of the cities, reporting on 350 camps, gave an attendance figure of 831,622 children. The 1960 figures show another jump. A total of 1,040 day camps were reported by 391 cities and counties, with an attendance figure of 1,291,421 youngsters from 178 of the cities and counties reporting on only 545 of the day camps. (In other words, only about half of the sponsoring agencies reported attendance.) It could be assumed, therefore, that somewhere around two and a half million youngsters attended some type of day camp conducted under municipal or county sponsorship by public park or recreation agencies in 1960.

In 1960, the American Camping Association reported an actual card count of 1,336 day camps with an enrollment of 1,036,068 campers per season. It is doubtful that there is very much overlapping between the figures of these two organizations (although there will be some). Between them, they give a conservative picture of a rapidly growing field of recreation-education. Both organizations feel quite sure that for every day camp reported, there is probably another one unreported.

It should be pointed out that there is a wide variation in these day camps. Some may be day camps in name only. Some operate a very limited program in a short period of time. Some are excellent, some are poor. (This fact is true of all areas of work, of course. Not every school is top-standard, not every teacher is the best. Not every home offers perfect love and security.)

The fact remains that day camping is not only here, it is here to stay. It is the subject of zoning ordinances, of insurance study, of health regulations, of public and private budgets, of leadership training, of college curricula, of experimental setups on many university campuses, and of private operation for profit.

It can no longer be regarded merely as a substitute for a resident camp, or as a type of well-planned playground program, or as a child care center. It has its own important part to play in the field of child development. It fills a hiatus—a vacancy that existed for many years—by providing a psychologically sound transition program during which the child can take his first place in nonhome-centered activities that introduce him to the world around him through a natural, informal, and stimulating program.

Much still needs to be done to help the day camp movement reach and maintain the best in standards. Research is needed. Leadership and leadership training are needed. Upgrading of program content is needed. Professional literature is needed. More co-operative efforts between public and private agencies, between parent, school, and community groups, are needed. These are all problems of the coming of age of any specialized program—and day camping is coming of age.

CHAPTER **2:**

# FACTORS AFFECTING
# THE ACTIVITY PROGRAM

Planning the activity program, like news reporting, involves the Big Five—Who, What, When, Where, and Why. Activities are not separate, individual facts that can be dropped one by one until a child's day fills up "like a barrel of potatoes." All camp activities should be more like building blocks, useless in themselves separately, but, along with others, capable of becoming wonderful structures when they are combined with knowledge and imagination.

"Cap'n" Bill Vinal once described this necessary, ongoing quality in his vivid style: "Camp activities grow out of a child's need. To visit the heron rookery on an island, he must be able to canoe. There can be no safe canoeing without certain ability in swimming. To go swimming he must obey certain . . . laws. Each step is a vital part of his existence. Out of such experiences comes growth."

A day camp deep in the heart of a city park, or on five acres of suburbia, may not be able to supply a rookery and a canoe, but Cap'n Bill's statement involves two factors that make the difference between inadequate, haphazard activity programs and really meaningful camp experiences. These are MOTIVATION and PROGRESSION. Activities that provide a natural motivation for the child are those which open new doors, provide new opportunities. Such activities must be capable of growing, expanding, leading on to new action, new creation, new experiments, new adventures.

Motivation for what? Progression to what? These questions can be answered only through the working out of specific objectives, geared to each individual day camp.

The most important statement in "Day Camp Standards," as

developed by the American Camping Association, is hidden in Part II—PROGRAM, Section B (see Appendix A): "The program should be so planned, administered and supervised as to lead to the achievement of the general objectives of camping and the special objectives of the particular camp. *It is recommended that these objectives be stated in writing.*" (Italics are our own.)

This point is emphasized because without specific objectives, worked out and understood by the entire staff, a day camp program can easily become a day-by-day rehash of activities available to youngsters in school, on the playground, or through other community resources. Constant referral to, and checking activities against, the written day camp objectives is one of the best ways to recognize and eliminate activities good in themselves but not contributing directly to the attainment of the stated objectives.

Introducing a child to the world of nature and guiding him into an understanding of his responsibility in it are tasks not to be taken lightly. Important lessons are learned quickly through play. Important physical and mental skills are developed by the challenge and adventure of play activities.

It is at this point that day camp activity programs often bog down. A good, well-balanced activity program is not always, or necessarily, a good *day camp* program.

Two simple rules of thumb can be used in selecting and in conducting day camp activities: (1) *Never conduct an activity indoors if it can be conducted outdoors,* and (2) *Can the activity selected be replaced by a more camplike activity. If so, replace it.*

If these two rules are followed, many controversial issues—such as how much, if any, of an organized sports program should be included in day camping—will work themselves out.

*Factors in Planning.* The activity program will be the direct result of interaction between campers and staff within the limitations of the camp site, facilities, and resources, and within the framework of specified policies and objectives. Major factors include the Big Five—Who, What, When, Where, and

Why. In day camping, these factors influencing the activity program involve Campers, Staff, Camp Sponsorship, Camp Site, the Weather, the Schedule, and Basic Values.

## The Campers

First of all—the CAMPERS. They may be boys, girls, or boys and girls. They may be average youngsters, handicapped groups, or groups in which handicapped and nonhandicapped are integrated. They may be members of a specific agency, a specific religion, one economic level—or the campers may cut across the entire socio-economic structure of the community. The average day camper in most day camps is between five and twelve years of age.

These factors of age, sex, physical condition, economic and sociological background have great implications for program. A five-year-old is very different in his needs and interests from a nine or a twelve-year-old. A twelve-year-old girl is usually much more mature than a boy of that age. A handicapped child has the same play needs as the nonhandicapped, but may require a different tempo and adaptation in some activities if he is to achieve the glow of success and accomplishment.

Decentralization and careful grouping are necessary if individual needs are met. Adequate leadership, too, is necessary. Usually the campers are divided into groups with an age range of two, sometimes three, years. Different agencies have slightly differing standards, but the ACA standards of a counselor for every eight youngsters under eight years of age, and for every ten youngsters eight and over, is quite representative.

*Age Characteristics of Children.* Children are not sardines to be packed tightly into tin-can generalities. In their interests, play, and behavior, they flow in and out of any designated age characteristics as freely as the tide. Like the tide, however, there are certain basic rhythms of growth. A new or inexperienced counselor can profit by knowing these basic rhythms and selecting those activities best suited to a given age range.

Counselors should realize, however, that such brief descriptions can be at best only generalities. No two children are alike, whatever their ages. The following descriptions are included not as expert guides, but as material for discussion and observation.

*The Fives* are the what-is-it, what-makes-it-go, group. They are observant, fascinated by what they see, wanting to find out about it. They want to poke, and stroke, feel, listen—not just read or hear about. They like to be useful. They'll sweep, and rake, and wash—not well, but they *think* it's well.

They like tools and learning how to use them. They like to saw, to hammer, to model clay. They like playing house, playing store, dressing up. They like to cut out, paste, paint, blow bubbles, cook. They like group games, but they don't understand losing; so games involving everybody taking a turn are better than competitive games. Circle games and singing games are best for the fives.

They like tunes, simple rhythms, simple musical instruments. They like to "play-act" their stories—and to make up their own. They like noise, cowboys, Indians, cops, picnics, surprises, trips —in fact, they even like adults!

*The Sixes* are perpetual motion. They don't really know how to function as a social unit, but they love to *be* a unit. They like to run in packs, to tease, to scrap, to be "sassy." They like *speed*. They never walk. They hate to lose—and still don't understand team play. They'll tattle, they may cheat; but they do it because it hurts to lose. Avoid competitive games, or games that have strict rules. Use group games that involve everybody, like tags, relays, and running games.

The sixes like drama projects—making and living in a pioneer village, making puppets, a puppet theater, and writing and putting on puppet plays—projects that carry over for days.

They like tools. They can use screwdrivers, drills, files, as well as crosscut and coping saws—but they're likely not to finish the project.

They like rhythm bands, "playing" on a uke, listening to records.

They love animals and enjoy table games; they are noisy, argumentative, and sometimes rude. They tire easily. Counselors should watch for signs of fatigue and provide restful, change-of-pace activities when needed. They are sometimes insecure. They sometimes are subject to intense fears. New or possibly frightening situations should be handled with care.

*The Sevens* have to "belong." They get into cliques, they are cruel to "outsiders"; they begin to be less responsive and communicative to adults. They have strong likes and dislikes—and change them frequently. They are fond of rules—and the games like marbles, O'Leary, jacks, are at their height in popularity. Running games are popular.

Drama and dramatic activities need "props," uniforms, and are best played in groups, not by individuals.

Sevens are sensitive, sometimes sulky. Games should be active, should involve everybody and not demand too much individual skill. They like humor—the slapstick variety. They are demanding in time and attention. They are also delightfully responsive.

They enjoy movement, but their dancing should be dramatic rather than rhythmic. They like stories, to read, listen to, or to tell. They like to draw with crayons and pencils, and they enjoy working with odds and ends "to see what happens." They like to play and build with sand, dirt, and mud; and they enjoy natural materials like pine cones, grasses, bark, rocks. They like collecting, magic, puzzles, tongue twisters, table games, card games, magnets, microscopes, fishing, and any kind of water play.

*The Eights and Nines* are young rebels, slangy, impertinent, acting, dressing, and talking like everybody else in the "gang." They love to work on difficult projects, like building a clubhouse—or a wigwam—and they need adult help in how to do it.

They love stunts, tricks, magic, all sorts of science experiments.

This is the age for learning knots, for using a jackknife, for starting metalcraft. It's also the tumbling, wrestling, climbing, hiking, biking age—the age to blaze trails, learn orienteering, practice firemaking, set up a weather bureau.

It's the age of pantomime, of making up and putting on skits, making costumes, singing folk songs. The girls like all types of dancing. The boys hate any dancing with the possible exception of Indian dances and masked or costumed animal or clown dances. On the whole, the eights and nines are like quicksilver, slipping from one activity to another, interested (for a while at least) in almost everything. Some nines become sensitive and easily hurt; preadolescent in a new shyness, very different from their previous exuberance and bounce. Counselors who know the eight-year-old should not be too startled by such a possible change.

*The Tens through Twelves* are the joiners. They like clubs, hobbies, trips, tours. They are skillful with their hands, strong, full of vitality. They are competitive, they like team sports, they need skill instruction in the individual and dual sports; they love guessing and magic games, quizzes, card games, vocabulary and number games, dramatic games, reasoning games.

This is the age to emphasize handcrafts, to go into ceramics, weaving, modelmaking, leatherwork, sewing, candle making, kite and birdhouse making.

Portable musical instruments to play while the gang sings are the most popular. They like to sing at campfires, hayrides, and other social occasions. They're ready to go into folk and square dancing.

They are ready to learn and to appreciate design, to make mobiles and stabiles, collages, dioramas, and group murals. They can handle tools, and have developed special craft and art interests.

This group, because it is so active, is likely to overdo. It needs relaxed activities in between times. It needs encouragement just to sit and talk, or just to lie down on a hill and watch the clouds. It needs opportunities to discuss problems, behavior, religious beliefs, world affairs without fear of sounding childish, or of being laughed at. They're on the outer edge of childhood. Leaders should try to smooth their entry into the troubled years of adolescence by not pushing them into maturity too early, and by not expecting too much, too soon.

**The Staff**

To the ten qualifications for all members of the program staff of a day camp, as listed in the ACA standards (see Appendix A) should be added two more, and two of the highest importance—those of *Curiosity* and *Enthusiasm*. A counselor may be the right age, he may have the proper training and experience, the highest moral integrity, and particular skills in some part of the activity program—and still not be the opener-of-doors, the catalyst that brings about a positive reaction between camper and camp, camper and camper, camper and counselor.

Curiosity and enthusiasm can go far in overcoming a possible lack of training and information in the area of nature. It is difficult to find a counselor who knows all about trees, or swamp life, or ants, or flowers, birds, bark, chipmunks, or garter snakes. An observant counselor with an "I wonder why" attitude—"I wonder why birds don't fall off a tree branch at night," or "I wonder why feathers smooth out when they're stroked," or "I wonder how much rain fell last night," or "I wonder how tall that tree is," is very likely to lead a group of youngsters into a magic world of personal discoveries.

Such a counselor may have had little experience in drama, but he will wonder who first set foot on the land, what he was like, how he lived, played, worked, and worshiped. Out of discussion will come research, at least to the extent of the children's ability. Then will follow an act-it-out project, involving not just drama, but crafts, games, sport, music, dance. In camp, the performing arts are all "kissing cousins" of the hand arts, as they were in earlier, less sophisticated eras. They become a part of everyday living.

The director of the day camp looks for these plus values in selecting the counselors, tries to stimulate these qualities by at least fifteen hours precamp training, provides reading material for supplementary study. He works with the counselors in developing the objectives of the camp, and in deciding upon the broad program areas. He leaves the selection of specific activities to the counselor and his group, except when activities involve other groups, or the entire camp. He guides but does not dictate. He leads but does not push. He encourages initiative, resourcefulness, experimentation. He not only believes in, but practices, democracy. He is not alarmed or dismayed when a counselor or a camper seems out of step with the others, or "hears a different drummer," as Thoreau put it.

The ratio of counselors to campers has been mentioned—a counselor for every eight children eight years and under; a counselor for every ten children over eight years. Supplementing the group counselors may be junior counselors, or counselors in training; specialists in areas such as nature, swimming, horseback riding, archery, sailing and canoeing, music, dance, arts and crafts, and drama; resource specialists called in for special purposes and on special occasions, such as rangers, naturalists, foresters, fish and game wardens.

The smooth-running day camp, depending upon its size, location, sponsorship, and other factors, may involve various other camp personnel vital to its health, safety, and successful operation and administration. Doctor, dietitian, nurse, cook, maintenance workers, bus drivers, and clerical workers are among such staff, but are not concerned primarily with the activity program.

## The Camp Sponsorship

The activity program of a day camp will of necessity reflect the policy and the objectives of its sponsoring agency. This sponsorship determines whether the camp will serve girls, boys, or mixed groups; whether it places any special emphasis upon one religion; whether it serves one, or more than one, age group, and whether it operates on a nonprofit or profit-making basis. The sponsoring agency's policy—and budget—also determine the hours per day and the number of days per week or month that the camp operates.

A day camp program operating three days a week, with a different group of youngsters every week, will have a very different program from the camp which the same youngsters attend for an entire summer.

Day camps operated by public recreation and park departments are sometimes organized on a weekly basis, with young-sters from the various playgrounds taking turns. Sometimes the public day camps are operated on a first-come, first-served registration basis, again usually on a weekly schedule.

The ACA Standards require a minimum of at least three days a week, for not less than two weeks, per camper.

### The Camp Site

The actual *location* of the day camp and its physical character-istics play a big part in the formation of the activity program. A day camp set up in a city park, one operating in a state or county park, or located in a mountainous area, or on a lake front, or on a desert's edge, a ranch or farm—each will be influenced by the location. The seaside camp's activity program will lean toward water sports, sand and water play, the wildlife of beaches, marshes, and the sea, sea chanteys, ship and pirate themes.

Travel *distance* is another factor in the camp site. When youngsters are transported by bus to a State Park from various pick-up points in the city, as is done in Milwaukee through its Department of Municipal Recreation, and in other cities, under different sponsorship, bus travel to and from the day camp consumes a sizable part of camp time. The bus, in such cases, becomes a part of camp, and activities in the travel periods must be carefully planned. Suggestions for those periods will be given later in this book.

The actual *acreage* also is a factor. No actual research has been made on a standard ratio between the number of day campers and the acreage of the day camp site. The ACA Standards do not include a specific recommendation. Obviously the resident camp standard of an acre per child is unrealistic for most day camps in urban settings. Equally obviously, some sort of "edu-cated guess" must be decided upon, until research has been done, and standards accepted. An essential quality of any form of camping, including day camping, is freedom of movement within as wide a variety of physical resources as possible. Chil-dren need *space*. Too many youngsters on too small an area can turn the day camp site into an outdoor slum.

### The Weather

In any type of program involving outdoor activities the weather plays a big role. In the first place, weather has a definite influence on behavior. The sensitive counselor knows that on a hot, humid day, with the feel of a thunderstorm in the air, the campers are likely to be quarrelsome, inattentive, and hard to interest. Wind, especially when it persists over a period of time, sometimes is reflected in a general restlessness and lack of concentration. A cool, crisp, brilliant day asks for special activities involving physical exertion, exuberant action.

Days that are too hot, or too wet, or too cold will require rapid changing of plans. The weather changes programs as well as people! The weather, however, should be used as an important asset in selection of activities. It should never be used as an excuse for a poor program.

### Basic Values

What basic values can the activity program give the camper? What lessons in living will the camper absorb without being taught? They will vary in number and degree with each camper. One camper may learn the joy of sharing, whether it is food, toys, talk, or friendship. Another may find out that he doesn't have to be a bully, or to tease to get his own way, because everybody takes turns and he gets his turn. Another may find that he doesn't always have to be the best in order to enjoy anything, or to get recognition. Still another may discover that it's fun to try something new, whether it works or not. A basic value emerges, as each individual shares his day with the others. *He learns a bit of democracy.*

He finds out that his idea may be good, but that Bill's may be better; that the others don't always agree with him, and that it's all right to disagree. He finds that what he does matters to the others, and affects them. If he skimps on his chores, he holds up his group. If he does something well, he can help Mary, who can't seem to get the knack of it. He learns to take a part in planning, but not to sulk when he doesn't get his way.

He takes a big step toward *self-direction and initiative*. His opinion is respected. He is encouraged to try—and try again. He is encouraged to ask questions and find out answers, to experiment, to observe and make sense out of what he sees, to use all his senses and his mind and his muscles in exploring to its limits this new world around him.

He finds out that he's a real *person*, not just a child, or a son, or a camper. He's a needed and valued part of the day camp community, with something of himself to give. He feels the sweet taste of achievement. "I made it, I found it, I did it, *me*, all by myself."

And all these values become a part of the boy or girl through the understanding efforts of a counselor, using a wide range of activities to provide fun, adventure, and new experiences.

## The Activity Program Schedule

Purists in day camp circles, as in camp circles, decry the schedule, or the division of the day camp day into definite segments. Under optimum conditions, with campers whose imagination and curiosity have been stimulated by parental understanding and the best of school situations, this attitude of letting activities develop without any type of direction might work. Even with them, however, certain areas of time must be blocked out.

For example, if youngsters are transported to a day camp site, whether by family car, public bus, school or camp bus, a travel schedule has to be set up, taking up a chunk of the morning and the afternoon.

Lunch should be at a regular time, and so should a rest period. Some sort of daily opening and closing of camp lends it a bit of drama important to childhood. When large numbers of children will use the same facilities, such as a swimming pool, archery range, nature museum, camp fireplaces or stoves, and the like, groups must be scheduled not only for safety but for a fair distribution of time. Also, just as any businessman knows roughly how his day will be divided into correspondence, conferences, appointments, and planning of work, so a counselor must have an idea of what the day will bring.

Depending upon the many factors discussed previously, the

framework or schedule skeleton may indicate "specifics" or "constants," leaving open, for individual counselor and group initiative, big blocks of time that can be filled in with flexibility. The framework might look like this:

| | | |
|---|---|---|
| 9:00 AM— | | ..Bus pick-up and activity |
| 9:30 AM— | | ..Arrival at day camp |
| 9:30 | —10:00 AM | ..Opening ceremony. Divide into camp groupings |
| 10:00 | —11:30 AM | ..Activity program |
| 11:30 | —12:00 NOON | Activities—featuring less active ones, preparatory to lunch |
| | | Wash-up |
| 12:00 | — 1:30 PM | ..Lunch and rest hour |
| 1:30 | — 3:30 PM | ..Activity program |
| 3:30 | — 4:00 PM | ..Closing ceremony |
| 4:00 | — 4:30 PM | ..Bus trip home—bus activity |

Except for that hour on the bus coming and going, such a schedule gives five-and-a-half hours for activities, including eating, washing up, opening and closing ceremonies, and rest period. Opening and closing periods are usually all-camp events, at least once a week, often every day. Any special event like a circus or a treasure hunt may be for everybody. Most of the other periods, however, should be on a decentralized plan, in which the youngsters form small age or interest groups that separate and combine depending upon the activity. Several may join for an exciting period of active games; separate to practice camp-craft skills; join for storytelling; separate for lunch, with simple table, magic, and guessing games; join for swimming; et cetera, et cetera—the degree of group independence and the extent of co-operative effort depending upon the experiences of the campers and the skill of the counselors.

However the schedule is filled out, it should show a fine balance between very active and quiet activities; between the plastic and the performing arts; between individual and group activities; and between small- and large-group activities.

*Activities should FLOW. Sudden breaks or changes are disruptive and frustrating to youngsters. Time should be allowed to make comments, to clean up, to get into the mood for something* else. *Pressure of time, pressure of too many things to do in too short a time should be eliminated. A day camper should be re-laxed—not loafing or lazy, but not hectic, overexcited, and over-tired.*

# Environmental Activities

You must not know too much,
    or be too precise or scientific about
    birds and trees and flowers and
    water-craft; a certain free margin,
    and even vagueness—perhaps igno-
    rance, credulity—helps your enjoy-
    ment of these things.

                            —WALT WHITMAN
                            *Birds*

CHAPTER **3:**

# NATURE
# AND
# SCIENCE

The following chapters of this section on Environmental Activities are placed purposely so that they follow the first short section on Basics For Counselors. This particular chapter is placed deliberately at the beginning of this section. The reasons are the same. Each has high priority.

The fundamental and basic difference between a day camp program and any other good outdoor, summer program is its emphasis on the natural camp environment and on the use of this environment in developing an interest in, and responsibility for, our natural resources.

This emphasis, however, is often the most neglected aspect of a camp or day camp program. Insecurity—a feeling of inadequacy on the part of counselors—is usually the reason.

A counselor does not *have* to be a naturalist, a scientist, a weatherman, a geologist or other specialist to open the doors of wonder. Campers are at the right age, full of interest, curiosity, eager to experiment with new sights, sounds, ideas, eager to ask and find out Why and What, When and How. All they need is the *opportunity* and someone who is willing to take time to learn along with them. The scientific spirit can be developed in anyone. All a counselor needs is

- a questioning attitude,
- a "feeling" for our natural resources and his responsibility toward preserving them, and
- interesting projects to do with the campers.

One other trait helps—a relaxed, informal manner, unhurried and patient, putting no outside pressure on the camper.

Every project and suggestion in this chapter, and those in the following chapters of this section, can be carried out by any counselor, scientifically trained or not. A day camp doesn't try to make naturalists of its counselors or campers, but it *should* create an attitude that encourages the scientific spirit through natural experiences.

## The Five Senses

Many city children have never really *seen* growing things, noticed birds, listened to small, outdoor sounds, touched little living things. Many youngsters, not just city children, have had very few opportunities for learning how to use and to enjoy their five senses. Activities that open up ways of using and enjoying the senses are wedges that will in turn open up nature and science to the youngsters—in fact, they are all parts of the same thing. The following are suggestions for stimulating the use of the senses.

### SIGHT

Sight is the sense most of us rely on even more than we have to. Often it fortifies or corroborates other senses. We hear and see traffic. We see, smell, and taste food. We see, hear, and feel rain.

Sight alone, however, can give us *color*—the brilliance of a sunset, the swirl of color in an oilslick, the petals of a flower, the blue of eyes, the red of a fire engine, the green of a leaf.

Sight tells us the shape and size of an object without our touching it. It identifies food without our tasting it. It warns us of smoke without our smelling it.

We take sight for granted. We look without really *seeing*. Check with the youngsters on simple things they have all seen, but not registered:

How many toes does a cat have? a dog? a bird?
Which direction does water turn when it goes down a drain?
How many legs does an ant have?

Answers should be found out by *looking*. Encourage the children to observe and then to question the others—a sort of "Stump the See-er" game.

Observation can be intensified by giving the youngsters an opportunity to see some of the small wonders that escape normal vision.

A *pocket lens* can be a magic mirror through which a child can step into his own wonderland. It is exciting to see

- the number of threads in cloth.
- the leg of a grasshopper. Just look at those jumping muscles!
- the "dust" on a butterfly's wing—tiny scales covering it like feathers on a bird.
- the head of a black ant. See those strong jaws and big feelers.
- the head of a butterfly. Try to find the sucking tube coiled up like a spring.
- the "barbs" on a feather. So *that's* why a bird smooths down his feathers! Those barbs all lock together like a zipper!

A *microscope* opens an even wider door. A drop of water that *looks* clear turns out to be a small sea full of water life. Blood, fiber, hair, salt, sugar—everyday things are suddenly strange and beautifully made.

If the day camp does not own a microscope, try to borrow one for at least one day a week. If that is not possible, work out some way to take the youngsters to a school, laboratory, clinic, or hospital to give them this experience while they are still in the age of wonder.

Traveling zoos, nature museums, slides, films, records, charts, magazines, books, and specialists in any form of outdoor life are all wonderful supplements to observation opportunities.

Activities like *games* can be used to stimulate observation too. When sitting together, or resting, or lying on the ground, the old game of "I Spy" is always fun. Someone starts by saying "I spy something red"—or other descriptive phrase. Each person tries to identify it by saying "Is it so-and-so?" The one who finally guesses it then selects something else, and the game goes on and on. Children from six to twelve find this game remarkably fascinating—and it is great on a really hot day!

*Treasure hunts* that require following small trail signals teach observation. *Laying* them is as important as following them.

*Color hunts,* in which youngsters are given a stated period of time in which to find and list as many things of different colors as possible, train the observation. They can be played individually, or in groups. The latter is a good method to use with young children whose writing and spelling skills are not so developed as their enthusiasm. Each member of a group can report his or her findings to a leader, and then the various groups can compare their findings later.

Building a vocabulary of descriptive words can be made into an interesting activity. How many words can you think of that describe some shade of red? green? yellow? blue? Keep a list and add to it as youngsters think of others. See how long it can grow during the summer.

Color charts put out by paint companies can be helpful to show the many gradations of color. Beg or borrow some. Then keep the interest up by being observant *yourself.* "I can see six different shades of green from where I stand." "What color would you say that tent shadow looks?"

### TASTE

What *is* taste? Does it help to hold the nose when taking a bad-tasting medicine? Does *sight* have anything to do with taste? Does smell?

Campers will enjoy experimenting to find out. Blindfold someone and have him hold his nose—so that he can't see or smell. Then give him a bite of something with a distinctive taste, like a small piece of a chocolate bar. Chances are he won't know what it is! His eyes couldn't help, and his nose couldn't help!

*Where* is taste? Campers can find out for themselves. Dissolve a spoonful of sugar in half a glass of water. Dip a toothpick in it and apply to different parts of the tongue. Where did it taste sweetest?

Try the same with salt; then with vinegar; then with an aspirin dissolved in water. With such experiments, the campers will find that the following facts are true:

- the tastebuds for sugar are on the tip of the tongue;
- for salt, the tip and sides;
- for vinegar, the sides;
- for aspirin, the back of the tongue.

Does heat or cold have anything to do with taste? Which seems the sweeter, hot or iced cocoa? A freshly picked peach or one that's been in the refrigerator?

What about texture? Does it have anything to do with taste, or with food preferences? Does it have anything to do with *sound?* Does the crunch of celery, raw carrots, or a crisp apple have anything to do with how it tastes? Why does a crisp cracker taste better than a soggy one?

What words are used to describe taste? Campers will enjoy trying to think of the *ways* foods taste—then name as many foods as possible in each category. What tastes *bitter? smooth? oily? sharp? sweet? sour?* What foods taste a combination of ways?

What are spices, and where do they come from? Many youngsters have never seen cinnamon bark (buy it at any drugstore). Cloves are flowerbuds. Bay leaf, mint, and basil are all leaves. Coffee is a bean; tea, a leaf; coconut, the inside of a nut; mustard is a seed; ginger is a root.

Very often children have never seen the real thing—just powders in small jars or cans on the kitchen shelf. Bring in samples—to nibble, look at, handle, smell, feel—and taste.

FOOD is a wonderful topic for discussion. Everybody likes to talk about it. Sentences like "It smelled so good it made my mouth water," or "It looked good enough to eat," or "Just the sight of it makes me sick," all are clues in how closely taste is tied up with other senses.

Sometimes such discussions of food likes and dislikes are good ways to encourage better eating habits. They also provide an atmosphere that encourages experimentation—and many children are very conservative in their food habits.

What *is* food? Where does it come from? Many campers have never really realized that the world of living plants provides a large part of our food supply.

*Food from Plants.* Many youngsters have never seen vegetables and fruits except in markets or in cans. A project that ties in the home and the day camp is *food identification.* Campers can bring samples, or samples may be brought by the leader, to be used for group discussion. Trips to farms and markets are good follow-ups.

• What *roots* do we eat? Add others:

|          |          |
|----------|----------|
| beets    | salsify  |
| carrots  | parsnips |
| radishes | potatoes |
| turnips  | onions   |

How food *looks* on the plate often has a great deal to do with appetite and food enjoyment. Nutritionists are concerned with food values, not just color, but they may advise "one yellow vegetable and one leafy vegetable," so that we get vitamin and mineral content in our food. Color combinations on a plate look pretty enough to eat—and so they get eaten!

• What *stems?*

|          |          |
|----------|----------|
| rhubarb  | broccoli |
| leek     | celery   |

It's a good idea to mention a queer thing about rhubarb—its stems are so good when they're stewed with sugar, but the leaves and the seed stalk are poisonous. Beet tops, yes, Rhubarb tops, NO!

How does celery get so white? It really isn't, unless the farmer keeps it covered so that it gets blanched. Lots of people prefer the celery that has been allowed to get green.

Look up the history of leeks. The Welsh wear a leek in their cap, as the Irish would put a shamrock, or the Scot a thistle.

• What *leaves?*

|            |         |
|------------|---------|
| spinach    | endive  |
| watercress | parsley |
| lettuce    | kale    |

Spinach tastes gritty unless it's washed and washed and *washed*. Look at a spinach leaf and see why it is so hard to get the sand or grit off.

How many kinds of lettuce do the youngsters know? Show them *leaf* lettuce and *head* lettuce.

• What *fruits* do we eat as vegetables?

| | |
|---|---|
| string beans | peppers |
| eggplant | squash |
| pumpkin | tomato |
| okra | cucumber |

Did you know that tomatoes came originally from the Orient, and were brought back by sea captains because the fruits were a pretty color? Their wives sowed the seeds to grow decorative plants, and for many, many years everybody thought tomatoes were poisonous. They were called love-apples in early days of our country.

• What *seeds* do we eat as vegetables?

| | |
|---|---|
| corn | rice |
| peas | lima beans |

Why does popcorn pop? Why does it pop *better* if it's soaked a few minutes in cold water?

What is *maize?* Why don't Europeans eat corn-on-the-cob? Their corn is really field corn, used for feeding farm animals. *Maize* is a plant of the New World, known and raised by Indians in North and South America. It was so important to them that many tribes have lovely legends about it. Find some and dramatize them.

• What *seeds* do we make into bread?

| | |
|---|---|
| wheat | barley |
| corn | oats |
| rice | rye |

What's the difference between white and whole wheat bread? between rice and brown rice? Which have the most food value?

- What *sap* do we eat?

  maple syrup                sugar cane

How do we make maple sugar, maple sugar candy, and regular sugar? What about beet sugar?

If there is a spice bush around, taste a twig. Do the same with sassafras. Our great-grandmothers boiled sassafras roots to make a very good tea.

- Open a lima bean very carefully. See the little plant all ready to grow? Cut through an onion vertically and see its layers of self-food.

- Cut a potato through the middle. Then cut a very thin slice, and hold it to the light. There's a lovely star—use it as a design in drawing. Use the cut potato for printing by cutting a design on it, inking it with stencil paint, and printing on cloth or paper.

- Taste a piece of fresh, raw potato. Chew it well. It has a fresh, wet, starchy taste.

- Peel a very ripe banana. Can you find the seeds?

- Cut an apple straight through the middle, horizontally. Look at the shape of the core, the location of seeds, the shape of the stem and the blossom end.

- Look at a lettuce leaf and a cabbage leaf. Do the veins run the same way? Is the color different? the texture? the taste?

Day camp sites are often not "woody" enough to provide many opportunities for finding and tasting wild foods. Exceptions are fortunate, and leaders should make the most of them. Others, however, can awaken a sense of wonder and curiosity about edible plants by using what is available. There'll be a carry-over.

### SMELL

The sense of smell, so closely tied in with the sense of taste, varies in different people, often because it is not cultivated. Many people say that it is the one sense that can recall an occasion more quickly than any other—the basis of many advertisements for perfumes! A brief whiff of lilacs—and a New England dooryard or a crisp, cool spring morning comes to someone's mind. Tar, cedar, pine, nutmeg, roses, plowed ground, new-mown hay—these and many other smells have the power to evoke memories. Children will need pleasant memories. They should have specific opportunities to *use* their sense of smell.

Let them think up answers as well as questions. What *is* smell? Why does mother keep a tight top on her box of spices? her bottle of perfume? Put a bit of ground coffee in a dish. How far away can you smell it? Let it stand an hour or so. How far can you smell it now? Not nearly so far. The molecules that carry the smell shot up in the air, spread out, got into the nose and made certain little nerves send an electric message to the brain. Every kind of smell causes a different pattern or signal.

*Enjoy* smells—the air after a lightning storm . . . fresh-cut grass . . . leather . . . tar . . . an ocean breeze . . . smoke . . . broiling meat . . . fresh earth . . . pine needles . . . clean hair.

As in the case of taste, opinions and reactions to smells that please or displease vary in individuals. Talk about favorite smells. Disagreeable smells. What words describe smells? What smells remind you of something special?

Have a *Smelling Bee*. Collect a number of small bottles that can be corked. Put a few drops or pinches of various well-known liquids or solids with distinctive smells in them, and label them only with a number. Keep a record of the items per number. Then let the youngsters take turns smelling and writing down what they think each bottle contains by number. This can be repeated a number of times during the summer, adding and subtracting different smells. Here are some easy ones:

| vanilla | vinegar | turpentine |
| cloves | lime | clorox |
| cinnamon | nutmeg | mint |
| lemon | cedar | sage |
| onion | garlic | lavender |

These tests work best by blindfolding the child who takes them, so that sight doesn't give him a clue. The bottles should be tightly corked after each sniff.

Smell is one of the easiest of the senses to encourage. "I smell something sweet. What is it?" and everyone stops, smells, and looks. With encouragement from an alert counselor who enjoys and appreciates his sense of smell, day campers will do the same—learn new terms to use in describing the smells and use their sense of smell to augment the other senses.

TOUCH

Touch is a sense we use often, but we don't give much thought to it. "Don't touch" is one of the first things a baby hears, and he hears it for many years. "Don't touch—it's hot"; "Don't touch—it's wet"; "Don't touch—your hands are dirty"; "Don't touch—it'll break." Children *need* to touch. It's a way of finding out, of recognizing, of estimating, of becoming aware of weight and texture.

The sense of touch is usually not so well verbalized as the other senses. This is a good activity area to emphasize. To be aware *plus* being able to put the feeling into words is a valuable trait.

Matching *words* with touch is a good way to experiment in finding just the right word. Discuss a list of articles with different *textures,* like these:

| fur | wool | bristle | rock |
| terry cloth | nylon | feather | cracker |
| soap | velvet | bark | pine cone |
| sandpaper | string | steel wool | glass |
| moss | hair | paper | foil |

Which word or words best describe them?

| crisp | dry | sticky | soft |
| stiff | thin | smooth | rough |
| scratchy | damp | slippery | sharp |
| gummy | squashy | warm | cold |
| silky | gritty | heavy | rounded |

The sense of touch, like the sense of smell and of sight, can be fooled. Try this little experiment:

Ask a youngster to close his eyes, and then to cross the middle finger over the index finger of one hand. Then rub a pencil between the crossed fingers, lightly touching both fingers. It will *feel* like two pencils. Try it and see!

Information *fortified* by personal experiences with one or more of the senses will have a reality that reading or talking can't produce. *Look* at the trunk of a shagbark hickory tree, a beech tree, ironwood, and birch. They all *look* different—in color and in shape. *Feel* each tree trunk. The bark of the hickory is sharp, jagged, thick. The beech is very smooth; the birch's bark feels thin and crackly. The ironwood feels like strong muscles under the bark.

Feel the edges or margins of leaves. Some will be smooth. Some will feel like little saws (the word serrate comes from the Latin word for saw). Feel the underside of leaves. Some will be silky, some fuzzy, some rough.

Blindfold games encourage using the senses of sound and touch. Encourage touching tests by blindfolding the camper. "What does it feel like?" "What is it?" Use the Touch Box (see Chapter 13, "Arts and Crafts") often, changing its contents frequently. Bring a piece of Braille writing for the campers to feel. Some may have seen "The Miracle Worker," and wondered about how Helen Keller learned to "read" through her sense of touch.

*Talk* about feeling and the sense of touch. Look at the "feelers" on a butterfly or other insect. What is the use of a cat's or mouse's whiskers? Does the feel have anything to do with food likes and dislikes?

SOUND

What *is* sound? If a tree falls in the forest, and no one hears it, did it make a sound? A vibration causes air to move like a wave. The wave reaches the ear and vibrates a special instrument, the eardrum. The *pattern* of that wave against the eardrum tells you whether the sound is loud or soft, high or low, sharp or shrill, pleasant or unpleasant.

Listening is a way to learn. Every child should learn to be very still, keep very quiet, and *listen.* There'll be all sorts of small sounds—wind in the trees, waves lapping the sand, a bird call, a squirrel scolding, a bee buzzing.

Establish a Listening Post—a tree, hilltop, or any quiet place where campers can go alone, or in small groups, and just *listen.* Then talk about what was heard. Find words to describe the sounds. What words come from sounds—like "buzz," "cheep," "whirr," "crackle," "moo."

Experiment with sound. *Tap* lots of things—walls, windows, tables, chairs, the head, the cheeks, the chest. What makes "pitch"? Does the length of wire or rubber band have anything to do with whether the tone is high or low? What happens to the sound if a drumhead (or rubber band, or wire) is very tight? is loosened? What is *rhythm?* What is *beat?*

What sounds do animals make? Try to imitate them. Try to imitate some bird calls.

Make musical instruments (see Chapter 13, "Arts and Crafts"). Make musical sounds on them. Beat out a familiar song and see if the others can identify it.

*How* do we talk? Try to talk while holding the nose . . . while keeping the teeth together . . . while not moving the lips.

If possible, make a tape recording of each camper's voice, and play it back. Were the words clear? The voice pleasant? *Listen!* Listen to your own voice; to the voices of other people. Practice talking clearly, with a *happy* voice.

### Walks, Rambles, and Strolls

Thomas Huxley once commented: "To a person uninstructed

in natural history, a country stroll is a walk through a gallery filled with works of art nine-tenths of which have their faces turned to the wall." A good day camp program can bring those pictures back into view.

Walks and rambles are not the same as hikes. Hiking is going from one place to another as quickly as possible, on foot, and usually for some specific purpose. The physical activity and the destination are the most important factors.

Walks, rambles, and strolls are relaxed, informal activities, full of Stop-Look-Listen, just for personal enjoyment. They are excellent ways to stimulate the use and enjoyment of the five senses:

## A SOUND WALK

How many sounds can be identified? The rustle of leaves, the scolding of a squirrel, the drone of a plane, the buzz of different insects, a bird call, the wash of waves? Keep a list.

Try to describe the sounds in words. How many words can you think of that are *based* on sound, like "whirr," "hum," "buzz." How do different sounds make you feel? What is the difference between a fire alarm sound and a church bell? Do birds and animals have special alarm or warning sounds?

Is there anything absolutely silent? Is electricity in a wire silent? A bird high in the sky? A flower opening?

## A FEEL WALK

What different *feels* can be described? A patch of moss *looks* green. It *feels* soft and damp. That pebble *looks* white and round. It *feels* smooth and cool. The margin of this leaf is smooth—but feel *that* one! It's like a saw! These pine cones are both brown, but one feels sharp, the other smooth. This stem is smooth, but that one is prickly. Which would make the safest place for a small animal to hide in? The ground here in the shade feels cool. A foot away, in the sun, it feels warm. Which feels moist?

## A NOSE STROLL

What smells can be identified? Warm hair? Tar? Leather?

Pine? Cut grass? Moist earth? A skunk? Mint? Salt air? Fish? A flower? Smoke? What *words* describe these smells?

## A ONE-WONDER WALK

Everyone wanders slowly along a path, or across a field, or through the woods, or along the shore. Each stays within sight and sound of the others. Each looks for something especially wonderful for any reason—its shape, color, movement, location, size, or whatever. When he finds his wonder, he marks it with a stake, or piece of facial tissue or some easily visible object (removed later, of course—no litterbugs in day camp!).

When everyone has found one wonder and marked it, they all visit each other's and discuss their findings, giving their reasons for selecting them. Wonders might include such items as

- a tiny woods flower so small it can scarcely be seen, but perfect in every detail
- a strangely shaped, fallen tree limb
- an odd piece of driftwood
- a leaf with an insect wrapped in it
- a cicada nymph shell
- a rock glittering with mica
- a clump of fern growing on a rock
- markings on a tree trunk
- a strange burr or seed pod
- an orange-colored mushroom
- a bird's nest
- a bird's feather

## A COLOR HUNT

This was described under "Sight."

## A BRING-'EM-BACK-ALIVE SAFARI

A trip during which the youngsters look for, find, and collect single specimens of small, living things, such as beetles, ants, worms, caterpillars, and the like.

Back at camp these are looked at carefully, using a hand lens if possible; looked up; studied; identified—and perhaps named.

If frogs, toads, and turtles are included, suitable living quarters should be provided, and the specimens kept only for a day or two. Respect for the lives of small things should be a part of any learning activity in day camp.

## GYPSY TRAIL

A combination of game, treasure hunt, and ramble, a gypsy trail encourages observation and learning to follow directions. The trail should be marked with 4″x4″ scraps of colored cloth, different colors meaning different instructions:

green - go straight ahead
blue - turn right
orange - turn left
red - danger

The campers divide into two groups of gypsies, one going ahead with a twenty-minute start, the other to follow and meet up with their band. The first group marks the trail, not too obviously. The second group follows the trail, collecting the markers as they go. When the gypsy band is together again, it's a good excuse for a cold drink or a picnic.

## SUPER-SNOOPER TRIPS

On these trips the youngsters should be in small groups if possible. The whole idea is to creep through the given area or route as silently and as unobtrusively as an Indian or a wild animal would go. Children place their feet carefully, so as to make no rustle of leaves, or clatter of pebbles. They go *around* rather than across an open area. They take advantage of tree trunks, boulders, shadows. They creep through tall grass. They cross the brook without a splash.

Such trips are fun in themselves because the child dramatizes himself and the situation. Practice often enough—and soon the youngsters will become skilled enough to move instinctively. Then they're likely to see some of the real inhabitants—a rabbit or a woodchuck; a grass snake sliding under a rock; a turtle in a cool, moist spot; the click of a scarlet tanager; a pileated woodpecker on a dead tree; a squirrel leaping from a bough, or coming headfirst down a tree.

When children see wildlife without being observed, they have their first, and very lasting, feeling of delight in being a part of it. Walt Whitman knew this when he wrote, "There was a child went forth every day; And the first object he looked upon, that object he became; And that object became part of him for the day, or a certain part of the day, or for many years, or stretching cycles of years."

## Plant and Animal Life in the Camp Setting

In addition to encouraging the use and enjoyment of the senses, basic to all activities, day campers need to extend their curiosity beyond their own physical enjoyment into the edges of nature education. This activity area is all too often one where counselors blanch and children learn to be bored. Emphasis in the past on collecting and on identification has been largely responsible for the lack of interest. Natural history, the study of plants and animals in their own setting, is fascinating to every child when properly presented and motivated.

The brief facts about plant and animal life given in this chapter are designed primarily to interest a counselor who has had very little training in the broad field of natural history. Such information may give him a starting place. Pointing out one interesting fact about a tree, or fern, or shell, or insect can start a discussion, stimulate more observation, and lead straight to other interesting facts. In other words, facts can motivate actions.

The ideas presented here will give only the tiniest peephole into the field of natural history, but even a glimpse may encourage enlarging that peephole into a door through which youngsters can enter the wonderland that lies all around them.

It is not particularly important to learn to identify ten trees by their leaves, or to name and identify ten birds, flowers, or other wildlife, or other stereotyped and unmotivated nature activities. It *is* important to learn that trees, flowers, birds, and animals are all mutually dependent upon each other, as is man—

and that man must learn to understand, preserve, and use them wisely, not wastefully, as he has done in the past.

If, for example, everyone in camp cuts down a sapling for a cane or a toaster or a tent pole, what will happen to the forest? In the early days and even in fairly recent times, it seemed as though the supply of wild areas was inexhaustible. Now we know how close we are to losing our heritage. Campers cannot learn too early the lesson

LOOK • LEARN • LIKE • LEAVE

Counselors sometimes underestimate children by oversimplifying language and information. Children enjoy being talked to in adult terms. Don't say "red bird" when you mean a cardinal, or "tree" when you know it's a maple.

Names are interesting. Many names *describe* the object

| | |
|---|---|
| grass*hopper* | *yellow* jacket |
| *honey*bee | *garter* snake |
| *sapsucker* | *poison* ivy |
| *katydid* | *measuring* worm |

(Sometimes people's names describe, too, where they once lived, or what they did—like Overbrook, Miller, Smith. Campers can think of many others.)

## Trees

Trees have played a big part in our history. Donald Culross Peattie, in his *A Natural History of Trees of Eastern and Central North America*, says, "First the trees were barriers and ambushes, then they became blockhouses and cabins, gunstocks and cradles, wagon wheels and railroad ties. Now they are airplanes and newsprint, plastics and prefabrications. . . . They are the best we have left of the wilderness, and witnesses of our finest moments; trees still standing could tell us how Boone and Lincoln, Lewis and Clark, Washington and Penn took shelter beneath them or laid a hand on the bole while speaking. . . . Almost every tree in our silva has made history or witnessed it, or entered into our folkways, or usefully become a part of our daily life."

Preserving what we have and planting for the future can both be day camp projects. What would our country be like without trees? What happens to a hillside when all the trees are burned, cut, or bulldozed down?

Trees are like people. They all have *family* names, and often there are many different ones in a family. For example, the oak family is Quercus, and in it are lots of different varieties of oak —the pin oak, the white oak, the chestnut oak, the red oak, and so on.

Some varieties of plants (trees are woody plants!) get their names in various ways:

from a person—like *Douglas* fir
from a region—like *Ohio* buckeye
from use—like *sugar* maple
from its home—like *swamp* maple, *mountain* ash
from some feature—like *white* birch, *shagbark* hickory, *weeping* willow

Trees are roughly divided into two groups, *evergreen* and *deciduous*—those which stay green all winter and those which lose their leaves in the fall. Evergreens, to children, are the trees used at Christmas time. Campers may have noticed that there are many different kinds of "Christmas trees."

Evergreen leaves are called "needles." Those needles can be different in shape—look carefully. Pine needles grow in little bundles, from two to seven in a bundle. That's the way to check on what *kind* of pine tree it is.

All trees have fruits. How many kinds can campers name? Then add more.

| | |
|---|---|
| balls—(sycamore) | pods—(locust tree) |
| acorns—(oak trees) | pome—(apple tree) |
| cones—(evergreens) | drupe—(cherry tree) |
| "wings"—(maple) | nuts—(walnut, hickory, pecan, etc.) |

The edges of leaves are called *margins*. Some are *smooth* to the touch. Some are *wavy*. Some are *lobed,* or indented deeply with smooth indentations. Some are *serrate,* meaning with little sawtooth edges. Some are *double serrate,* indented with little and big sawtooth edges. These different margins are a way of finding out what tree family it belongs to. Campers can find all these, and test the margins with their own fingers. Look at and feel the margins.

Look at the *shape* of a leaf, too. It is one of the best ways of identifying a tree in the summer. There are two major types of leaves, *simple* and *compound.* Look at the tiny bud at the base of the leaf. It will be next year's leaf! A simple leaf, like oak or maple, has this bud at the base of each leaf. A *compound* leaf may have a number of little leaflets along a central stem, but that little leaf bud will be at the base of the central stem.

If two leaves are attached across from each other, they're called "*opposite.*" If the leaves are stair-stepped, first on one side, then the other, they're called "*alternate.*" Trees that have *alternate* leaves are easy to remember. They're "MAD-horse" trees—M for maple, A for ash, D for dogwood, and "horse" for horse-chestnut or buckeye.

On the next stroll, or ramble, look at leaves and see if you can find simple and compound ones, and ones with different kinds of margins. Bring a sample back, and look it up so that next time the tree can be called by its real name. It's nice to recognize a *family,* like oak, or maple, or ash (baseball bats are ash!), or willow, hickory, pine. It's even *more* fun to recognize the right *member* of the family—*red* oak, *soft* maple, *mountain* ash, *black* willow, *shagbark* hickory, *white* pine.

If there's a newly cut stump, look at the rings, and try to see how old the tree might have been. Why are some of the rings wider than others?

*Measure* a tree at shoulder-height. Which is the largest around? the tallest? (See Chapter 8.) Make a camp leaf scrapbook. Make spatter prints and crayon prints. Collect acorns, cones, and other tree fruits and use them in making "woods pretties," as they're called in the Blue Ridge. (See "Arts and Crafts" for more projects and directions.)

Lie down under a tree and look up through the branches.

Notice the movement of the leaves. Listen to the rustle. Look at the shifting of the shadows. Think of things that may have happened under that tree. Make up a play, a story, a poem, a song, a dance about it.

### Flowers

Most camp sites even in midsummer will have daisies, black-eyed Susans, asters, goldenrod, milkweed, Queen Ann's lace, dandelions, and other varieties typical of the geographic location. Everybody takes them for granted. Very few have really *examined* them. They are all worth a careful look, and a magnifying lens will add even more enjoyment.

Most flowers have four parts: the *pistil* that is in the center, a number of *stamens* around it, *petals* circling these, and *sepals* that seem to hold the petals in shape, and which form the calyx of the flower. The tops of the stamens have little sacs filled with grains of pollen. At the bottom of the pistil is a tiny plant egg. The top of the pistil is often slightly enlarged, and shaped a bit like a cross. The pollen grains from the stamens must be taken by wind, or bees, or butterflies to the stigma, where they grow down into the pistil, uniting with the egg to develop into a seed. This process varies with flowers of different kinds and shapes, but the process is fundamentally similar—and a wonder to children who have never seen the plant egg, or touched pollen, or examined a stamen or pistil carefully.

Flower *petals* are sometimes separate, sometimes in one piece, like a morning-glory flower, sometimes with different shape, like upper and lower lips.

Many summer wild flowers are called *composites* because what we call the *head* is really a bunch of tiny individual flowers.

The dandelion is a good flower to study because every child knows it—or thinks he does! Also, it can usually be found in all stages—buds, flowers, and seeds.

Try to find a young dandelion plant. Taste a small, new leaf.

It has a bitter, fresh, "salady" taste—and pioneers used to go out eagerly in the spring to pick it, eat it as a salad or as a spring tonic, or cook it like spinach. In fact, many people *still* collect young dandelion leaves in the spring. Supermarkets in some cities carry canned dandelion greens.

Find a young plant with the buds tucked in it at its base. Open one of the buds and find the flower all there, curled up, waiting to open.

Pick a dandelion blossom. Look at the stem. It's so hollow that it makes a good sipping straw. Look at the "flower." Is it really a single flower, or a cluster of tiny flowers? Pull out one of the tiny yellow "petals," and see if it looks like a lion's tooth—for which it was named.

Queen Anne's lace, or wild carrot, is another flower that has a long growing period in a wide geographical range. Is *it* a single flower? Look closely. There are *dozens* of tiny flowers in that flower head, each one with five tiny petals. Note how the flower stalks all come out of the same place. Watch for one that has gone to seed and see how it looks like a bird's nest.

The familiar white daisy is the perfect example of a composite. The white petals that tell whether "he loves me, he loves me not" are called ray flowers, and the yellow center of the daisy is a mass of tiny *disk* flowers. Pull out a white ray. The bottom is shaped like a tube, and has a pistil in it. Look carefully at one single disk flower. It is a tube with stamens and pistils.

The black-eyed Susan, or coneflower, is another composite. Let the youngsters take a flower head apart, and examine the rays and disks. Feel the stems, too. Look at the shape of the leaves. These are all ways of finding out the proper name of a flower. All these things are "keys" to plant life. Most are so small they go unnoticed—but when noticed, they arouse wonder.

A counselor need not be a botanist to accomplish this. A few specimens, curiosity, careful inspection, and a good flower book are all the tools he needs to arouse the interest of a young camper.

Introducing campers to culitvated, as well as to wild, flowers is good program. Some campers will have flower gardens around their homes. Neighbors are glad to help out. In fact, samples are easy to come by, and a few for appreciation and for inspection can be brought to camp at frequent intervals.

When this is done, encourage the senses. Let the youngsters *feel* the thorn and the velvet of the rose, smell it (some smell like tea!), taste a petal. Learn its name—rose, yes, but what *kind?* climbing? trailing? floribunda? hybrid tea? Then its *popular* name—Blaze, or Pinocchio, or Peace, or Queen Elizabeth, and so on. Try letting youngsters suggest *their* names for a variety before telling them its name.

Summer garden flowers that every child should know include such favorites as these:

| | | |
|---|---|---|
| roses | marigolds | zinnias |
| cosmos | bachelor's buttons | petunias |
| stock | larkspur | delphinium |
| peony | verbena | sunflower |
| lantana | chrysanthemum | portulaca |
| hollyhock | phlox | alyssum |

Bring a flower catalogue to day camp. Look up the different flowers, let campers see how many varieties there are, and what interesting and descriptive names they hear.

For the counselor who knows nothing about wild flowers, a simple book that identifies first of all by *color* is a help. Soon he will find other and more scientific methods, and can progress to a more comprehensive book. The *start*, however, is the important thing.

Walt Whitman had encouraging words for a counselor not too familiar with the whole wide area of nautral history. He said, "You must not know too much, or be too precise or scientific about buds and trees and flowers and watercraft; a certain free margin, and even vagueness—perhaps ignorance, credulity—helps your enjoyment of these things."

Enjoy them, and campers will do the same. That is the first step toward knowledge.

SEEDS

Summer is a good season, and day camp a good setting, for

examining the marvels of seeds. Why do weeds pop up where they do? Why do some plants seem to move forward every year from where they were last year?

Parachutes and space capsules are not new! Plants have been using them for centuries. Examples are all around.

The dandelion is a fine example. Every child has held the stem of one that has gone to seed, and blown it to see the tiny parachutes drift through the air.

Try to find a milkweed pod and split it open carefully. Show the youngsters how carefully the seeds are tucked away. Pull out one of the compartments and show how much is packed in such a small space. Count the seeds. Each seed has little fuzzy hairs to carry it through the air. Try to count the hairs. Watch some of the seeds fly in a good breeze. Will they float?

Any cattails around day camp? If so, cut one and put it in a jar without water. What happens in a few days? Take the seeds outdoors and see if they fly as well as dandelions and milkweed. Youngsters can figure out for themselves why cattails grow near each other, yet dandelions and milkweed pop up almost anywhere.

If campers come back from a hike or stroll with cockleburs or beggar's lice sticking to their clothes, examine those seeds with the eyes, and with a magnifying lens. What held them to the cloth? Some of the youngsters have had experience getting burrs off their dogs. *Those* seeds traveled, too, without a parachute. They were *carried*.

The pods of the jewelweed or touch-me-not are a fascinating first experience to every youngster who has never touched a ripe pod before. *There's* a plant that *throws* its seed!

Collect all sorts of flower and tree seeds, and let the youngsters figure out where they're likely to go, and why. Western youngsters will be familiar with tumbleweed, for example. It has another way to spread its seeds—to roll as a dry plant, dropping its seeds as the wind blows it along. What are other ways that seeds get carried?

SPORES

Some plants don't have flowers or produce seeds. They're all around—the fungi, the mosses, mushrooms, puffballs, and ferns. Campers have seen them, but the way they grow, produce, and spread their spores are mysteries to youngsters.

Find a mushroom. Cut off the top, and lay it very carefully, bottom side down, on a piece of colored construction paper. Cover it with a glass dish, or a box, so that no air can touch it. After a day or so, lift the dish or box off *very* carefully, and see the design the spores of that mushroom made as they fell on the paper. Spray it with shellac or plastic to make a collection.

See how many different colors of spores can be found by this method. Some spores are pink, some white, purple, brown, and black. Use a gray or blue paper so that the design will show up.

Those mushrooms are *gilled* underneath. The campers may find some that don't have the little partitions, but look somewhat like a sponge. These have *pores,* and the spores of these fall down through the tube-like pores.

*Puffballs* grow from the size of marbles to ones as big as basketballs. Why are they called puffballs? Try to find a "ripe" one and press it. That brown dust that puffs out is made up of *trillions* of spores!

*Mosses* are fun to study because they can be allowed to dry, put in an envelope, kept till needed again, moistened—and they seem to spring to life again! Campers can find many different kinds if they really *look.* Some are deep and thick; some feel like velvet; some are delicate grays, and every shade of green. Let the campers find the *"capsules"*—the little hats that sit on top of thin stalks that grow above the moss. Those capsules contain the spores—and have all sorts of clever ways of letting the spores sift out at just the right time. Show them to the campers, using a magnifying glass. What safety devices can they find that protect the spores and let them fall out at the best time? Look for different colored capsules, too.

The campers are sure to find *ferns* that have brown spots underneath the fern leaves or *fronds.* These aren't dried out, or diseased. Those tiny little brown dots are really clusters of tiny capsules, *much* smaller than the moss capsules. On dry days, those dots (called *sori*) will break, and thousands of spores will be flung out.

The sori vary in position and shape on different kinds of ferns. Cut a frond from each of different kinds of ferns and compare the leaf shape, edges, size, color, and the sori. Look them up in a fern book and learn their names. They're too interesting to be all lumped together under one name, "fern." Don't pick or dig up wild ferns unless their new home is just like the old one, in shade, moisture, soil. Enjoy them where they are.

## Insects

Insects are found in every part of the world and in vast quantities. There are more different kinds, or species, than all the birds, mammals, fish, and reptiles combined. They are very ancient, existing today not too different from what they were like millions of years ago.

Most insects are harmless. Many are very useful to man. Some, like flies, are pests, but they too have their uses in nature as scavengers. Some, like mosquitoes, hornets, and wasps, can sting. Some, like the bee, can sting, but play an important part in crop pollination as well as making the honey that we all enjoy on our pancakes.

Insects have six legs, often used for more than just walking. A honeybee carries pollen in "baskets" on its rear legs. A grasshopper's back legs give him that tremendous spring forward, and some water insects have legs shaped like little oars.

Insects have antennae, just as a television set has, but these antennae are used for many purposes, varying in different kinds of insects. Sometimes they hear sound vibrations, or taste food, or help the insect to find its way in the dark.

Insects also have three major body parts—a head, a thorax (meaning chest), and an abdomen, each separated by a narrow waist. The legs and the wings are attached to the thorax.

Bugs, beetles, butterflies, moths, bees, hornets, flies, ants, grasshoppers, ladybirds, fireflies, dragonflies, waterskaters—they're all insects. A *bug* is a special kind, however. Bugs are those insects which have hollow needles that pierce plants and suck their sap, like the chinch bug, and squash bug.

Some insects are called *social* insects, because they work together and are dependent upon each other. Bees and ants are the best known. Many books have been written about the complex pattern of their lives, and scientists have spent years studying them. Here again, a counselor does not have to be an entomologist. He should, however, be able to arouse interest, and to encourage observation and study. The following brief bit of information about bees shows how readily available simple information is—and what a marvelous world of insects is around us.

### HONEYBEES

Professor von Frisch, an authority on bees, and author of *Bees, Their Vision, Chemical Senses and Language,* has found that bees can distinguish colors. They can see yellow, blue-green, blue, and ultra-violet the best. Red looks black to them.

He also has found that bees communicate with each other in a very complicated way, not through sounds, but through intricate dances! He has even been able to work out the "choreography" of the dances one bee uses to tell other bees that it has found a new food supply, where, and how far away.

If there are any flowering plants, cultivated or wild, in the day camp site, campers can watch honey bees busily engaged in going from flower to flower collecting pollen and nectar. Nectar is sweetened water. Children can taste it for themselves by sucking the end of a honeysuckle flower. When the bees store it in their sealed-off cells, this nectar is converted into honey, one of the few foods digestible without change in the human body.

A bee colony is like a city. It has a population of around 30,000 to 75,000 bees. It has streets and alleys. It has air conditioning— bees that fan constantly to keep the hive always at the same temperature. It has a sanitation department—bees that keep the hive clean. It has a standing army and air force—bees that guard the hive against intruders. It has nurseries—bees that nurse and feed the larvae. Every bee has its own job, and does it.

The queen is the largest bee, and there is only one to a hive. If another is allowed to grow, the hive divides; and the old queen goes to another colony with part of the bees. This happens when the hive is becoming too small for the number of bees in it.

The queen lays all the eggs—from 300 to 1,000 a day! The food that is fed to the larva determines the kind of bee it will develop —coarse food makes a worker, the finest food a queen. The drone, or male bee, is fed and taken care of. He does no work and he dies after mating with the queen. He is driven out of the hive at the end of a summer season.

Farmers raising vegetables, grain, or orchard fruit depend largely upon bees for the pollination of their crops. Many raise bees for this purpose; others *rent* bees during the flowering season.

A *hive* is the home of one colony of bees. An *apiary* is a collection of hives operated by a beekeeper for the honey, or for crop pollination.

Very often a nature museum or a country fair will have an exhibit showing a bee colony at work. Also, in most places a local beekeeper can be found. Such a person can be visited, or invited to camp to talk about his work or hobby.

Glassed-in hives that can be sealed in a window can be purchased and are not very expensive. These hives have an entrance spout on the outside of the window, so that the bees can come and go. The colony-life of the hive and the process of honey making can be watched through the glass walls of the hive. For day camps with indoor facilities, a "hobby hive" will give new meaning to bees and their importance to man. A source for such a hobby hive ("City of the Bees") is given in "Selected Resource References" in the rear of this book.

The life of the bees in a colony has so many aspects in common with human life, yet is so different, that it has fascinated people for thousands of years. Modern youngsters are no exception.

ANTS

Ants are amazing, social insects. Like bees, they have a queen, the only ant that lays all the eggs for the ant "nest." She stays *always* in the nest, where the others feed, and wash her, and carry away her eggs to the "nurseries." Ants divide up the work, just as bees do. Some stay with the eggs. Some go out searching for food. Some are fighters.

They perform amazing feats. Compare the size of an ant to the size of the anthill. Or the size of the ant to the length of the grass stalk it climbs over while it is carrying food or eggs to a new nest. Watch ants move a big, dead insect. Try to follow one ant. See if it will lead to its nest.

An ant nest is not hard to build. If space is available, it can be left at the day camp and observed throughout the season. (See Chapter 13, "Arts and Crafts" for instructions.)

BUTTERFLIES AND MOTHS

These are the most beautiful of the insects. Butterflies are daytime insects; moths mostly fly at night, so that most of the "flying flowers" seen by day campers are likely to be butterflies. A good way to tell the difference is to watch one land. If it keeps its wings high up in the air, it's a butterfly. If the wings droop like a tent, it's likely to be a moth. Moths usually have much thicker, hairier bodies. Butterflies are often brighter colored.

The butterfly has antennae that end in little knobs. Look for them. Moths have marvelous, fancy antennae that are feathery and very beautiful. Both have long, hollow tubes that are kept rolled up under their heads, but that can uncoil and reach deep down into a flower, so that the nectar can be sipped up.

If milkweed grows in or near the day camp site, the youngsters may see a beautiful black and orange butterfly. It is the Monarch. It is remarkable because it is one of several butterflies that migrate, like birds, in the fall. It leaves Canada and the northern states and goes to Florida or Mexico, and it goes in big flocks. In the spring, the Monarch returns. The female lays eggs on the leaves of a milkweed plant—nothing else will do. When the eggs hatch in a week or so, out comes a caterpillar with black, orange, and white rings about its body. It eats and eats and eats. Then in around two weeks it spins a sticky pad, attaches itself to it, sheds its skin, and becomes a *pupa*. Finally this case splits, and out comes a moist, funny-looking shape. In a few hours, though, the wings begin to open, and to move up and down, the butterfly begins to walk, then off it flies—a beautiful Monarch. *Use* the Monarch designs in arts and crafts. Examine one close-up. Note the "dust" from the wings. These are really tiny scales and are removed if the butterfly is handled carelessly. Admire the delicate beauty—and let it live.

SPIDERS AND INSECTS

Spiders are often grouped with insects, but they're *not*. Insects all have *six* legs. Spiders have eight. Insects have *three* body parts. Spiders have only *two*. Insects have wings. Spiders do not. *Both* belong to a big family of animals that wear their skeletons on the outside, and that have jointed legs. (Crabs, lobsters, centipedes, and shrimp also belong to this big family of creatures with outside skeletons and jointed legs.)

Almost every child has seen the web of the garden spider, especially visible and beautiful in the morning when dew is on it. Speculate on how much rope and how much space a person would need to have in order to build a similar structure.

Often, even in city parks and playgrounds, thin silk lines can be seen floating through the air. They are kites made by the spider. It spins a long thread and lets the wind blow it. When it's long enough for flying, the spider lets go from her leaf or twig, and swings out into the air at the bottom of the thread. They have been known to float for hundreds of miles.

Spiders cannot eat solid food. They paralyze their prey with their poison fangs, immobilize it by covering it with a silken thread, and then suck the victim dry.

Aside from the tarantula found in the South, which can give a very painful bite, the only spider poisonous to man is the black widow. It is a shiny, long-legged spider with a spot of orange or red, shaped like an hourglass, on its underside. The black widow is seldom found except in dark, hidden places that a camper is not likely to be in. The venom of other spiders is not strong. They destroy many flies, mosquitoes, and other insects. Even if you don't love them—let them be.

The daddy longlegs is a familiar and harmless creature, unlike a spider because it cannot make silk. Its legs are very long. Its knees are far above its body, so that the body is suspended fairly close to the ground. Look at one carefully. Watch how daintily it moves those thin legs. If it loses a leg it can grow another. Look at its head with a magnifying glass. Its eyes are up on a little platform, so that it can see all around. The daddy longlegs feed on aphids, those tiny green plant lice that can be found on the stems and leaves of plants, and which some ants protect because of the sweet honeydew they produce.

### Birds

As is true of trees and flowers, too much emphasis on identification of birds can be boring. When campers become interested in a bird, as in a new neighbor, they'll *want* to know its name. Arousing interest should come first. First of all, a bird is the *only* animal with feathers.

Every youngster in this space age is interested in flight. Aerodynamics may be a big word, but it is not a strange one to the modern child. It provides the best possible motivation for observing birds, watching their different kinds of flight, and figuring out *why*. Some birds soar, catching the air currents like gliders. Some, like the black-capped chickadee and the little goldfinch, fly in "scallops"—a wavy pattern. Some work hard at flying, flapping their wings constantly. Some move their wings, then coast.

What effect do different-shaped wing and tail feathers have on flight? Which act as landing flaps? Of what other uses are tail feathers to a bird? Many campers know the woodpecker. How does he use his tail feathers when he is eating suet at a feeding station or on a tree trunk?

Often a camper can find a wing feather in the woods or fields. If not, a chicken feather can be used to find out why something that looks so delicate, and that is so light, can take such hard use. A feather is a wonderful thing to see under a magnifying glass. Up the middle of it runs the *shaft*. It is hollow and rounded, but very tough. The side branches of the feather are called *barbs*, and these flat barbs make up what is called the *vane*. (Is there a connection here with "weathervane"?)

Each barb has many tiny hooks called *barbules* that hook over those of the next barb, almost on the principle of a zipper. So every barb is a light, delicate thing hooked together into a strong, fanlike whole. Pull one barb apart, and the vane will separate. When this happens to a bird, it "preens" its feathers—runs its bill over those barbs so that they hook together again.

Not all feather are flight feathers. What is *down?* a pinfeather? What is a plume? Campers who have had canaries or parakeets as pets know that birds *molt* or shed their feathers usually twice a year. This gives them a chance to replace feathers that might have become sticky, or ragged, or injured in some way, and thus be dangerous to flight.

How many campers have ever looked carefully at a bird's foot? How many toes does it have? Most birds have four toes, three forward, and one, the big toe, behind. What keeps birds from falling off their perch? The toes automatically lock when the body is lowered. It *can't* fall off!

Some birds, like the woodpeckers, have two toes forward and two toes back. Is that an advantage in clutching the trunk of a tree?

Birds have no teeth. Their beaks are used to tear, crush, seize the insects, seeds, or flesh upon which a species lives. The shape of the bill is one way to identify the type of bird. What sort of bill is needed to crack a seed? To dig a worm out of a tree, or an ant from its nest? To go deep into a flower, like the humming-bird? To tear the flesh of a mouse, like an owl? To eat a fish at one gulp, like a pelican?

What sort of food a bird eats is often a give-away to where it can be found. A seed eater like a sparrow will be where seeds are plentiful. A flesh eater, like the shrike, will be where mice and small game are abundant. Birds that eat insects and spiders, like the phoebe, usually perch on a tree limb or wire or fence and dart out to grab insects as they go by. Some, like the little chickadees, eat both seeds and insects, and so can be found where seeds or insects abound.

Which birds are most likely to migrate—the seed eaters or the insect eaters?

And so, the *silhouette* of a bird, the shape of its beak, the pattern of its flight, where it is found, and what it eats, all are clues as important as its color and markings in finding out its name. Its song, too, is an identification.

The birds along the shore of the ocean or lake are often more conspicuous than the forest and field birds in the summer. Why do so many of these birds have *webs* between their toes? Do gulls dive under the water? Watch and see. Why do ducks waddle? Does the fact that their legs are set far apart make them better swimmers? How does a gull crack the shell of a clam? What sort of beak does it have?

A few birds don't fly. The Australian kiwi is one of these. It *runs*. The penguin *swims*. Look at pictures of these. Why can't they fly?

Birds are important to man, not just for their beauty and their song. They destroy all sorts of harmful insects and rodents that are destructive to crops. Some provide feathers and food. Man in the past has destroyed some birds in such quantities that species like the passenger pigeon, the great auk, the Carolina parakeet, and the Labrador duck are now extinct. Some, like the whooping crane, are almost extinct.

Today, however, it is not the hunter but the bulldozer that is the big destroyer. Take away a bird's habitat and his food supply, and that species will eventually die out. Cutting down forests, draining swamps, and polluting the water with industrial waste are things that man is doing now without thinking of its consequences not only to the birds and other wildlife, but to himself as well.

When interest in birds has been aroused, trips to nature museums, museums of natural history, and zoos will be meaningful ways of providing "close-ups" for further observation and discussion.

## Mammals

Mammals include those animals which are warm-blooded, which breathe air, have a backbone and hair, and which give birth to their young. (The platypus and echnida lay eggs, and are strange exceptions to the rule.) Mammals usually have four feet and a tail. The feet may be flippers in the case of the whale. The tail may be almost or completely gone, as in bears and in humans.

Day campers are not likely to see many of the wild mammals. Some are nocturnal. Most are very shy. *Chipmunks* and *squirrels* become used to humans, however, and will come close for handouts of food. *Rabbits* can be glimpsed racing for cover. Sometimes a *woodchuck* will be seen sitting up eating the top of some plant, or sunning himself near his hole under a rock wall. *Field mice* and the pretty little *white-footed deer mouse* can be seen occasionally. The ridges of earth in the woods or field indicate the runs that *moles* have made in their search for earthworms, insect larvae, and edible roots.

Only one mammal can fly—the *bat*. It flies only at dusk or night in its search for insects. The bat is much maligned. It will *not* get in the hair. It does *not* carry bedbugs. (It has been reported that bats in certain areas have become rabid. If a bat attacks or bites anyone, especially in the daytime, it should be killed and tested for rabies. The victim should be treated medically—and fast. Such a case, however, is very unlikely.)

Campers may see a bat hanging upside down by its feet in some dark barn. They may see one flying rapidly but silently if they stay late some afternoon for a cook-out or overnight. Encour-

age them to study pictures of the bat and to read about its special "depth perception" like our sonar. Compare the picture of
a bat with that of one of the prehistoric flying monsters.

Every youngster has seen a *rabbit*, even if only as an Easter
bunny. Most nature museums and children's museums have rabbits that can be touched and observed. Should a rabbit be picked
up by its ears? How *should* it be picked up? How does a rabbit
signal danger? Who has seen a rabbit thump with its strong
back legs?

Their hiding places are called "forms." Can you guess why?
*Hares* and *jack rabbits* are larger than those we call rabbits, cot-
tontails, and bunnies, and they have longer ears and legs. They
can move very rapidly, and will race away from danger. A rabbit will usually try to hide.

What kind of teeth do rabbits have? Why? What do they eat?

The *squirrel* family includes not only the *gray, red,* and *fox
squirrels,* but *woodchucks, chipmunks, prairie dogs,* and *ground
squirrels.* How does a chipmunk carry its food? Does a squirrel
carry its food away like that? Watch and see. What kind of teeth
does the squirrel family have? They are mostly vegetarian. Does
that have anything to do with the shape of their teeth and jaws?

*Carnivorous* animals are those that eat the flesh of meat or
fish. Our two favorite pets, *cats* and *dogs,* are carnivorous. How
do they use their teeth? *Skunks* and *raccoons* are mostly nocturnal
and not likely to be seen by a day camper. *Foxes* are usually too
wary to show themselves.

Most animals, except pets and farm animals, avoid being seen
whenever possible. Day campers may see—and look for—*signs* of
them, such as tracks, droppings, holes, nests. Campers may find
the place under an evergreen tree where a deer spent the night,
or see its delicate hoofprints along a forest trail. The telltale signs
of life are everywhere; and sharp-eyed youngsters, if they try,
can find them.

A visit to a farm, a game preserve, a children's zoo—even a
really careful examination of a pet dog, cat, rabbit, or hamster—
can be used to find many things about animals. How many claws?
Do a dog's claws show in its footprints? a cat's? What sort of

footprint does a rabbit make? Do horses have eyelashes? What is a dewlap?

*Nature's signs are small and hidden. A child dashing from swimming pool to baseball diamond is not likely to see the squirrel flick behind the tree trunk, the partridge taking a dustbath in the road, the butterfly on the flower. He will miss the line of ants carrying their eggs to a new nest, and the spider-web stretched across the path.*

*When he learns to go slowly, to stand still, to look, to listen, to enjoy without touching, to look and leave, he'll begin to understand nature's signs. He should not be hurried, pressured, or bombarded with activities he can enjoy at home or on the playground. Time in day camp should be savored, not rushed through like commuters racing for a train.*

*Will the child become interested in, or impatient of, the world of nature? The day camp counselor is often the one who can cast the deciding vote.*

## Turtles

The history of the turtle goes back to the days of the dinosaur. It is a reptile with a shell, and with four legs. Those which live in the sea have legs that are flippers. They all have lungs, breathe air, but even those that spend most of their time on land can stay under water a long time. They have no teeth, but some, like the snapping turtle, can do damage with their horny jaws. All species lay their eggs on land, even the big sea turtles that are getting fewer and fewer in number as man has either killed them for food or invaded their habitats.

Turtles make interesting pets—if the owner will give them a cool, moist place to live, water to swim in, deep enough to submerge when eating because some won't eat except under water. They require feeding about twice a week—a bit of raw, ground meat, or fish, or worms, with a little green vegetable once in a while.

In some states it is against the law to keep native wild turtles in captivity. In any state, a wild turtle should be returned to his native habitat after a short visit for observation. Most turtles kept as captives in aquariums were bought from pet shops.

The shell of a turtle should *never* be painted. The paint keeps the shell from growing. If a turtle with a painted shell is bought, the paint should be scraped off carefully.

As swamps are drained, brush piles and fallen trees removed, fields cleared, and wild areas made into building lots, turtles, like birds, may eventually be killed off. What millions of years have not been able to do, man may do unknowingly in a short period of time.

### Lizards and Salamanders

These strange creatures go back into the world's past. They do not belong to the same family, although they're often confused.

The *lizard*, like the turtle, belongs to the *reptile* family. Unlike the snake, most lizards have ears, eyelids, non-expandable jaws and four legs, each of which has fine clawed toes. The lizard also has several rows of scales on its underside. A snake has no ears, no eyelids, highly expandable jaws and just one row of scales on its underside.

Lizards have teeth, used more for holding their prey of worms, snails, spiders, and other lizards than for chewing.

They are usually seen around old stone walls, brush piles, rocks, clearings. They can stand heat and they like a hot, sunny day and place. They keep under cover when it's cool or cloudy.

If a lizard has smooth, polished scales, it usually is a skink. If the lizard has spiny scales, it is usually either a fence or a horned lizard, and there's only one species that is horned. Any lizard seen in New England is likely to be the five-lined skink. Those found south of Pennsylvania are likely to be the broad-headed skink. The prairie states have the Great Plains skink, with diagonal markings. These are the most common.

The *salamander,* unlike the lizard but like the frogs and toads, belongs to the *amphibian* family. It lives the first phase of its life in the water and develops legs, like a frog.

Salamanders, whose early life is like the frog's, develop and *keep* their tails. They have a moist, smooth skin, only four toes, and those without claws. The eastern part of the United States has more salamanders than any other place in the world.

These amphibians avoid sunlight and heat. Their skin must have moisture. Some live in caves, in wells, in trees, on mountain cliffs. Most of them are nocturnal, and day campers may not get a chance to see them. They may find a shiny black salamander with broad white bands hiding under a log or rock. It is the marbled salamander. If the salamander is orange-red with red spots, and is on land, it is a newt. If the salamander is large, dark, and has yellow blotches, it is the tiger salamander.

One fascinating thing about lizards and salamanders is that if they lose a tail, another one will grow. In fact, a salamander can grow a new leg as well! Mud puppies and hellbenders are salamanders that live in the water.

Lizards and salamanders have a part to play in the balance of nature. They are shy, interesting, and useful. Look and let live.

## Frogs and Toads

Most youngsters, unless conditioned by adult reactions, enjoy finding and picking up frogs and toads. Many have brought strings or clusters of the eggs home in the spring, to watch the tiny black cell develop into a tadpole and then into a frog. Many youngsters, too, are unknowingly cruel in trying to make pets of these wild things without understanding very much about their life cycle and their requirements.

Frogs, toads, and salamanders all belong to a large animal family called *amphibians,* meaning "two lives." They are formed from cells that grow into tadpoles that have gills and live the first stage of their lives like fish in the water. The tadpole develops lungs and legs, and becomes land-living. Amphibians never lose their need for water, however. Their skin must stay moist. They return to the water for mating and egg laying, and many of them hibernate in the mud in the bottom of ponds.

Because of their sensitive skin, many stay close to water and wet places. That's where campers must go to find the big bull-frog, or the pretty green and leopard frogs, or the tiny "peepers." The wood frog and the toad are not quite so dependent on water. They can be found in moist woods, fields, and gardens.

Toads and frogs have no tails. They belong mostly to three big groups of amphibians—*toads, frogs,* and *tree toads.* The tree toads are the "peepers" of early spring. Their feet have little disks that cling by suction to reeds, tree trunks, or twigs.

*Toads* are the members of the amphibians most likely to be seen by the campers, although they *might* get a glimpse of a bullfrog on a lily pad, or see a green frog jump into the pond. Toads have bumpy, warty skins—which accounts for the super-stition that they cause warts. *They don't.* Those warts cover glands that secrete a fluid which is poisonous or annoying to an animal but which does no harm to humans.

A toad can be adopted as a pet *if* the owner is willing to take the time and trouble to supply it with a vast number of *live* insects. A toad must fill its stomach four times a day—so it's best to watch it, pick it up carefully, study it—but let it live in its own habitat. Toads burrow into the ground during the heat of the day, to keep moist. Look for them in shady places, early in the morning, or later in the afternoon.

Toads are a gardener's best friend because they eat such pests as flies, beetles, caterpillars, and cutworms. The tongues of toads and frogs are remarkable. They have rough, sticky tips, and are fastened near the *front* of the mouth, instead of at the back where the tongues of most animals including humans are fastened. Be-cause of this, the tongue can be flicked far ahead, to catch the unwary insect and flop it back into his mouth. Toads will eat something *only* when it is moving—another reason why it's best not to take them home for pets. Feeding them can be a real chore.

In the spring, toads lay their eggs in long strings of jelly. The bullfrog, leopard frog, and green frog lay theirs in large masses of jelly. The little "peeper" eggs are laid singly. Remind campers that when they find such egg masses, they must take only a few, and keep them in *pond*, not *tap*, water to watch the evolution. The pond water must have growing water plants in it to supply food for the tadpoles, and when the forelegs appear, the tadpole should be transferred to a shallow aquarium with a shore accessible to it, or taken back to the edge of the pool and liberated. They belong to two worlds—the world of water and the world of land. Interfere with their life cycle, and they will die.

## The Seashore

A day camp on, near, or with access to, a beach can have nature programs centered around the plant and animal life of the sea. Here again the counselor need not be an expert, but should possess curiosity and wonder. He should also take *time* to look, touch, question, and seek the answers.

Aside from swimming and playing in the water, the most popular beach activity is looking for shells and collecting them. Shells are the skeletons of mollusks. Inside the shell, the living animal has no head, trunk, or legs. It does have a mouth, a stomach, a simple nervous system, a heart, and muscles. Those with one shell, like snails, are called *univalves*. Those with two shells that open and close, like oysters and clams, are called *bivalves*. The seashore at low tide is the best place to find shells. Smart day campers will find that *digging* is a good way to find shells they might miss otherwise.

Those who have the collecting instinct should be encouraged to find, discard, find and discard again, replacing chipped or scarred shells with better ones. Shallow boxes lined with cotton make good and safe exhibit cases. Each shell should be labeled.

Collecting one variety of shell, from the tiniest form to the adult, largest stage, is an interesting hobby. Some hobbyists collect only univalves; some only bivalves. Learning the *names* of shells is not difficult. Many are descriptive—baby's ear, cup-and-saucer, dove, angel wing. Many books have wonderful color prints of the different shells, making it easy to identify them.

The pretty and interesting spiral shells are the skeletons of various sea snails. Some are *limpets*—small, conical shells like little caps, spotted with brown, green, and white. *Boat shells* are fun to find. They are dull white, and there's a little seat running across the inside, just like the seat in a toy boat. *Oyster drills* are about an inch long, and sharply pointed, like a drill. *Periwinkle shells* are often found in piles. They're about a half-inch in size, and dark, sometimes bluish-black, or greenish-black. The *whelks* are large snails. The big, curved shell that children hold to their ears to "hear the sea" is a whelk shell. Whelks range from a few inches to eight or nine inches long. *Moon shells* are pretty, rounded, plump shells, smooth, gray or brown. The snail shells are univalved.

The bivalves have two shells (called valves) hinged together by one or two very strong muscles. They are mostly vegetarians, extracting food in tiny particles from the sea water. The *hardshell clam* is the one made famous by New England clambakes. Their shells are white or grayish blue, usually oval or round. Those shells, bluish on the outside, white inside, found all along the beaches are the common *mussel* shells. *Scallops* have pretty, flattened shells, quite circular, and with a projection on each side of the hinge. There are many varieties in a wide range of colors. *Cockle shells* have wavy edges, and are minus the projection the scallop has at its hinge. The pretty little shells around an inch long, and with a hole in near the top of one of the valves is the *jingle shell*—and youngsters love to string them into necklaces.

The two valves of the *oyster* are always different in size. The *inside* is often very lovely in its iridescent coloring. The outside is likely to be ugly.

If there's a tidal pool on the beach, the campers can watch other marine life—the sea anemone that looks like a flower and is an animal, sea urchins that look like pincushions, living limpets on the bottom of the pool, perhaps a starfish.

*Seaweed* can be found in shallow waters, tidal pools, and tossed up upon the beach after a storm. *Sea lettuce* is often to be found, looking like a lettuce leaf, from an inch to several feet in length. *Ribbonweed* looks ugly on land, but is graceful in the water. It waves like ribbons, but is rounded, like tubes. *Silkweed* or *mermaid's tresses* is the third green seaweed. As its name describes, it waves in the water like green hair. These seaweed get the sun's rays, and are green.

The brown seaweed seen on beaches comes from farther out and deeper, where it never gets enough light to be green. The kind with bladders along the outside are called—guess what?—*bladderwrack*. They'll pop when squeezed or stepped on.

*Kelp* is the brown, tough, blade-like, smooth plant that grows sometimes ten feet long—often found washed up by a storm.

Collecting specimens of seaweed is an interesting activity. They should be collected in a bucket of seawater, washed thoroughly to get rid of all sand and other debris. Then they should be floated in shallow water so as to get them spread out into thin natural shape. Slip a piece of heavy paper under the specimen and lift it carefully out of the water, keeping the plant in its same position. It is so gelatinous that it will stick to the paper. Press and dry it between blotting paper and soft cloth like cheesecloth. When dry, mount it. It will last for years. Preparing such specimens is a good craft project.

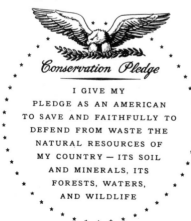

*Conservation Pledge*

I GIVE MY
PLEDGE AS AN AMERICAN
TO SAVE AND FAITHFULLY TO
DEFEND FROM WASTE THE
NATURAL RESOURCES OF
MY COUNTRY — ITS SOIL
AND MINERALS, ITS
FORESTS, WATERS,
AND WILDLIFE

CHAPTER **4:**

# FIREMAKING
# AND COOKING

The average child of day camp age has had few if any personal experiences with fire, firemaking, or outdoor cooking. These activities, because of their danger elements, are among the most closely guarded of all adult activities, and for that very reason are especially attractive to youngsters. Mothers say, "No! Don't touch!" whenever children reach for a match, a stove burner, or a cooking pan. Fathers work getting fires started in outdoor grills and fireplaces while the children stand around in an admiring and envious circle.

The attraction of the forbidden, the fun of outdoor eating, and the camaraderie of the fireside circle place firemaking and outdoor cooking high in camper popularity.

## FIRE AND FIREMAKING

Fire, water, earth, and air—these are the four elements that children delight in, and that are necessary for our life. In the area of firemaking and cooking, these elements are all present. Perhaps that is the basis of the fascination that fire has for everyone, from the early caveman down to the most sophisticated modern man.

Some day camps provide excellent opportunities for firemaking and cooking. Others must use outdoor fireplaces provided in a park or on a playground. Still others have no facilities for firemaking and outdoor cooking. Since these are two of the fundamental campcraft skills, every effort should be made to include them in the activity program. This may mean getting special permission, or special permits, clearing with sponsoring agencies, parents, and the local fire department, but specific and well-made plans can usually get such approval.

Day camps using public facilities, such as city parks and playgrounds, can improvise adequate fireplaces or provide mobile grills. Bricks, concrete blocks, cinder blocks, or stones can be brought in and arranged as a safety circle or piled up to make sides for a grill. Any metal wheelbarrow makes an excellent fire site, if the bottom is covered with about four inches of sand. A sandpile can be set aside as a fire site. A cement walk, or a corner of a multiple-use concrete court, provides a safe place for a fire. Stoves and reflector ovens can be improvised easily. Instructions are given later in this chapter.

When facilities are limited, the various units in the day camp must take turns, or be assigned specific days, for firemaking and cooking. Every age group should be included.

Many children have had no experience with fire beyond lighting Dad's cigarette. Many have had no experience with outdoor fires and cooking except perhaps on charcoal or electric grills, and even this experience is usually limited to watching. Most city youngsters know practically nothing about trees, or kinds of wood and their properties, let alone being able to identify them in a woodlot or a woodpile.

Firemaking as a campcraft skill cannot be held back and made dependent upon tree identification. Joseph Lee, the godfather of playgrounds, used to say that the right time to learn how to dance was whatever age you happened to be. So it is with fire. The right time to make a fire is when you *need* a fire, whether you know the difference between pine and oak, birch and eucalyptus, or not.

The wonderful thing about firemaking is that it serves as one of the most potent motivations for *learning* about the various kinds of woods, where they come from, what they are good for.

It also serves as a motivation for several aspects of conservation. Green wood doesn't burn—therefore a sapling should not be cut down for firewood. If wood crumbles, it's rotten—and rotten wood doesn't burn, so leave it on the forest floor. Limbs on the ground are likely to be damp. They'll dry out for future use if stacked, but it's best to look for dead limbs still on the trees for immediate use. A fire that's too big makes too much heat to cook over—so save the fuel and make a *small* fire. A tree that took twenty years to grow can be killed in twenty minutes by a fire too close to its trunk or roots, so location of the fire is important.

So it goes. More than most campcraft skills, firemaking and cooking are wonderful *teaching* situations, because the youngsters not only are eager to learn—they are also eager to succeed because success brings food!

Day camp counselors sometimes think that firemaking is too dangerous an activity for young children. If a child is too young for one of the most important (if not the most important) campcraft skill, then he is too young for day camping, and the activity program should be called a play program, or some other term. It will not be day camping, and it will not be a day camp.

All activities in a day camp are conducted under supervision. Firemaking is no exception. A counselor should *always* be present during firemaking and cooking. The steps should be taught carefully and practiced with many "dry runs" before a match is lighted. Equipment for handling a fire if it should get out of hand, and procedures for getting help, should be familiar to everyone in camp.

All camp skills that involve fire should emphasize that fire is a friend when it is controlled; a terrible enemy when not controlled. It is useful when managed properly; destructive when it gets out of hand. It is not a plaything. It should always be treated with respect.

From the very beginning, safety rules should be taught, illustrated, and emphasized:

- NEVER play with fire. It is not a plaything.
- NEVER play with matches. *They* are not playthings.
- NEVER leave a fire unguarded.
- NEVER build a fire near the trunk, roots, or limbs of a tree.
- ALWAYS clear a wide area before building a fire.
- ALWAYS enclose a fire in some way—with stones, bricks, a trench, or a rim of sand.
- ALWAYS have fire-fighting material around—a pail of water, broom, sand, shovel.

- Build SMALL fires. A big bonfire or ceremonial fire is needed only on very special occasions—very seldom if at all in a day camp program.
- ALWAYS make *sure* a fire is really out before leaving it. Throw soil on it, throw water on it, and feel the bed of ashes with your hands to make positive there are no live ashes or coals. Don't rush this. Many forest fires start from fires that campers *thought* were out.

Fires, even small, carefully watched ones, *can* escape. A sudden spark, a sudden breeze—and dry leaves and grass outside the fire area can catch fire. Safety rules should be obeyed in such cases:

- If the fire is very small, and equipment is on hand for fighting it, get busy. Smother it with wet burlap bags. Beat it with brooms. Cover it with sand. Confine it in one area by digging a trench around it. If there's the slightest doubt about controlling it, send for help.
- Fight the fire face to face. In other words, always have the wind in your face. Otherwise, you just help spread it.
- If the fire gets out of hand, or if you run across a big fire in the area, send someone to telephone the nearest fire warden or fire department.
- Get the youngsters out of the area. Teen-agers can be useful, but small children should be taken at once to a safe area or home.
- If, by any chance, a youngster should catch his clothes on fire, put him on the ground, roll him, and smother the flames with a blanket, poncho, coat—anything. Such accidents are very rare, especially since children's play clothing has become so much more utilitarian or abbreviated. Shorts and blue jeans are much safer than the wide skirts of yesterday.

## Building the Fire

Once the site has been selected or found, and the area enclosed for safety, building the fire can begin. Fire requires two things to burn—fuel and air. The proper arrangement of the fuel will provide air space, so that flames can go up.

A good firemaker uses three types of material—tinder, kindling, and fuel.

- *Tinder* is dry material no thicker than a match stick. It can be a fuzz stick, shavings, tiny pieces of bark, small dry twigs. Dry grass isn't much help.
- *Kindling* is wood from matchstick-size up to the thickness of a thumb, and from a few inches to a foot long. It should be so dry it will snap when broken.
- *Fuel* is the real food for the fire. It can be logs split or unsplit, or charcoal, coal, peat, but for camping it is almost always wood, sometimes hard wood, sometimes soft wood. Hard wood comes from trees that take a long time to grow, such as oak, maple, and eucalyptus. Soft wood trees, such as pine, cedar, hemlock, white birch, grow rapidly.

    The hard woods make long-lasting coals; the soft woods burn fast to make a quick, hot fire. Both are useful. Both, to be good firemakers, should be cured and dry. (Sumac is one of the few woods that will burn easily when green, but it has little value in cooking.)

The trick, in firemaking, is to get a good start. Anyone can keep a fire going once there is a good bed of coals! Starting it, however, takes care and patience. Take it step by step.

- Place a handful of tinder within a little enclosure of twigs. The twigs are used mostly to support the kindling just at first, so that it doesn't fall into and smother the lighted tinder. They also support the tinder. It should be loose, but each bit of it should touch some other piece. Leave a little "cave" for air. That's where you stick the lighted match. Use *plenty* of tinder.
- The tinder will usually flare up, and then comes the step that is the hardest, but the most fun. Piece by piece, delicately, the kindling should be added, not too fast, not too slow. Always add it so that air can get to the fire. Feed the fire bit by bit, small kindling first, until there's a good, brisk

fire, with some coals, and the fire is burning thumb-size kindling. Use plenty of kindling, too.

- The last step is adding the fuel, slowly as needed, arranging it for the kind of fire required for the type of cooking being planned.

## Open Fires for Cooking

For day camp use, two major types of cooking fires are sufficient. They form the basis of all other fires.

### THE TEPEE FIRE

The tepee fire, so called because its shape is like an Indian wigwam or tepee, is built after the foundation fire is burning well, by placing the wood into a leaning, cone shape, keeping it tall and narrow. The tepee fire, since flames and heat go upward, gives a quick, hot heat useful for boiling.

### THE CRISSCROSS FIRE

The crisscross fire will burn a long time and make a fine bed of coals. After a good foundation fire has been built, wood is added piece by piece, building up from larger wood in the bottom layers to smaller wood at the top. This sort of fire needs air from below, and the opening should face the breeze. It is excellent for most types of cooking.

When placed against a rock, or other type of reflector, this fire is used for baking in a reflector oven. (The usual fireplace fire, where andirons take the place of foundation logs, is a slight variation of the reflector fire. The backlog and the back of the chimney make the reflector that throws the heat out into the room.)

The tepee and the crisscross fire can be built in an open, cleared area; in an outdoor fireplace; in an indoor fireplace; even in a charcoal grill, in a wheelbarrow with a bed of sand, or in other improvised areas. They are fun to build, pretty to look at, useful to cook with—and wasteful of wood! For quick results, using far less fuel, tin can cooking is often used. Both types are important to know.

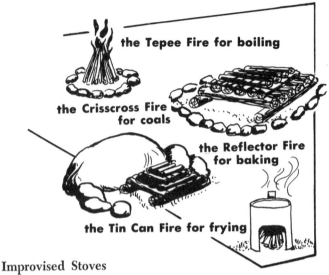

the Tepee Fire for boiling

the Crisscross Fire for coals

the Reflector Fire for baking

the Tin Can Fire for frying

## Improvised Stoves

Stoves are merely devices for containing fire and conserving its heat. They may be improvised, for outdoor cooking, out of tin cans from one-pound coffee-can size to big oil drums, or other metal containers. (Tin is a misnomer. What are called tin cans are really steel.) Making them into stoves is an excellent camp-craft. *Using* them is another campcraft skill. The following are some of the easiest to make and to use.

Tin Can Stove

### TIN CAN STOVE

This is fairly good to cook on, simple to make, and it requires very little fuel; in fact, the fire must be kept small, or the stove will get red hot.

This stove is made by turning a five-gallon oil or other type can upside down, and cutting a 4-inch opening on one side at the bottom. This opening is for feeding the wood into the fire inside the can. At the top of the can, on the opposite side of the bottom opening, cut a 2-inch opening for a chimney. Fry food directly on top of the can, or use a pan.

*Variation:* A five-gallon can with straight sides will give a larger cooking area and can be used for pancakes, toast, coffee, hamburgers, and so on. Set the can on its side. Cut a 4-inch opening at the bottom for fuel and air, and several vents at the top of the other end for a chimney. (Triangular can opener makes good air holes.)

### TWO-STORY TIN STOVE

This stove is so simple, and so small, that each camper should make and use his own. It requires two coffee cans (or cans similar in shape), a two-pound can for the bottom of the stove, a one-pound can for the top.

Turn the large can upside down, cut a door at the bottom, about 4 inches long and 3 inches high—or just big enough so that small pieces of wood can be added to the fire inside. Using a triangular can opener, cut vents all around the top of this bottom can, for the heat to go through.

Two-Story Tin Can Stove

With an icepick, make holes around the top rim of the big can and the bottom rim of the top can, and wire the two cans together. With the can opener, cut a row of triangular vents along the top of the smaller can, on the side opposite the lower can's fuel hole. These will serve as a chimney.

When using tin can stoves, the fuel opening should face the breeze, and the fire should be kept small. The stoves should be set on a layer of sand, or rock, or soft earth, and the area around them should be kept clear.

They require constant feeding. One person should feed the fire while another cooks. The little stoves get very hot, so gloves and pot holders should be available to prevent burned fingers.

### REFLECTOR OVEN

A very efficient reflector oven can be improvised from a five- or ten-gallon tin can. Cut the can in half diagonally, leaving the bottom in one piece and enough metal at the top to curl over for a safe edge. String wires back and forth through holes bored diagonally from the center of each side to the bottom edge. These wires make a grill shelf.

Prop the oven against a log or rock so that the shelf is level. Set the oven so that it faces the fire, moving it nearer for fast cooking, farther back for slow cooking.

### DISHPAN OVEN

A new idea from the West Coast, and an easy one. Let a good fire die down to hot coals. Scoop out a hollow in the coal bed, and set an inverted pie plate in the hollow. Put the food to be baked on the plate. Cover the plate with an inverted, metal dishpan, and heap the hot coals around and over the dishpan. Let the food cook there until done.

### SOLAR GRILL

This is a new idea, and manufactured solar stoves of aluminum may now be bought. To make a solar grill and try it out

is a fine cooking experiment. It may not work in all areas. It works best and fastest, of course, in hot, dry areas—and it works *only* when the sun is shining. But try it!

Cut a triangle of flexible cardboard, and cover it *very* smoothly with aluminum foil.

Bend the triangle carefully into a smooth cone. Stick a hot dog on a wire, or thin stick, run the wire or stick through the bottom of the cone, and into the ground, pointed in such a way that the cone points directly into the sun. If the sun's rays are strong enough in your area, the hot dog will begin to ooze its fat, and finally will cook through.

Use this project, too, in other campcraft areas, to illustrate scientific principles of heat and of the power of the sun, leading into discussions of the effect of sunlight on our world.

### Matches

Matches deserve a special comment. They have a fascination for some youngsters, probably because their use has always been forbidden. Also, small hands often have not learned to handle matches. The children should be taught how to strike a match properly, how to hold it so that it will burn, and how to put it out.

Wooden matches, of the large, kitchen type, are best to use in teaching. The counselor should demonstrate how to strike the match *away* from the body—and explain why. He should explain that a flame goes upward, so that the match should be slanted just enough to catch fire from the flame, but not enough to burn the fingers. He should demonstrate how to insert the lighted match carefully into the tinder in starting the fire. Once the youngsters understand how to strike and hold a match, the smaller box variety can be used also.

It is a good idea, too, to teach how to strike a match from a matchbook—tearing it off, *closing the book,* and then striking the match away from the body. Book matches absorb moisture easily, and are not suitable for efficient camp use. However, since they are so prevalent, and so familiar to youngsters, their proper use should be included.

One safety measure should be emphasized. NEVER throw a match away until the head is cold to the touch, and until the match has been broken in half.

## OUTDOOR COOKING

Some day camps serve a well-balanced meal prepared by trained kitchen workers. In other day camps, youngsters bring their own lunches, and are served milk and fruit juices. Regardless of the official policy, outdoor cooking is the logical follow-up of learning the basic skills in firemaking. Failure to provide opportunities for both will result in an incomplete program.

Outdoor cooking, in a day camp, can range from the most simple, such as toasting bread, to the elaborate, such as the pit cooking used in clambakes, depending upon the ages of the campers, their previous experience, and the fire and cooking facilities available. Any day camp program, however, can provide experiences in several types of cooking, including hot ash and hot rock cooking, stick cooking, skewer cooking, tin can cooking, reflector oven cooking, and foil cooking. The use of prepared mixes makes cookie and pancake making simple.

A point to remember is that the younger the child, the quicker he expects results. The very young ones will enjoy toasting food, but usually they cook it too fast, too near the coals. Foil cooking is too slow for them, and reflector-oven baking, skewer cooking, one-pot meals, and the like are too difficult. For these, the youngsters can help with the preparation, but can go off to storytelling or some other activity to take up that long hour of waiting. Or their meal can be supplemented by one cooked-over-the-fire item—perhaps a special dessert like "s'mores." Don't underestimate children's ability to learn, however. Restrictions of opportunities should be on a safety basis only.

Foil can be used to eliminate many pots and pans. It provides good individual servings when items like thinly sliced potatoes, onions, or meat are wrapped up securely in foil folded the way a druggist folds his paper, and allowed to cook slowly in ashes, or along the edge of the fire grill. Foil saves charred outsides, or food full of ashes or soot. It is not easy for youngsters to handle, however, so provide practice in folding and twisting. Also, provide tongs or gloves, or other means of handling and opening the hot foil to prevent blistered fingers. And provide a litterbag so that the foil can be carried away for disposal. It does not burn and it should not be buried.

## Recipes

The recipes that follow are only a few of the many ways of cooking different kinds of food outdoors. These are simple recipes, particularly suitable for youngsters in day camp programs, when time is much more of a factor than in the resident camp. Learning to build the fires necessary for their cooking, to prepare these foods, and to clean up afterward are big steps in campcraft. When day campers become as skilled as this, they are well prepared for added enjoyment of resident or family camping.

### ANGELS ON HORSEBACK

An old camp favorite. Cut American cheese into cubes about twice as large as a pat of butter. Cut a slice of bacon in half, and roll each piece around the cheese, one piece in each direction, so that the cheese is completely covered. Fasten the bacon with toothpicks. Put on a toasting fork or a stick and broil over coals until the bacon is crisp. Serve on a toasted bun.

### BREAD STICKS

Youngsters love them. Use a biscuit mix, and cut down on the milk or water, so that the dough is fairly stiff. Roll into long strips about a half-inch thick. Wrap a strip spiral-fashion around a straight green stick about the thickness of a thumb, after flouring it to prevent the dough from sticking. Leave a small space between each spiral, so that the heat can get to the sides of the spiral. Press the ends of the dough strip against the stick to hold the strip in place.

Hold the stick over hot coals, turning frequently until evenly brown. Or press the end of the stick into the ground at an angle that lets the heat reach the dough evenly.

*Variation—and fun to use:* Press the dough around the end of a thicker floured stick from which the bark has been removed. Then cook as above—and stuff the "cup" made by the stick with jelly, sausage, egg, or some other filling.

EGGS IN A FRAME

Tear a hole in a piece of bread and put the slice on a lightly greased pan or griddle. Break an egg into the hole. Fry until the egg is the right consistency, then turn bread and egg over and cook the other side.

ROAST POTATOES

Roasting potatoes, using medium-size ones, usually takes about an hour, so allow plenty of time. After scrubbing them well, place them in the hot coals and cover them over with the embers. If foil-wrapped, they'll cook faster, and won't get quite so charred.

If time is a problem, boil the potatoes first—or bring them partially boiled from home. Roasting will give them that good roast-potato flavor.

ROASTING CORN

Corn-on-the-cob is a real American dish. (Europeans don't grow maize, our kind of "roasting ear" corn. Their corn is what we call "field corn.")

Pull the shucks back from the ears and remove the silk. Then cover the ear with the shucks, and soak in cold water for about half an hour. Roast it over low coals, on a low grill, turning it often. It will take a half to three-quarters of an hour.

An easier, more modern way is to shuck the corn, remove the silk, spread the ear with butter, salt and pepper it, and wrap it in foil, twisting the ends. Then put it on top of a grill, over coals, turning it frequently. It will be all ready to eat in about fifteen minutes if it has been in the center of the grill, half an hour if it has cooked more slowly around the grill's edge.

DOG-WITH-A-STICK-IN-HIS-MOUTH

Much better than the toasted hot dog! Split a frankfurter half-way through, lengthwise, leaving the ends closed. Put a long strip of American cheese inside the split. Tie the frankfurter together by wrapping it diagonally in a slice of bacon, completely covering the cheese, and fastening the ends with toothpicks. Cook on a stick, or on a grill, over hot coals, until the bacon is crisp and the frankfurter is hot all the way through. Serve on split, toasted buns.

Try a slice of dill pickle instead of the cheese, too.

#### BEAN POT

A one-dish meal—and *good!* For four servings, use 6 frankfurters or sausages, 2 cups of cooked corn kernels, 4 cups of baked beans, and a medium-size onion, chopped fine. Cut the franks or sausages into small pieces and fry with the onion until brown. Pour off excess fat. Add the corn and beans. If too thick, add a bit of water to prevent sticking. Season to taste, and add ketchup if desired. Serve hot.

#### KABOBS

An outdoor favorite. Provide cubes of meat, fruits, and vegetables, to suit individual tastes. Such foods as small cubes of beef, lamb, or ham, slices of onions, tomatoes, green peppers, apples, bacon, pineapple, cheese, are often used. All should be sliced or cubed so that they will stay on a stick or metal spit. Alternate the slices on the stick, leaving a little room between to allow for heat penetration. Cook slowly over hot coals, turning frequently. Baste with barbecue sauce if desired. When done, push off onto a plate and serve with a toasted roll.

#### S'MORES

A special camp dessert. Toast a marshmallow slowly until it is big and brown, and put it on a soda or graham cracker. Cover it with a piece of milk chocolate, add a top cracker, and squeeze gently.

#### BAKED BANANAS

Easy! Just wrap a banana, skin and all, in foil, and put it in the hot ashes for about ten minutes.

BAKED APPLES

Core each apple, but don't cut through the bottom. Pare about an inch down from the top, but leave the rest of the peel. Fill the hole with brown sugar or honey, add a dash of cinnamon and a small dab of butter. Set each apple in the middle of a square of foil, bring the foil up over the apple and twist lightly. Bake in reflector oven, or on edge of grill, or in bed of coals. Takes from a half-hour to an hour, depending upon the size of the apple and the degree of heat.

CLEANING UP

Camp chores should be rotated fairly, and made so much a part of the program that they are accepted cheerfully. In fact, it is often through working together at a common task that friendships are built up between campers, and understanding between camper and counselor.

If the sides and bottoms of pans are rubbed with yellow soap before placing over a fire, the soot will come off easily when they are washed.

If food has stuck, soak the pan in cold water before washing. Scouring a pan with sand is a great novelty to city children.

DISPOSAL OF GARBAGE AND LITTER

A good camper always leaves a camp site better than he found it. Litterbags can be made as a day camp project, used on the bus and in camp, and extra ones made to take home for the family car. All candy and chewing gum papers, paper handkerchiefs, napkins, ice cream cone left-overs, lollipop sticks, and things of that sort should be put in the litterbag, *never* thrown out of a bus or car window, or left at the camp site.

Garbage that is dry can be burned in the fire after a meal. If it is "wet," made of things like lettuce leaves, fruit peeling, soggy napkins, it can be dried out over the fire and *then* burned, or put in a waterproof container for later disposal.

All tin cans and foil should be flattened, and taken home. They don't burn, and they don't disintegrate when buried; and so they interfere with plant growth. Glass bottles and jars used in wilderness camping are often buried in a deep, narrow hole after being broken first—but breaking glass can be dangerous. Better take them home, too. Day camp sites are not wilderness areas.

Many day camps provide covered garbage cans for wet garbage, cans, and bottles, and open litter baskets for discarded papers. Train campers to use them. Explain what happens to this refuse, and let the disposal of it be a part of camp chores.

Any chore is less onerous if it makes sense. Discuss the *science* of fire. What happens when something burns? Which burns faster, a crumpled sheet of newspaper, or a folded sheet? Why? What is charcoal? Why does the wood of an open fire burn up into ash, and not into the pieces of charcoal used in cooking, and in drawing? What different ways are best to put out different kinds of fires? When is water best? What is best to put out a grease fire? If an electric wire burns, how should it be put out? Often a local or nearby fire department will be glad to demonstrate.

CHAPTER **5:**

# KNOTS AND
# LASHING

Inexperienced counselors sometimes feel incapable of teaching this campcraft skill. Actually, it has a built-in motivation—*need*.

Rope is useful. It is one of the best friends of campers. It holds down a tent; hoists food out of the way of animals; holds poles together for tripods, beds, and other outdoor furniture; moors boats and canoes; hoists flags and sails; rescues a swimmer or a mountain climber. Little girls jump it; little boys make lassoes out of it; both climb it and swing from it.

## KNOTS

Knotting is a skill that camper and counselor can learn *together*, if the latter doesn't know it. Its requirements are few:

- A *piece of rope* long enough and thick enough to handle easily and to see the steps used in making the knot. From four to six feet is a good length. The diameter of the rope should be ¼ to ½ inch, so that the shape of the knot can be seen. Clothesline will do, because it's smooth and flexible, but a heavier, laid rope of hemp, sisal, jute, or cotton is better. Don't use string or twine. Each person should have his own rope for use and practice.

- *Instructions, either visual or oral*—or both. "A picture is worth a thousand words" is an old Chinese axiom. A *knot board,* on which samples of knots are displayed is even more helpful.

- *Practice and more practice,* until the fingers acquire a "memory" independent of sight. Practice should be realistic, too. If a knot is to be used to tie a rope to a post, practice with a post, for example. Teach knots for their *use,* not just for skill in tying.

There are two kinds of rope, *laid* and *braided.* Laid rope is made of hemp, sisal, jute, or cotton, twisted into *yarn.* Two or more yarns are twisted into *strands,* and several strands are "laid" together to form rope. Most ropes used in pioneer and marine work are laid ropes.

A braided rope is made of strands of cotton, linen, or other material, interwoven into a complicated pattern. Clotheslines and sash cords are usually braided. Braided ropes are soft and flexible. They are often used for life lines and lariats.

Like tents and like flags, ropes have their own language: "laid" and "braided" are examples. The "lay" of a rope is the direction in which the strands are twisted. Most rope is "right-laid." Hold a piece of rope in front of you, vertically. If the strands spiral upward to right, it's right-laid. "Ply" indicates the number of strands. Standard rope is three-ply.

In learning how to make the different knots, it is important to know and to use the correct terms:

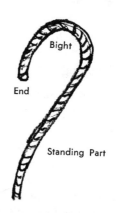

- The *end* is the end of the rope with which you are working when you tie a knot.
- The *standing part* is the inactive length of the rope. (It is helpful if this is kept spread out away from the "end.")
- The *bight* is the central part of the rope between the working end and the standing part.

In directions for making a knot, several terms are important to know and recognize:

- An *overhand loop* is made by crossing the end *over* the standing part.
- An *underhand loop* is made by crossing the end *under* the standing part.

OVERHAND
LOOP

UNDERHAND
LOOP

A TURN

A ROUND
TURN

- A *turn* is taken by looping the rope around an object such as a post, or even another section of itself.
- A *round turn* is taken by looping the rope *twice* around an object.
- *Over-and-under* sequence. When two sections of rope cross each other, one must go *over* and the other *under*. The right sequence *has* to be followed, or else the knot will not be the right one—or even a knot.
- *Drawing up* means tightening the knot, *slowly and evenly,* once it has been made, to make sure that it keeps its proper shape.
- *Whipping* is a method of binding the ends of a rope so that it won't unravel. A good rope is worthy of good care.
- *Splicing* is a way of joining two ropes, or ends of a rope without making a knot. Splices can be used to make one smooth rope or to make a rope grommet (a good way to make your own quoits).

### Whipping a Rope

Before using his rope for knots, each camper should protect it by whipping the ends so that they won't unravel. A three-foot length of strong twine, cotton fishline, or marline is enough for a rope ½ inch in diameter.

Place the end of the twine at the end of the rope, and lay a loop of the twine along the rope. (Sketch 3a)

Wind the twine tightly around both loop and rope, binding them together. Wind to a distance about equal to the diameter of the rope. Put the winding end B through the loop. (Sketch 3b)

Pull the other end, A, until the loop is drawn out of sight. Then cut both ends of the twine short to make a neat finish with no ends visible. (Sketch 3c)

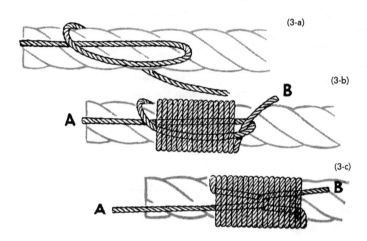

Little girls can make decorative handles for jump rope by using bright-colored cord and making a smooth lashing long enough to hold comfortably.

## Which Knot to Tie?

Knots are designed for special uses. There are many different kinds of knots from which to choose the right knot for the right job. Learn when to use which, and why.

Overhand Knot (4-a)

Figure Eight Knot (4-b)

### STOPPER KNOTS

Stopper knots keep a rope end from slipping through a hole or a pulley, or through a loop of another knot. (Lazy people sometimes tie them in the ends of ropes, instead of whipping the end to keep it from raveling.)

The easiest is the *overhand knot,* usually used with small cord or twine. TO TIE: Make an *overhand* loop, pass the end *under* and up *through* the loop. Draw tight. (See No. 4a)

The *figure eight* is stronger than the overhand knot and easier to untie. TO TIE: Make an *underhand* loop. Bring the end around and *over* the standing part. Pass the end *under* and then up through the loop. Draw tight. (See No. 4b)

Square Knot (5)

### BINDING KNOTS

Binding knots tie one or more objects together.

The most often used is the *square knot or reef knot.* It's the popular knot for bandages and for bundles. It's used at sea for reefing and furling sails. It is *not* a good way to tie two ropes together because it loosens when either end is given a jerk. (See No. 5)

TO TIE: Pass the left end *over* and *under* the right end. Curve what is now the left end toward the right. Cross what is now the right end *over* and *under* the left. Draw tight. NOTE: In the square knot, two ends are *under* one loop and *over* the opposite loop. Don't be fooled by the granny knot.

### LOOP KNOTS

Loop knots hold fast, will not slip, and can be used over and over again because they'll keep their shape. They are usually made in the hand and then placed over the object.

The *bowline* (pronounced bowlyn) is one of the best of all the knots. It can be made in the hand or around the object. It can be used to moor a boat, to hitch a horse, or tied in the end of a rope for hoisting. Variations of it are used to make a seat sling, to lift an injured person, or to haul a climber up a cliff. It is a very useful and important knot.

TO TIE: Make an *overhand* loop the size needed, with the end held toward you. Pass the end up through the loop, then up *behind* the standing part, then down through the loop again. Draw tight. (See No. 6.)

Bowline Knot (6)

The *double bowline* makes a good seat sling. TO TIE: Make an overhand loop with the end held toward you, just as in the Bowline. The difference is that you pass the end through the loop *twice*, making *two* lower loops, A and B, as in Sketch 7-1. The end is then passed *behind* the standing part and down through the first loop again as in the Bowline (see Sketch 7-2). Pull tight. Outside loop B goes under the arms. Inside loop A forms the seat, as shown in Sketch 7-3.

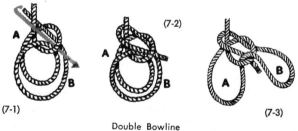

Double Bowline

The *man harness* is a loop knot used to rope mountain climbers together, or to make loops in a rope for hand- or footholds for climbing. For the former, it must be tied large enough to go over a person's shoulders, leaving the arms free. For the latter, it must be the right size for a hand or a foot to fit into.

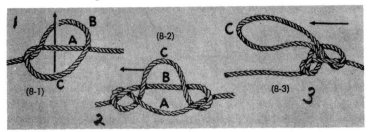

TO TIE: Make a loop in the rope and fold it forward and slightly to the right to get a loop like Sketch 8-1. Then take C up and under A, and over B, as in Sketch 8-2. Give C a good yank, as in Sketch 8-3, to finish the knot.

### NOOSES

Nooses are used to tighten a rope around an object. They are an important part of many snares. They are used to make a lariat or lasso. Any loop knot can be made into a noose by pulling the bight of the rope a short distance through the loop.

The *running bowline* is just a bowline tied around a loop of its own standing part. Use it to recover rigging or logs, or oars that are floating in water. Use it, too, in tightening the string or cord at the beginning of tying a package.

Running Bowline

### HITCHES

Hitches are temporary fastenings that untie easily. They are very much like loop knots, except that they are tied directly around the object. (Loop knots are usually tied in the hand and then placed over the object.) They are quick, temporary ways of fastening to an object. Remove the object and they're usually very easily untied.

The *half hitch* is used frequently for fastening to an object for a right-angle pull. It is a temporary fastening, and not always safe. It is the beginning of other, more secure hitches.

**1**
*Untrustworthy*

Half Hitch

**2**
*Fairly Reliable*

TO TIE: Pass the end of the rope around the object and tie an overhand knot to the standing part. If this hitch is used alone, the end should not be left close to the standing part because it will work loose. Nip the end under the turn of the rope some distance *away* from the standing part. If the pull against the half hitch will not be steady, don't use this knot.

Two Half Hitches

*Two half hitches* is a better knot, more reliable, yet easily tied. It is the knot usually used in mooring a boat or tying a line to a ring hook in fishing. It is just what the name says—a half hitch tied twice.

Clove Hitch

The *clove hitch* is the hitch most often used ashore. It is the hitch that holds the tent lines to the pegs; that lifts a plank, ties a bag, lashes two uprights. TO TIE: Make a turn with the rope around the object and over itself. Take a second turn around the object. Pull the end up under the second turn so that it lies between the rope and the object. Tighten by pulling both ends.

The *neck halter* is a variation, given here because it is a useful knot to use in tying a rope around an animal's neck so that it

Neck Halter

won't slip and choke him, yet is easy to untie. Campers who learn this can practice on their dogs or horses. TO TIE: Make an overhand knot in the end. Then tie a figure eight loosely in the bight, far enough back to go around the animal's head. The knotted end is then passed through the knot in the bight, which is then tightened.

### THE BEND

A bend is used to tie two ropes together. It is a temporary measure only. If the longer length is permanent, the two ropes should be *spliced*, not knotted. A spliced rope is much stronger and safer than ropes knotted together for length. Use a bend only with ropes that are alike in size and type.

The *sheet bend* is the most commonly used for joining light

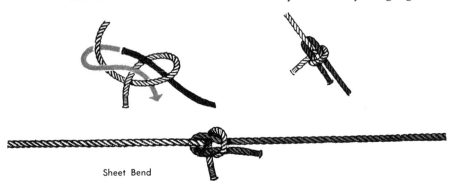

Sheet Bend

and medium ropes. (The carrick is used for really *heavy* ropes.) The sheet bend is very much like the bowline, only instead of the end being tied to its own bight, one end is tied to the bight in the end of another rope.

TO TIE: Make an overhand loop with the end of one rope. Pass the end of the other rope through the loop thus formed, then up behind its standing part, then down through the loop again. Draw up tight.

The *fisherman's bend* is strong and very useful, not only to anglers but to anyone who has to join pieces of string or twine together to tie up a package. It's easy.

TO TIE: Lay the two ends together, each pointing in the opposite direction. Tie an overhand knot in the end of each, *around* the standing part of the other. When drawn tight, the two knots will slide together and won't slip.

Fisherman's Bend

SPLICING

Splicing is the best method of joining two ropes of the same size and type, or of joining the end of a rope to itself to form a loop or a grommet. A spliced rope, if done expertly, will be around 90 per cent as strong as an unspliced one, and much stronger than a rope made from two ropes knotted together. It is really a reweaving of the strands.

Splicing takes time and patience. It is not likely to be really *needed* in day camp, and, for that reason, it is suggested that this skill be left to resident camping, or to those older day campers who have developed a real interest and skill in knot work. Most books, manuals, and pamphlets on knotting include splicing.

## LASHING

Lashing is a way of binding sticks or poles together by using twine, cord, or rope instead of nails or screws. It makes use of knots, especially the clove hitch. It is a real campcraft skill and, like knot tying, it provides the camper with the honest motivation of filling a need.

For example, in really rustic day camp settings, there'll be a need for a place to hang towels or wet bathing suits. A stick lashed between two trees won't hurt the trees, and makes a good towel rack. Poles lashed together at the top, and then spread out, make the "bones" of a tepee. Three shorter ones can be lashed into a tripod from which a pail of water or a pan of stew can hang over a fire. Logs or twigs lashed together make a raft —a real one or a toy one. In fact, twigs lashed together with string can be made into interesting toy furniture, log cabins, and other models for craft programs.

It is easier to learn how to lash, and to practice it, with sticks or dowels a half inch or an inch in diameter, and with binder's twine, so that the various steps are clearly visible.

Each camper should have three of these sticks and a 2- to 3-foot length of twine. The sticks should be at least two feet long.

The first step is to learn the language of lashing:

- *Square* lashing means crossing the sticks at right angles and tying them.
- *Diagonal* lashing means crossing two sticks into an X shape, and then tying them so that they'll *stay* in that position.
- *Shear* lashing means joining sticks as they lie parallel—a good way to make a *longer* stick out of two short ones. When spread, a set of two pairs of these sticks can form a base like a sawhorse. Three sticks can form a tripod.
- *Continuous* lashing means tying a series of smaller sticks at right angles to a longer stick. It might make a back to a camp chair, or the framework of a camp bed.
- *Tripod* lashing means tying three sticks or poles together in such a way that the bottoms or tops can be spread, so that the framework will stand alone. Most tripod lashing is just shear lashing with three poles.
- A *turn* means wrapping the cord once around the stick. Turns should lie neatly close to each other and be tight.

• *Frapping* is a way of tightening the binding by winding the cord *between* the two sticks, so that the binding is pulled tighter together. It is usually one of the last steps in making a lashing.

Making improvised camp equipment out of curved, forked, or odd-shaped pieces of wood is a fine craft project. Part of the fun is *finding* the pieces. Part is deciding what they are best fitted for. Finally, part of the fun is lashing them in place, and then *using* them—for example, coat hangers, towel racks, shoe holders, benches, frames, racks, stools.

Some day camps will find lashing a not very important activity. Others, emphasizing rustic, pioneer skills, will enjoy it. Day campers can learn the *techniques* by practicing with twigs, making miniature articles. Practicing with the larger poles and stronger twine is an excellent lead-up activity for resident, family, or wilderness camping. It is a good conservation craft, too, since it does not require the use of nails and screws into living wood.

As in knotting, it is helpful to make samples of the different types ahead of time, so that campers can see what they look like. Lashed *objects* make fine interest-arousing supplements to these samples. Something that has a purpose is more interesting to look at than two sticks tied together, no matter how neatly.

Lashing is an activity that can be *demonstrated*. Camper and counselor should stand or sit together, so that they get the same view. Practice the hitching knots, especially the clove hitch first —then tie it, and start lashing. Untie, start again, and again. Skill and smoothness come with practice.

*Square lashing* starts with a clove hitch around the upright pole at A, just below the horizontal pole. Twist the short end of the rope around the long end for neatness. (See No. 16-1.)

Pass the rope over B, then around behind and under C, over D, and under A. (See No. 16-2.)

Follow the rope "trail" two or three times more, keeping the rope tight. At A and C, run the rope *inside* the previous trail, but at B and D run it *outside* the previous trail. (See No. 16-3.)

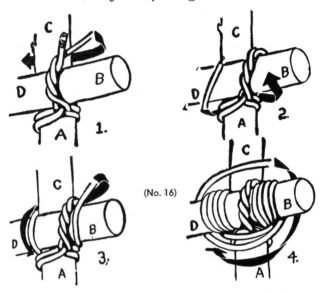

Square Lashing

Make three frapping turns, passing the rope between the poles and around the turns already in place. Pull tight and finish off with a clove hitch at B. (See No. 16-4.)

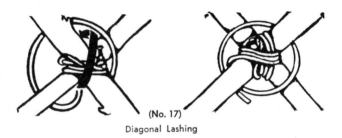

Diagonal Lashing

*Diagonal lashing* starts with a clove hitch around both poles that are crossed in an X shape. Make three or four turns with rope around the same fork of the poles, then three or four turns around the other fork. Take two frapping turns, tighten, and finish with a clove hitch around either pole. (See No. 17.)

*Shear lashing* is versatile. It can be used with two poles instead of diagonal lashing if a sawhorse shape is needed. With three poles, it can be used to make three-pronged or three-legged shapes.

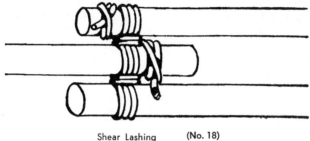

Shear Lashing      (No. 18)

For a tripod, lay three poles on the ground, as in sketch. Begin with a clove hitch around an end pole. Take three loose turns around the poles, passing the rope over and under, and back and forth. Make two loose frapping turns between each pair of poles. Finish with a clove hitch around the center pole.

Hoist the tripod into place, and adjust the lashing if necessary, to make it looser or tighter. The use to be made of the tripod will determine where the lashing should be made, and how much of a "spread" is needed. (See No. 18.)

*Continuous lashing* joins small, shorter sticks or poles to larger, longer poles in a ladder effect. Usually the larger poles are notched so that the smaller ones fit into place accurately and are then lashed. The lashing starts with a clove hitch at the end of one of the long poles. This hitch is made in the middle of the twine, so that the two ends are even. They then "lace" the short poles to the long one, very much as a shoe is laced, keeping all the crossed ends on the under side of the long pole. Finish off at the top with two half hitches and tuck ends in neatly. Repeat the process on the second long pole.

These "ladders" can be used for such purposes as table-tops or racks. Made of really sturdy poles and side pieces, they are good frames for beds. They also can make good "boardwalks" over muddy paths, or newly grassed areas, or sandy strips.

### Why Lashing?

Lashing, like knot tying, is an excellent manipulative activity, encouraging co-ordination of mind and muscle. It is capable of all sorts of adaptations, and fits beautifully into other types of camp activities—stage sets for the drama or council ring programs, cooking equipment, service projects for camp beautification or improvement, miniature models for craft programs, and the like.

It also encourages observation, in finding limbs and twigs with odd and useful shapes—and imagination in putting them together to form useful, interesting, or beautiful objects.

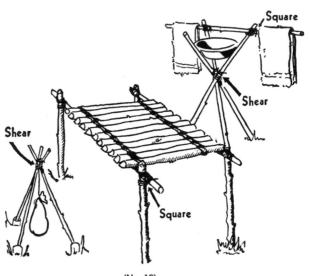

(No. 19)

# CHAPTER 6:

## SHELTERS

Shelters of some sort are provided on most day camp sites. They range from comfortable cabins, lodges, and houses especially planned for long-term use to improvised facilities such as a roof-top, a gymnasium, a barn or a schoolroom. Many use shelters more appropriate for camping, such as lean-tos, tepees, tents, and the like. Many use combinations of both types.

Learning to live in the out-of-doors without sacrificing personal comfort, yet without destroying or injuring natural resources, is an objective of camping. Though the opportunities for "overnights" may be limited, youngsters should get the opportunity of seeing how primitive shelters were made, how sleeping bags work, how a tent can be improvised—in other words, to learn the beginnings of another campcraft skill. It is always good to be authentic, but it is not always possible. Youngsters can improvise and "play like" when the real camping equipment is not at hand. They should be aware of the difference, however. They should have the opportunity of seeing pictures or plans of the real tepee, the real igloo, or hogan, or log cabin, and to discuss how they were constructed, and why.

This chapter is not designed to discuss camp site buildings that are erected and used for the program, and that include toilet facilities, infirmary, storage cabins, office space, and other special buildings such as a boat house, stable, woodwork shop, and the like. Those are provided *for* the campers. It will include simple shelters of various kinds, the construction and/or use of which can be part of the day camp activity program. Shelters, "hide-aways," treehouses, and other places where they can go to get out of the rain, sun, heat, or cold—or away from adults, for their own private daydreams—have always fascinated children. Give them the simple "makings," provide motivation through discussions—and the day camp site will blossom out with all sorts of

improvised shelters, ranging from a hide-away under the sweep-
ing limbs of a hemlock, or a scooped-out crouch-space behind a
rock to treehouses, playhouses, sod huts, tepees, lookouts, and
others never before dreamed of.

Such shelters are not ends in themselves. They are designed
and built by children *to be used*—and so they lead openly into
creative dramatics, games, and other camp activities. The best
activities are always those which are not only enjoyable in the
doing but which also lead into new paths of interest and activity.

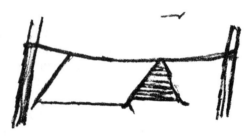

### Improvised Shelters

The simplest shelter, and probably the most-used from early
childhood, is some sort of cloth *over* some sort of framework. Indoors, the small child plays in a "tent," or "house," or "boat,"
or "store" or other imaginary place made by a blanket or large
cloth thrown over a dining table or card table. Outdoors, in the
back yard, a blanket over a clothesline, the ends held out by
weighting them with stones, makes a similar hide-out.

A tarpaulin is as great an aid in day camp as it is in resident
or wilderness camping. It can be used as a roof to keep out
rain or sun, as a carpet or floor to keep out ground dampness.
If its edges are bound, and equipped with tapes, a 10½ foot
"tarp" will make a number of different-shaped shelters. Sometimes a poncho doubles as a "tarp." An old army blanket also
can be used, but is not waterproof. Canvas, denim, parachute
cloth, and ticking are inexpensive, lightweight substitutes.

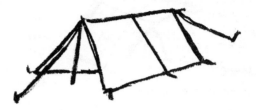

PUP OR A-TENT

Stretch the tarp over a rope between two uprights. They may be poles or trees. Use pegs and tapes to hold the sides out. For a breezy tent, an open end should face the wind. (If used as an overnight shelter, the camper would be warmer if the open end did *not* face the wind.)

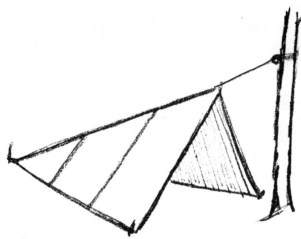

EXPLORER'S TENT

The explorer's tent is very much like the A-tent, but it has only one entrance, requires only one upright for support, is taller at the entrance. It gives more shelter. The tarp is fastened by its tapes to a rope running from a strong peg in the ground up to a tree trunk or other upright. The sides are held in place by tapes and pegs.

Open Wigwam Frame

Closed Wigwam Frame

### WIGWAM

The wigwam is a dome-shaped shelter made by covering a curved framework with tarp. Many tribes of Indians used different types of wigwams— some open at both ends, some covered with thatch, some with sod. An easy and useful wigwam can be improvised by using a heavy net (landing nets from military surplus stores are good) over ropes suspended by uprights, and covering the nets with tarp or other type of cloth.

Some wigwams were completely circular, rather like the Eskimo igloo. Others were vaulted. The type depended upon the tribe, and the use being made of the wigwam. Chicken wire can be used to experiment with different shapes of framework.

### TEPEE

The tepee is a pointed shelter made by setting poles in a circle around a center pole, fastening them at the top, and covering this framework with canvas or other cloth. The inside diameter can range from ten to thirty feet. Indians, of course, used hides to make their tepees, and were known as "3-pole" or "4-pole" people, depending on whether the tribe used three or four foundation poles, around which the other twelve to twenty poles were set. Smaller tepees for children will require fewer poles.

The tepee door usually faced East. Crossed poles in front of a door indicated that the owner was not inside, or was busy. No one ever entered when the crossed poles were in place.

The height of the tepee depends upon the height of the tepee cover. The poles should extend several feet above the cover. The foundation poles are set in a triangular shape, and tied together at the top, where the cover will come. The other poles are then fitted into that crotch.

The wall of the tepee can be made from a piece of cloth whose length is exactly twice the width. Sew smaller pieces together, if necessary, to get a piece large enough. Cut a semicircle, leaving the folded side intact except for cut-outs that will make a small door, and a cut-out to go over the top of the poles. Extra pieces can be used for door and smoke flaps. The edges should be taped so that the base can be pegged to the ground, and the opening edges pegged together. Tapes (or a rope) also hold the top to the crotch of the poles.

Making a doll-size tepee first is good practice—and a good craft project. Use heavy brown paper for the cover, and make the poles at least 12 inches long. It they protrude 4 inches, then the cover will have to be 8 inches wide, as will be the diameter of the tepee. Paint Indian designs on this "model" and decide which will be best on a full-size tepee.

Making such models, including wigwams and log cabins, is not a substitute for making life-size, useable ones, but it *is* a useful technique in experimenting with shapes and methods of construction.

A flap makes the door, and it and the bottom walls can be rolled up for coolness. The sides of a tepee can be painted to identify the tribe, or to represent some special Indian symbol. Red, black, green, yellow, blue, and white are colors usually used in real Indian decorations.

Tepee Framework

Tepee Cover

Folded Side

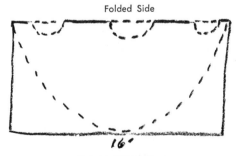

16"

Cut on Dotted Lines

TREEHOUSE

The most exciting of all types of shelters, to the agile, adventurous child, is a treehouse. It also makes good use of the campcraft skills of knotting and lashing—and provides excellent motivation for learning them.

The treehouse is usually a simple platform made of planks or logs bolted or lashed together, and built with a specific location in mind. This location might be in the crotch of two big, healthy limbs of one tree; between the trunks of several trees that grow close together; or in a tree with one straight trunk. The platform for the last would have to be built so that it would fit around the trunk.

The platforms all require protruding edges or poles so that they may be lashed securely to the limbs and trunk for base and overhead support.

Once the platform is securely in place, a railing or wall should be added, and lashed *very* securely in place. Sometimes a simple, raised roof can be added—but look-space should be kept open. A treehouse is a fine place from which to watch birds, squirrels, and other wildlife.

A knotted rope, or a rope ladder that can be raised or lowered, gives the treehouse added adventure. The rope should be securely attached by a timber hitch—a knot that tightens as weight is put on it. A taut rope ladder that is pegged securely to the ground is easier to climb.

Nails, of course, are never hammered into trees. All braces and supports should be made secure by proper lashing and strong rope. The timber hitch and square lashing will be needed the most often.

Even if time prevents the youngsters from making a treehouse, the camp site, whenever possible, should provide it. It is one of childhood's joys.

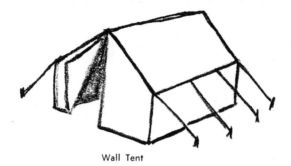

Wall Tent

**WALL TENT**

This type of tent is more than just a shelter. Floored or not floored, it provides indoor space for cots or sleeping bags, and has sides that can be rolled up or down, will withstand bad weather, and can be heated with a stove.

It is heavy, however, and takes considerable time and effort to pitch. Young campers will need lots of help, or their experience can be limited to learning the names of the various tent parts, and what they do:

- *Ridge pole*—the long pole that makes the very top of the tent.
- *Uprights*—shorter poles that hold up each end of the tent.
- *Grommets*—metal eyelets or rings through which rope or tapes can be tied.
- *Fly*—the slanting roof of a tent.
- *Wall*—the sides of a tent.
- *Guy ropes*—the ropes that hold the tent in place. Sometimes called tent ropes.
- *Pegs*—the wooden or metal pieces that are hammered into the ground, and to which the guy ropes are attached.
- *Side rails*—logs or bars to which the guy ropes can be attached instead of to pegs.
- *Ditch*—a trench dug around any tent without floor, to prevent water from running across tent area.

- *Handles*—small wooden pieces attached to guy ropes so that they can be tightened or loosened without changing the pegs.
- *Platform*—the floor of the tent. Loops at the corners of the tent wall go over pegs in the platform to hold the tent in place over it.

Even though day campers will not sleep in it, a day camp site should provide a tent that can be used for practice. Campers should learn how to pitch (not put up!) a tent, and to strike (not take down!) a tent. Even if permanent tents are used for shelters at a day camp, extras for practice will add another campcraft skill. All the sketches, books, or directions in the world cannot provide the look of utter confusion that a folded tent has, the "feel" of the various steps necessary to pitch or strike it, or the immediate and dire results of any carelessness or error. They have to be experienced. Pitching a wall tent should be limited to the older youngsters, however, and under supervision of an experienced counselor.

Umbrella Tent

UMBRELLA TENT

This square-shaped tent is much easier to pitch than the wall tent. It is pitched somewhat the same way an umbrella is opened. Its center pole has four arms that go out to the tent corners and which support it. It is easy to carry, takes up very little space, has plenty of head room, rolls into a smaller bundle and usually has a built-in floor. It's a good tent for auto travel—and a good tent for youngsters to pitch and strike. They can raise the center pole and stake down the corners of this tent.

It makes a good playhouse, too, if taken down in very windy or bad weather. It is not nearly so sturdy as the wall tent, but is portable and very useful. A very attractive adjunct to a day camp.

# CHAPTER 7

# THE WEATHER

The relationship of weather to man is a wonderful topic for group discussion. Crops depend upon weather. Meat supplies depend upon grass and grain supplies. Thousands of men and women depend upon farming and the thousands of other industries that are involved in feeding, clothing, and housing people.

Houses are built to protect man from the weather—from heat, from cold, from rain, snow, and storm. Clothing is worn to protect man from the weather. Man has not been able to change weather to any great degree, but he has learned ways of adapting himself to it, and of diverting some of its bad effects.

## Weather Is Important

Weather wisdom is fascinating. From the days of the cave man to our own time when weather planes fly into the hearts of hurricanes, weather satellites orbit the earth, and rain is spotted by radar, forecasting the weather has been important to man.

Forewarning systems now save thousands of lives and millions of dollars every year. Lightning rods have prevented the loss of many barns and houses by fire. Dams are built to prevent flooding.

Identifying clouds, measuring rain, estimating wind velocities, understanding weather flags and symbols, making their own weather "prophets" from chemicals—all these are not only interesting, but also useful, campcraft skills and day camp projects.

Every day camp can have its own Weather Bureau. Every day camper can be a weatherman. An official weatherman, who keeps a written record (or log) of his "official" forecasts each day can be elected. He should add a sentence to the log the *next* day, telling what the weather really was. Forecasts should be made at the same time each day.

Every youngster in day camp can learn how—and should have the opportunity—to use

a *thermometer* to measure temperature
a *barometer* to measure air pressure
a *weathervane* to learn the wind direction
an *anemometer* to measure the speed of wind
a *rain gauge* to learn the amount of rain
a *weather map* in the local newspaper
*newspaper symbols* for local forecasts
*weather flags*—to learn what they mean
*storm flag warnings* for daytime use
*storm light warnings* for night use
the *Beaufort scale* for checking the wind

Weather projects involving making and using various devices for measuring and forecasting the weather are absorbing to youngsters. They are very practical because results *show*. A weathervane moves; a chemical weather prophet changes color; a rain gauge can be measured; the water in a camp-made barometer rises or falls. To a child, these projects are like magic. Also, the weather is *important* to them. They *want* to know. A Weather Station at a day camp can be one of the most popular places—and can be used in teaching one of the best campcraft skills.

## Weather Projects

The following are all simple, fundamental projects that can be understood easily, and will serve at the same time to arouse and to satisfy curiosity. Interest in weather is a lifetime interest for almost everyone, and the more we know, the more interesting the hobby grows.

### KEEPING A WEATHER SCORE

A simple but fun-to-do project is to keep a daily record of sunny and rainy days (add cloudy, too, if you like!). Youngsters can make cloth or oilcloth bags—a yellow one for sunny days, a blue one for rainy days. Every sunny day, the weatherman drops a pebble or marble (or penny, or lollipop!) into the yellow bag; on rainy days, into the blue bag. No one else handles or lifts the bags.

At the end of summer, on the last day of the day camp, everyone has a guess as to how many sunny and how many rainy days there have been. The person whose guess is right, or nearest right, gets the bag and its contents.

WEATHER FLAGS

A weather flag should be run up at the Weather Bureau or Station every day. These flags are symbols that any weatherwise camper learns to identify and understand.

The flags are easy to make at day camp. They can be made of unbleached muslin, solid black denim or other strong cloth, and solid blue denim or other cloth. The *weather* flags are squares (make them about 12 inches in size). With them, a *temperature* flag can be used. It is a triangle.

The color and placement in weather flags determine what they mean:

- A white square means FAIR.

- A square, white on top, blue at bottom, means SHOWERS.

- A blue square means RAIN.

- A white square with a small blue square in the center means COLD WAVE.

- A black triangle weather flag flown *above* any weather flag means WARMER. If flown *below* any weather flag, it means COLDER.

WEATHER FLAG DAYTIME STORM WARNINGS

In 1958 the United States Weather Bureau adopted the following symbols for daytime storm warnings along the coasts of the United States (including Hawaii and Alaska), the Great Lakes, and Puerto Rico. These are *red* and *black*—not to be confused with the regular weather flags.

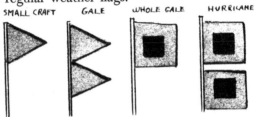

- A red triangle means SMALL CRAFT WARNING.
- Two red triangles, one under the other, mean GALE.
- A red square with a smaller black square in the center means a WHOLE GALE.
- Two of these, one under the other, mean HURRICANE.

STORM WARNINGS AT NIGHT

Red and black flags could not be seen at night, so the official night signals for storm warnings are red and white lights:

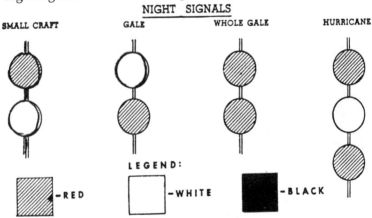

NIGHT SIGNALS

- Red light above white light—SMALL CRAFT WARNING
- White light above red light—GALE

- Red light above red light—WHOLE GALE
- Red light *above and below* white light—HURRICANE

NEWSPAPER WEATHER SYMBOLS

Besides the weathermap in the local newspaper, showing the various "fronts," there are square symbols that indicate the degree of rain, almost like Indian sign language!

- Empty square—FAIR
- Square with one black dot—OVERCAST
- Square with two vertical dots and a triangle pointing down—VIOLENT RAIN
- Square with two dots horizontal—CONTINUOUS SLIGHT RAIN
- Square with four "commas"—CONTINUOUS DRIZZLE

Counselors should make a special point of studying the daily weathermap in the local newspaper. They should encourage campers to clip the weathermaps and bring them to day camp for discussion and study.

THE BAROMETER

Air has weight. A barometer measures this weight, called *Pressure*. Let campers prove this by making a simple barometer. All they'll need is a bottle, a cork to fit it, a piece of glass tubing, and some water.

Fill a clear glass bottle about one-fifth full of water. Run a piece of glass tubing ¼ inch in diameter through a cork that fits the bottle top tightly. The glass tube must be long enough to reach down into the water.

Mark the water level with a fine, thin line of paint, or a string. Then look at the bottle every day.

When it's fair, the air pressure pushes down on the only opening—the top of the glass tube—and makes the water level rise because of the pressure on it. As long as it stays high or rises, the weather will be fair.

If the weather is changing, the air pressure gets lighter and the level of the water will *fall*, meaning rain is ahead.

RAIN GAUGE

"How much rain fell last Tuesday?" "Which was the wettest day all summer?" Campers can find out, and keep their own rain records. Set up an official one for day camp, and encourage making individual ones for home, to be used on week ends.

The gauge requires a can about eight inches wide, a tall, narrow bottle (like an olive bottle), a ruler, a bit of paint, and a fine paint brush. Pour water into the can until it measures one inch. (Be accurate. Stick the ruler in the water and hold it straight.) Then funnel the water carefully into the bottle, put a thin black line on the bottle, and write "1 inch." Empty it. Then put water into the can until it measures ½ inch, funnel into the bottle, and mark the water level "½ inch." Repeat the process, this time for ¼ inch.

Then empty the can and set it in an open place, braced so it won't fall or blow over. After the rain, funnel the contents into the olive bottle and find out *exactly* how much rain fell. Keep a record. Find out which day had the most rain.

IN WHICH DIRECTION IS THE WIND BLOWING?

Perhaps there's a natural weathervane that can be observed at day camp. If there is smoke from a tall chimney or smokestack, or a flag flying from a high pole, the campers can check the wind's direction.

(Wind is always named for the direction it blows *from*, not *to*. A north wind blows *from* the north, *to* the south.)

Each camper can make his own personal weathervane by following simple directions from the National Audubon Society.

Assemble a pencil with an eraser on the end, a soda straw, a paper feather, and a straight pin. Stick the pin carefully through

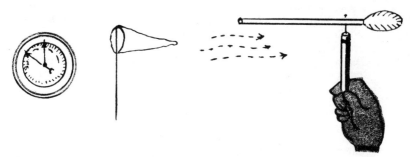

the soda straw and into the eraser of the pencil. Stick the paper feather into one end of the straw. Make sure the straw moves easily around the pin. Hold the pencil up in the air, and the *open* end of the straw will be pointed in the direction the wind is coming *from*.

Discuss wind resistance. Why doesn't the *feather* point the direction the wind is blowing from? Which would be most likely to be uprooted in a hurricane—a thick evergreen or a tree without leaves? Why?

Tie wind direction in with compass reading. Make a simple windsack.

HOW HARD DOES THE WIND BLOW?

An anemometer is used to measure wind velocity—how many miles per hour it blows. Without such an official instrument, however, it is possible to get a very good and quite accurate reading by using the Beaufort scale. Hopefully, the wind won't reach Whole Gale, let alone Hurricane proportions—but using this scale encourages observation, interpretation, and correct usage of words to describe the wind.

| WHAT THE WIND DOES | MILES PER HOUR | NAME OF WIND |
|---|---|---|
| Smoke goes straight up | Less than 1 | Calm |
| Smoke bends slightly | 1- 3 | Light air |
| Leaves rustle, weathervane moves | 4- 7 | Light breeze |
| Leaves and twigs in constant motion | 8-12 | Gentle breeze |
| Raises dust and paper; moves small branches | 13-18 | Moderate breeze |

Small trees sway ................19-24 .....Fresh breeze
Large branches in motion .........25-31 .....Strong breeze
Whole trees sway, walking difficult ..32-38 .....Moderate gale
Breaks twigs off trees .............39-46 .....Fresh gale
Damages chimneys and roofs .......47-54 .....Strong gale
Trees uprooted ...................55-63 .....Whole gale
Widespread damage ..............64-75 .....Storm
Most destructive of all winds .......over 75 ....Hurricane

**WEATHER PROPHET**

Chemicals that forecast wet or dry weather by changing color can be used to make excellent weather projects. From the local drugstore get a solution of these ingredients:

> 4 ozs. water
> 1 oz. chloride of cobalt
> ½ oz. table salt
> ¼ oz. gum arabic
> 75 grains of calcium chloride

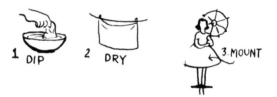

Dip a piece of paper toweling, or white cotton cloth into the mixture. Let it dry out, then use the cloth on a cardboard or plywood cutout. Campers can make their own "prophets," using the paper or cloth as sails on a boat cut-out, the skirt of a ballerina, the petals of a flower, the ears on a white rabbit, and so on. When the strip turns pink, the weather will be wet; when it turns blue, there'll be fair weather.

**CLOUDS**

Watching clouds drift by, seeing castles in them, finding animal shapes, watching the beautiful colors of sunset, all are lovely activities for every camper to enjoy. In addition to their beauty, however, clouds have their own specific names, and their own meaning in terms of weather.

Campers love big words, and they enjoy knowing the right names for things. Encourage them to observe the clouds not only for beauty but also to forecast the weather. Here are a few cloud names:

- *Cumulus*—"cream puffs" with rounded domes and flat bottoms, usually in a blue sky. They mean fair weather.
- *Fracto-cumulus*—like cumulus but thinner, with edges continually changing.
- *Alto-cumulus*—high, heavy, white or gray masses, partly shaded underneath and with edges overlapping.
- *Cumulo-nimbus*—thunderheads—overgrown cumulus, with black bottoms portending rain.
- *Cirrus*—high, feathery, wispy "mare's tails"—usually in a blue sky. If in a gray sky, rain will probably fall in 24 hours.
- *Stratus*—"Layer" clouds, forming a horizontal sheet usually wide and even. Look like lifted fog.
- *Cirro-stratus*—white milky sheet or tangled web.
- *Nimbus*—any cloud from which rain is falling.

FORECASTING

Counselors should encourage every camper to observe and record accurately, put two and two together, and use their powers of reasoning. Before forecasting, each youngster should check various factors:

What is the wind direction?
What is the wind velocity?
The temperature?
The barometer—rising? falling? steady?
The clouds—what kind are they?

Then—FORECAST.

CHAPTER **8:**

# MEASURING TIME
# AND DISTANCE

Long before clocks and watches were invented, people worked out many ways of telling *time*—not only the time of day, but also the time of the seasons.

*Distance*, too, has always interested man. Methods of finding out the height of a hill or a horse, the depth of a lake or a sea, the length of a piece of cloth, the area between two places, all have been devised for centuries. Some of the oldest methods actually are still in use—the pace, the span, the hand, the foot, and so forth.

As methods for transportation were invented, speed became a factor in measuring distance, and we speak of miles per hour. Power, too, became a factor—and it's called "horsepower"!

Methods of measurement are interesting to children who have taken words like "mile," "yard," "depth" for granted. No child can keep his hands off an hourglass, or not be fascinated by a metronome ticking away without a pause. Even more fascinating to everyone today are the time and distance factors involved in space travel.

Experiments in, and discussion of, ways of measuring time and distance provide excellent activity projects for day camp.


### MEASURING TIME

Campers will enjoy making a sun clock and a season clock. With the one, they tell time as people have done through many centuries. With the other, they can measure the coming of autumn, as each summer day grows a bit shorter. The season clock should be built during the first week at day camp, so that

126

it will record the length of the sun-shadow for each week at camp.

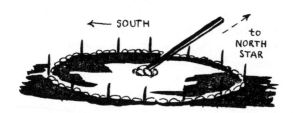

### The Sundial

A sundial measures time by the length and position of the sun's shadow. The shadow stick is called a gnomon (no-mon) which means "one who knows." A broom handle, a dowel, or a piece of pipe, all can be used.

Select a level, sunny place, out of traffic lanes on the day camp site. Slant the stick into the ground so that its *lower* end points south. Check this with a compass.

Slant the stick at an angle that is the same as the local latitude. Look this up on a globe or map of the area. Use a protractor to get the correct angle. If correct, the upper end of the stick will point directly to the North Star.

Using the base of the stick as the center, mark off a circle around it, on which to check the hours. Be sure your watch is correct. Every hour drive a stake in the circle at the point where the shadow falls. The sundial will measure only daylight hours, but it will be accurate. Don't forget that it will show standard, not daylight-saving time when you mark the hour stakes. Outline the circle in stones or bricks, heavy rope, or lime, and *use* it. Check the time frequently, letting the campers read the sundial.

### A Season Clock

A short stick set in a fixed vertical position in the sun will make a shadow that will vary in length with the seasons. June 21 is the summer solstice when the sun is at its highest, and therefore the shadow will be the shortest. December 21 is the winter solstice, when the sun is the farthest away from the earth. From June 21 to December 21, the daylight hours grow shorter; from December 21 to June 21, they grow longer.

The vertical stick may be placed into the ground in a sunny, level place, out of traffic lanes, or it can be set into a cement, plaster, or wooden base. The taller the stick, the larger the base. A stick about 3 feet long from base-level to top is a good size for a base about 12 feet long and 6 feet wide.

On the baseboard keep weekly *noontime* (standard time) records of the length of the shadow, marking them at the exact time each week, with a crayon or thumbtack. After the final week's marking, a curved line can be drawn, connecting the weekly readings, showing graphically how much longer the days are growing.

Campers can make a season clock to take home, and place in a south window, keeping their own record not only for the summer, but for the coming fall and winter seasons as well.

## MEASURING DISTANCE

Units of measure are fascinating to talk about, check, and experiment with. Some of the units still used in England and in the United States go back far beyond the time when rulers and yardsticks were invented. The *inch*, for example, hundreds of years ago was legally the length of barley corns placed end to end. Henry I, according to legend, proclaimed the yard as the distance from the point of his nose to the end of his thumb when his arm was outstretched. Clerks in department stores still use this as a rough measurement in taking cloth off a bolt to measure it out by a yardstick. Youngsters can measure their own "yard." Whose comes nearest to the real yard?

Do the same with a *foot*. If twelve inches hadn't been accepted by everyone as a foot, then everybody's measurement would be different. Campers can measure their own feet and see which is nearest to 12 inches.

A *span* used to be the distance between the end of the thumb and the end of the little finger when the hand is stretched out. It varied too—until nine inches was accepted as its standard.

Measure individual spans. Whose is nearest the standard?

A *hand* is used to measure the height of a horse at his withers (the ridge between the shoulder bones). It used to be the width of a hand. Now it is set at four inches. Campers can check the vital statistics of some of the famous horses and see how many hands high they were.

Horses aren't used very much any more to pull heavy loads, but the word "horsepower" is still used. What does it mean when an auto salesman speaks of a car having a 90-horsepower engine? Do campers know that 1 horsepower is the amount needed to lift 33,000 pounds a distance of 1 foot in 1 minute? (Actually this is about 1½ times what a horse can do.)

Many countries use the metric system, based on the International Prototype Meter, a platinum-iridium bar kept at the International Bureau of Weights and Measures in Sèvres, a suburb of Paris. In this system, a *millimeter* is about four-hundredths of an inch. A *meter* is about 3¼ feet, and a *kilometer* is slightly more than 3/5 of our mile. Our mile has 5,280 feet; a meter is about 3.28 feet; a kilometer is a thousand meters. If a camper drives 5 miles to day camp, and a little French boy drives 5 kilometers to his, which camper goes the farther?

Campers try to *estimate* distances, lengths, and heights, then measure to get the correct answer. "How many inches around that tree trunk?" "How long is that shadow?" "How long is a dollar bill? How wide?" Such guesses—and comparisons—are good training in observation and help to develop correct judgment.

If campers were traveling on a ship, they'd be going *nautical* miles. A nautical mile is longer than a mile—it's 6,076 feet. And speed of ship is measured by nautical miles per hour. A *knot* is the speed of one nautical mile per hour. Campers can look up the speed of big liners or of boat races.

Depth of a sea, ocean, or other large body of water is measured in *fathoms*. A fathom once was the distance between a man's arms when they were completely stretched out sideward. It too was finally standardized at 6 feet—twice King Henry's yard!

Though not a measurement of time or distance, the English *stone*, still a measurement of weight, fits into this type of program. A stone is now accepted as *fourteen* pounds. Wouldn't it be interesting to know what and where was the original stone used to weigh things? If a boy weighs 5½ stones, how many pounds does he weigh? Each camper can figure out his own weight in stones.

Also, though not a specific measure of time or distance, *numerals* are interesting to talk about. A foot is *twelve* inches. Where did those words come from—one, two, three, et cetera? Can anyone say them in French, or Spanish, or German, or Japanese, or any other language?

Discussion of Roman numerals fits into this sort of project. Campers can work out dates for others to figure out, or bring back dates copied from local monuments or cornerstones. Such dates are really a sort of shorthand, or even a code, with different symbols for different values. They're easy to decode, with just a little thought. In fact, they correspond quite well with our penny, nickel, dime, quarter, half dollar, and dollar! A letter in *front* of a letter is subtracted. I (1) in front of V (5) makes IV (4). X (10) in front of C (100) makes XC (90).

A letter *after* another letter *adds*. M (1,000) followed by D (500) makes MD (1,500). V (5) followed by I (1) makes VI (6).

The "code" is easy:

| | | |
|---|---|---|
| I- 1 | XL-40 | C- 100 |
| V- 5 | L-50 | D- 500 |
| X-10 | XC-90 | M-1,000 |

Roman numerals are used primarily in dating books, buildings, monuments, tombstones, and other permanent markers. They are used for *dates*—therefore they are measurements of time—if their use here is questioned.

## How to Measure Height

"How high is the flagpole?" "How tall is that tree?" Campers can find out by applying a very simple formula used by the Boy Scouts and other youth groups.

Start from the tree, or flagpole, or whatever is being measured, and walk 11 steps. Push a stick into the ground at that point, or get someone to hold it. (The taller the tree or flagpole being measured, the longer the stick should be. The line of vision from the ground line to the tree or flagpole top must *cross* the stick so that the crossing point can be marked on it.) Then walk one more step away from the object being measured, and mark *that*

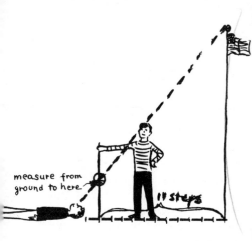

measure from ground to here

11 steps

point. Lie down on the ground with your eyes as near that point as possible, and sight across the stick to the top of the flagpole or tree. Note and mark where the line of vision crosses the stick.

Measure the stick from the ground up to where the line of vision crossed it. That distance in *inches* is the height of the flagpole or tree, in *feet*. Sounds impossible, but it works!

### Projects in Measuring Distance

Each camper can compare his personal measurements of a hand, foot, inch, yard, fathom, and span with the standard.

Each camper can work out his own measurements of distance of one place to another by measuring his own step. This is done by walking back and forth several times so as to get a fair average. Then measure that same distance with a yardstick or measuring tape. Divide the correct distance by the number of steps, and the answer will be the average length of the step.

Try to bring at least *one* pedometer—more if possible—and see how many miles are walked just in moving around the day camp all day. Run a guessing contest. The camper with the nearest correct answer gets to wear the pedometer the next day.

Campers learn to work out distances on road maps. (See Chapter 10, "Markers, Maps, and Compass.")

CHAPTER **9:**

# COMMUNICATION
# SIGNALS, SIGNS,
# AND CODES

Methods of communication by signals, signs, and codes have been developed and used by every civilization. The sign language of the American Indians and the rebus of the ancient Egyptians are two of the best-known examples.

The letters and numerals of modern languages are the result of primitive attempts to work out systems of communication.

Activities that include opportunities for learning and practicing ancient and more modern skills fit well into the day camp environmental program. They do not require highly specialized skills in the counselor. Even the Morse code, which has to be accepted and learned as it is, can be learned with the campers. These trailing, stalking, directing, and writing forms are ways to adventure. Through them, each young camper becomes personally *involved* in his environment.

## Trail Signs and Signals

Most trail signs and signals are *directional*. A twig is stuck in the ground so that the angle points in the proper direction; a bunch of grass is tied together so that its top points in the right direction; a small stone placed to the right or left of a large stone indicates the way to turn. A trail sign pointing *up*—stick straight in ground, grass tied to point up, stone on top of stone—these mean "Keep on. This is the trail."

132

Crossed sticks, a cross marked on the ground, or a circle within a larger circle, all mean "Stop."

Danger on the trail, or a call for help is shown by *three*—three sticks in a line, three rocks on top of each other, three tied grass clusters. They mean "Danger" or "Help." (See Distress Signals.)

## Tracking and Stalking

Following trail signs made by wildlife is one of the most exciting activities that youngsters in the "injun" age can do. The Boy Scouts recommend making a "whiffle-poof" for practice in tracking. It is just a piece of wood studded with nails driven only partway in, and dragged by a string or rope so that it makes a track. The bigger the log, the bigger the track, of course. One boy pulls it around a given area; another boy tries to follow the trail it has made.

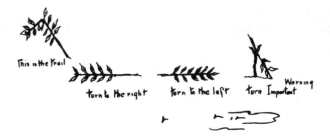

This is the trail    turn to the right    turn to the left    turn Important    Warning

Once youngsters learn to observe the grass, look for bent twigs or bruised or broken leaves, footprints, droppings, or other indications, they are well on their way to stalking. Here they learn to move quietly and smoothly through woods or fields, to fade into the landscape by not wearing bright colors or making any noise; to test the wind to see that their scent is not being blown ahead of them; to take advantage of trees, bushes, shadows; to "freeze" if the animal becomes alarmed.

Most day campers will not be hunting with guns. It takes stalking skill, however, to get near a bird, or follow a deer track, or play trailing and stalking games, or photograph wildlife. Tracking and stalking are useful outdoor skills, and they bring the same thrill of accomplishment that primitive man felt when these skills were necessary for his existence.

### Picture Writing

Writing a message by using pictures is the primitive way to overcome the language handicap. Indians developed it to a fine art, so that a tribe in one section of the country could understand the tribe from another section through signs, even though they could not speak the same language.

Picture writing uses the very simplest of lines, easily recognized by anyone. A simple stick figure of a man becomes a woman by drawing a triangle for a skirt. It becomes a baby by drawing a simple cradle around the figure; a chief by putting a feather in its head; a preacher or priest by adding a cross above his head.

Clouds can be shown by curved lines; rain, dashes below the cloud; snow, dots below the cloud; lightning, a zigzag.

Several tepees can indicate a village; put several tepees in an enclosed area and it can be a city. Different kinds of houses can be indicated by a smokestack for a factory; a cross for a church, a flag for a school; railroad tracks in front for a station.

Working out picture-language directions or stories is engrossing, because no one has to be an artist. It is excellent for group discussion. It develops observation and imagination.

"Here's a stick figure of a man. He's angry. How can we show it?" Do the same for happy; for sad. "How do we feel when we're sad?" And so, by thinking, and even acting out, sadness becomes a droopy figure; happiness, a dancing figure; anger, a figure with arrows around its head.

What about *hungry?* "My stomach feels empty"—so hunger, or feeling hungry becomes a figure of a body with a hole in it! Sleep? "My eyes close"—so sleep, or a person sleeping can be indicated by a closed eye.

Trees and mountains are easy. *Several* trees make a forest; several mountains make a range. Water can be a ripply line. Put it in a frame, and it can mean a lake. Let the frame be open at the top, and it can mean the sea or ocean.

Combinations are interesting. Water can be a ripple; short, straight lines can be grass. Put a ripple under the grass—and it can mean marshy, swampy land.

What pictures can be devised for words like hear, see, write, pray, think, speak?

How can words like day, tomorrow, month, year, food, fast, slow, walk, noon, midnight, fish, bird, stars be indicated?

Think up sentences to write in pictures. "An Indian chief and his wife walked for three months. They came to a lake, so they made a canoe. On the other side, the chief shot a deer. His squaw built a fire, and they had food. Then they built a tepee, and slept until sunrise." And so on, until the campers add their own adventures, or make a guessing game out of it by trying to read each other's stories.

Work out meaningful designs for tepee decoration, for camp log book, for beadwork, leather tooling, posters, and other crafts. Use picture writing for invitations to a special powwow or party. Use them for clues in a treasure hunt.

Try drawing them in sand; on the ground; on bark (from dead trees, of course); on canvas, leather, foil. Use colored chalk, crayons, and soft pencils on construction paper or newsprint. Try a picture-writing mural.

Campers might like to devise a sign or totem of their own— or for each other. What Indian names or word combinations can describe the girl with the pretty laugh; the boy who likes to eat; the camper who talks all the time; the best swimmer; the friend- liest one? Making one's symbol on a circle of leather to hang around the neck is a good craft project.

### International Morse Code

This is the only code used and understood all over the world. Other methods for sending and receiving messages have been developed and are faster, but they are not in universal use, and do not have the flexibility of the old Morse code.

This code depends upon a series of dots and dashes—long and

short sounds or flashes—for every letter of the alphabet. Before any message can be sent or received, campers must learn and practice sending and receiving the code. Boys and girls enjoy doing this, and day camp should provide ample opportunity to do it.

The thing that makes the Morse code so useful is its adaptability. It can be transmitted by *sound,* using the telegraph key, or drums; by *sight,* using semaphore flags by day, the right hand signaling the dots, and the left hand the dashes; or by flashlight at night, using short and long lights for dots and dashes. It can also be sent by reflecting light from a mirror, covering the mirror to indicate dots and dashes as in the case of flashlights.

The campers should also learn a few of the conventions. The person sending the message alerts the other person by sending AAAA as one word, until he gets K from the receiver, meaning that he's ready to take the message. If the sender makes a mistake, he quickly signals eight dots. When he finishes the message he signs off with AK, and the receiver shows that he understands by sending R. Here is the code:

INTERNATIONAL MORSE CODE

| | | | |
|---|---|---|---|
| A • — | | N — • |
| B — • • • | | O — — — |
| C — • — • | | P • — — • |
| D — • • | | Q — — • — |
| E • | | R • — • |
| F • • — • | | S • • •  . |
| G — — • | | T — |
| H • • • • | | U • • — |
| I • • | | V • • • — |
| J • — — — | | W • — — |
| K — • — | | X — • • — |
| L • — • • | | Y — • — — |
| M — — | | Z — — • • |

One of the very best sources of information on the uses of the Morse code for campers is the Boy Scout Handbook.

## Distress Signals

Distress is always indicated by three equally spaced sounds, signs, or signals. A hunter lost in the woods signals for help by firing three shots, waiting a while, and firing three more. Campers needing help should shout, or blow a whistle, three times at intervals, or send smoke signals in threes, or use a mirror or flashlight in flashes of three. It is interesting to note that S O S in the Morse code consists of three dots, three dashes, and three dots.

Campers should practice using distress signals so that they learn how—but should never use them in play, when on a trip or hike. Distress signals should be saved for real emergencies. The time might come when they are a matter of life or death.

CHAPTER **10:**

## MARKERS, MAPS, AND COMPASS

To most city children, finding their way means streets, recognized by street signs that name them at an intersection, or the signs on a bus or streetcar giving the final destination, or road signs seen from the family car.

Most day camp youngsters have never seen a compass. Most of them have never really looked at a road map, have never even *heard* of a topographical map, and have never looked inside a bus or train schedule.

Learning how to use the compass, how to read a map, how to find places on a map, figure distances, and read a timetable are highly useful and important steps in growing up. Most youngsters enjoy such activities. They present a challenge, and provide real satisfaction in entering what up to then has been a mysterious field known only to adults.

These projects are so simple, too. They require no equipment except a compass—and *that* can be made, although it will not be a real substitute for a good instrument. Road maps are free at every filling station—maps that anywhere else in the world are sold, and are not readily available to all. Train and bus schedules are free. All that is really needed is interest and enthusiasm.

The use of a compass is an important campcraft skill. It, and other ways of finding a given location, of not losing the way, and of finding the way back if lost are important safety and survival skills. Every youngster should learn them.

Becoming familiar with, and obeying when necessary, the many different road and traffic signs and symbols are other important projects for day camp. Making such signs and symbols is a good campcraft project.

138

Straight lines indicate the road and any intersection:

- a crossing of two roads
- a road on the right
- a road on the left
- a road angling in from the right
- a road angling in from the left

The main road is usually indicated by a wide line; the side roads, by a narrow line.

Whether using arrows or lines, the diamond-shaped signs mean Be Careful.

An arrow by itself is often seen on city streets and in entrances to public buildings or parks. It indicates *direction*. "Follow the arrow." It means go *only* in that direction—a one-way street or traffic lane.

An octagon-shaped (eight-sided) sign is accepted by the United States Department of Roads as the official STOP sign. Usually the word is printed on it, but not always. It means what it says: Come to a full and complete stop before going on.

A railroad crossing is usually marked by a round sign with the letters RR on it, separated by crossed lines meaning danger.

Roads may have local names, like "the old river road," or official names like the "Lincoln Highway." State and federal roads and highways are identified their entire length, however, by numbers. The markers for United States, or federal highways, are always in a shield-shaped sign with US printed on it. Those for state roads are usually on round signs.

Road markers always tell something: Deer Crossing, Hospital Zone, School Zone, School Bus Stop, Soft Shoulder, Steep Grade. What markers can campers find on their way to camp?

Map and marker reading are highly educational, as well as being useful skills. They help to make geography interesting. They lead into history through marking historic places. They teach spelling. They help make arithmetic a useful skill in judging distances. Most of all, they lead a youngster into an understanding of his country—his immediate city, places near it, other states, and finally the great complex of the United States.

The road doesn't end there. Other countries open up by sea, land, and air routes—and space itself is waiting to be conquered. Maps are magic carpets. Learning to read and understand them is all that is necessary to put the magic carpet into the air. Armchair travelers usually end up by going places!

**Road and Traffic Markers**  **WARNING**

Learning to see and to identify road and traffic markers is a good bus trip project. Reproducing them on paper or cardboard, and learning their meaning are not only craft but safety projects.

The diamond-shaped road marker is one of the most often seen, and important to obey.

### DIAMOND MEANS DANGER

They are always warnings. Arrows or straight lines inside the diamond are symbols of what *kind* of warning. Arrows indicate which way the road will turn by the direction of the arrow and the sharpness of its angle.

- to the right
- to the left
- sharp right

- sharp left
- first right then left
- first left then right

**Maps**

There are all *sorts* of maps—treasure maps, star maps, world maps, airplane maps, topographical maps, road maps, railroad maps, and bus maps. Maps are drawn to show how to get to places, or to locate them in terms of distance and in relation to other places, or to indicate the topography of the area. They are easy to read—if the ABC's of map reading are learned.

Get a map from an airline and compare it with a road map. Each shows the same United States, but the airline map shows more what it looks like from above—the shadings of green, brown, and blue showing the topography. The road map shows all the little villages and towns, and the mazes of roads that connect them.

Railroad and bus line maps show their routes. Often restaurants, shopping centers, and so on, give out maps showing how to get to them.

Making a map of their neighborhood and of the camp site are good projects for day campers. Make a *relief* map too—one that is made of clay or papier mâché, that shows the *shape* of the area three-dimensionally.

A road map is full of information for those who can read it. The first thing to do is to find the "legend," the explanation of the symbols used on the map. The legend gives the scale of the map, or so many miles to the inch. That is useful in figuring distances.

The legend also shows how various kinds of roads appear on the map—such as thruways, turnpikes, hard-surfaced roads, roads under construction. It also shows the symbols it uses to indicate airports, historic shrines, national and state parks and forests, camp sites, fish hatcheries, and other places of interest.

Different symbols by towns and cities indicate their population. Figures between towns give the mileage; between several cities, the combined mileage is given by putting a small star at the beginning and end of the area measured. In states with major turnpikes or thruways with limited access, the exits and entrances have symbols.

When a state has a very large city, there's usually a square in the corner of the map showing the major roads or streets through the city.

In another place on the page, there's a listing of counties, cities, and towns, arranged alphabetically. Each is followed by a letter and a number. These letters and numbers are guides for finding that city on the map. The letters are arranged down each side of the map. The numbers are at the top and the bottom. If a city has D 10 after it, D will be between two lines along the sides of the map; 10 will be between two lines at the top and bottom of the map. Follow these lines until D's and 10's intersect. The city will be in the square formed by those 4 lines.

Mileage is indicated along the roads shown on the map. It also can be measured by using the scale of distance shown in the legend. On most maps, however, the distance between major cities is shown in a special square. In this square, the cities are listed alphabetically across the side and across the top, with horizontal and vertical lines separating them. In each small square there's a number. By following the horizontal line of one city until it crosses the vertical line of the second city, the correct mileage can be found.

Campers can practice measuring distances between cities with a ruler, and comparing their figures with the chart.

Road maps make wonderful quizzes, contests, and games. They're good to test youngsters on following directions. "I'm in Hartford, Connecticut, and I want to get to New London to see a submarine launching. How can I get there? How far is it?" State maps are best to start with, but use city maps, and a U.S. map, too. "I'm going from Washington, D. C., to Yellowstone National Park to camp. What's a good route? Where will I cross the Mississippi? What big cities will I go through?"

Road maps, airplane maps, bus and railroad maps, city maps, all are concerned primarily with transportation. The *topographical* map is concerned with the shape of the land itself—woods, hills, mountains, fields, waterfalls, lakes, dams, marshes, bridges, houses, roads, trails. *Contour* lines show the area's shape, and by their distance apart they show whether the land is flat, has hills, valleys, mountains. The closer the contour lines, the steeper the slope of the land.

The U. S. Geological Survey, Washington 25, D. C., has excellent topographical maps. Order the largest topographical index map of your state, then decide upon what part or quadrangle you need and order it. Mount it on muslin to preserve it.

These maps are exact—much more so than road maps that can become out of date with each new road. They are invaluable for wilderness campers or canoe trips. Their interpretation makes a good day camp project, even if they are not actually used until later, in resident or wilderness camping.

Ask locally, too, because local topographical maps of specific areas are often available.

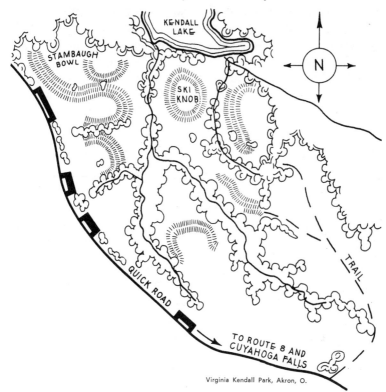

Virginia Kendall Park, Akron, O.

*Train, bus, and plane timetables* show not only *where*, but also *how* and *when*. They belong to the map family, and should be included in map projects.

Many adults would rather telephone for information about the arrival and departure of trains and buses than to look it up in a timetable. There are times, however, when it's important to read a timetable. The best time to learn how to do this is when it's not necessary, but is fun.

Trains are romantic to many youngsters. In fact, traveling by train is a real adventure to many who have never been on a train. It is quite possible, in these days of speed and mobility, to find youngsters who have flown all over the world—but who have never been on a train!

The *names* of trains are romantic, too—the Crescent Limited, the Humming Bird, the Gulf Wind, the Yankee Clipper, the Orange Blossom, the Chief, El Capitan, the Corn Belt Rocket, the Hiawatha, the Zephyr. Not all trains are *named,* but they all have numbers.

Railroad timetables show the *line*—Pennsylvania, Union Pacific, Baltimore and Ohio, New Haven, Chicago, Milwaukee and St. Paul, Santa Fe, Illinois Central, Southern, and so on. Each line issues a series of tables, with columns indicating the various trains by number and by name, if they have names (the Hummingbird is No. 5 southbound, No. 6 northbound; the South Wind is No. 15 southbound, No. 16 northbound). These columns also indicate, going down the page, the time of departure of each train. A big column lists each city or town along the route, with *lv* (leave) on the left and *av* (arrive) on its right. In the case of trains going north and south, the city column is read *down* for southbound and *up* for northbound.

Timetables use many symbols and abbreviations, and in each there is a column of "reference notes" explaining the meaning of each symbol. For example, symbols will indicate such information as "no checked baggage," "connecting service," "central standard time," "stops 30 minutes for breakfast." It's important to look up any symbols before deciding upon any one schedule.

The main factors in reading a railroad or bus timetable are to select the correct table, look at the several departure times, compare their arrival times at the destination, and select the one that is most convenient. In case of overnight, check pullman accommodations. Most modern timetables now include a table of fares and pullman fares between various cities. They also include a column or page of general information, such as railroad policies about children, redemption of tickets, stop-over, baggage regulations.

Timetables take study, but they are *very* interesting. *Reading* them can become a game or drama activity. "My wife and I want to go from Chicago to New Orleans to see the Mardi Gras. What trains can we take? When can we leave? When will we arrive? What cities will we go through? What is the fare? Is there a diner? A parlor car?" Timetables tell all these things.

As campers learn how, the trips can become more extensive.

"Let's go from Philadelphia to Los Angeles, but let's stop over in Chicago, go to Seattle, and come down the coast. What railroad lines will we have to use? Can we work out a schedule?" Before long there'll be railroad buffs among the campers!

Bus and airline timetables are arranged very much like railroad schedules. Learn the key, then unlock the travel door. Doing your own checking is a form of independence—and some day you might *have* to!

## The Compass

No piece of camp equipment is so popular or romantic to a camper as the compass. It is so inexpensive that every child can have one, and camp equipment should include at least one really good, although not necessarily elaborate or expensive, compass. (Military surplus stores and sporting goods stores sell them.) Compasses should be *used,* too, consulted often; and activities planned around them.

Compasses are just thin, sensitive pieces of steel magnetized to point to the magnetic pole (*not* the North Pole!). Even if the campers own compasses, it is an interesting project to *make* one.

*A sewing needle compass* is easy to make. A steel needle, a little water in a saucer, a magnet—and there's an emergency compass! Magnetize the needle by rubbing it on the magnet. Run a finger along the side of the nose to get skin oil, then rub the needle across the oily finger to coat it with the oil. Then hold the needle very lightly with the points between thumb and index finger. Lower it *very* carefully, horizontally onto the water. (It must land flat, or it will break the surface tension of the water and sink. Several trials may be necessary.) If put on top of the water properly, the surface tension will hold it there, and the needle will turn by itself to face North!

Campers can test its accuracy with their "store" compasses —and they'll find it's right.

*A watch or wristwatch* can be used to find directions, too, if the sun is shining. Put the watch flat on the ground in the sun. Hold a broom straw, or thin sliver of something, vertically over the center. Turn the watch v-e-r-y carefully until the shadow of the sliver falls over the hour hand. North will be halfway between the hour hand and 12 on the dial, going the shortest way to the 12. Try it and see!

*To read a compass* hold it flat in the hand. Face the direction you want to find out about. Wait for the needle to stop quivering—and don't be in a hurry. When it comes to a standstill, the needle will point to the North. Then turn the compass very slowly so that the marker of north on the compass case and the needle pointing north coincide. Put a pencil, or better still, a thin sliver marker *across* the compass, pointing in the direction you're interested in. Read the marking on the case, and there's the direction you want. Practice! This is an important skill.

*The North Star* or Pole Star is a good night compass. The Big Dipper is easy to find. The two stars that form the very end of the dipper, farthest away from the handle, are the "pointers." Follow a straight line with the eyes, up past the top of the dipper, and the line will run straight to the North Star. This star has been the guide of seamen and wilderness scouts for ages.

When North is known, then it's easy to find the other directions. Facing North, South will be behind, East will be to the right, and West to the left.

Day campers may not have a chance to see the North Star, but if they take part in any evening ceremony, or in a campout, or overnight, finding and recognizing the North Star should be a part of the program.

*The sun* is another important, although not absolutely accurate, way to check directions. Face the morning sun, and the direction will be roughly East. Behind you will be *West, South* will be to your right, *North* to your left. In the afternoon, reverse this. Face the setting sun in the West. East will be behind you. North will be to your right, South to your left. These directions will not be exact, because the earth's orbit around the sun varies with the seasons.

Maps, markers, timetables, and direction finders are *tools*, not just information. They should be put to use—in planning trips, in playing games, in creative dramatics, in camp bus travel, in hiking, and in other day camp activities. Skills develop through practice.

CHAPTER **11:**

# HIKING

Hiking, according to the dictionary, means to "move with spirit; to march; to tramp." It is different from a walk, a trip, a hunt, or a ramble in three aspects: it assumes a reasonable, consistent degree of speed, it assumes a specific predetermined destination, and it is taken on foot. Its main accent is on walking-to-get-somewhere. It can, of course, be a part of other activities. A hike to a lake may be followed by a water program of swimming, boating, and other water sports. A hike to a farm may result in seeing farm machinery in action, petting a baby calf, finding out how butter is made, and what vegetables look like when they're growing, before they get cellophane-packed in the super-market. A hike might take a group to a fish hatchery, a fire tower, a nature museum, or the top of a mountain.

Of course, hikers enjoy the area through which they go. They also enjoy the pleasure of easy movement, of singing, of being together, of anticipation. Hiking technically is a sport. It requires specific body skills, proper clothing, and even a standard time. The average comfortable hiking speed is considered about four miles an hour—although this depends upon the age of the camper, his physical condition, and the terrain.

Hiking, when conducted as a sport and not as sauntering, is excellent exercise for developing physical fitness. Many young-sters, unfortunately, have never learned to walk properly. Day camp, with its outdoor areas that stimulate creative play, is a perfect place to teach walking properly. Going through wooded areas quietly, putting the feet down without rustling a leaf or making a twig crack, are skills that awake the Indian in every youngster. Balance plays a large part, too. A few hints by a counselor, not on walking, but on how Indians walked—and a young camper becomes conscious of these skills.

The head is up, chin in, chest out, shoulders and back relaxed,

147

arms hanging loosely from the shoulders, stomach tucked in, buttocks tucked in. Knees are loose, to cushion any jar. Legs move in an even, rhythmic stride, a comfortable step, not too long or too short. Feet touch heels first, with a slight spring as the weight is transferred on the ball of the foot, *one foot at a time.* This makes for rhythm. The weight of the body flows easily from one foot to the other. Toes point straight or slightly in. (Stalking games and games that require movement while carrying something on the head, like a book, tin cup, or stick, are good practice for learn-through-play.)

A mistake often made by counselors is the introduction of hiking before campers are ready for it. A hike that is too long and too fast, for campers who are too young or too soft, can be a very disagreeable experience; and no one likes to repeat a disagreeable experience. Counselors forget sometimes that a child's short legs have to move much more often to cover a distance than an adult's longer stride. It is sometimes a very good idea to go by car, bus, wagon, or other means and return by hiking, or hike out, returning by other transportation. Sometimes it's fun to be met halfway!

*Clothing* is important. No camper should ever start on a hike barefooted. Stubbed toes and stone bruises are only the most minor of possible bad results. Most youngsters wear sneakers in the summer, and for ordinary daily use they are satisfactory. They are not the best footwear for hiking, however; in fact, they should not be used for really active hiking, especially in mountainous country. In planning this type of hike, notify the youngsters to wear lightweight wool socks and sturdy shoes that day. Wearing band-aids will prevent heel blisters.

Slacks or jeans and a blouse or T-shirt are much better than shorts and halters. They'll prevent many a scratch, insect bite, and sunburn. If the hike will be a sunny one, a cap, hat, or light scarf will not only help to keep the sun out of the eyes, but will keep the head cool. A handkerchief tied across the forehead will keep sweat from running into the eyes. It's an old trick used by tennis players.

If anything is carried—lunch, bathing suit, or whatever—make it into a pack and carry it over the shoulders. Arms are useful for balancing properly. They should be free.

## Hiking Suggestions for Counselors

- Younger children aren't likely to need this, but sometimes, when hiking, the hands swell from being in a downward position for a continuous length of time. Practiced hiking groups often make a point of holding the arms up in the air at intervals.
- Small pebbles, if clean and smooth, will keep the mouth moist when carried in the mouth. Don't use this hint with the younger campers, especially preschoolers. They might swallow them accidentally! Chewing gum helps, too.
- If going far, and water supply is uncertain, carry water, or fruit juices, or fruits like oranges and tomatoes. *Never* allow youngsters to drink from streams, or other source of untested water.
- Avoid soft candy, especially chocolate. It gets messy *and* it makes you thirsty. Sour fruitballs are the best if youngsters have to have something.
- Be sure any knife or axe is sheathed.
- Use a pedometer. Youngsters love to find out how far they've gone. Make it a guessing game—how far to that rock?, and similar questions.
- Use a compass. It's good practice and adds interest.
- A counselor should always be at the head of a hiking group, and another at the end, to watch over the stragglers.
- Vary the speed once in a while. Walk twelve steps, run twelve steps. It helps prevent fatigue.
- Sing or whistle. Use songs with strong beats. Set the tempo to the length of the campers', not your, steps.
- Use the hike as an opportunity for informal talk with individual campers. It's a good time to establish friendly, personal contact.
- Be on the lookout for places or things that can be used for further exploration—an unusual rock formation, wild flowers, bird's nest, good camp site, stream for fishing.

- Plan the destination points carefully in terms of distance—from short ones made highly pleasurable to arouse interest to longer ones as youngsters learn hiking skills and develop stamina.

### Outdoor Manners

Outdoor manners are important. A discussion of ownership, responsibilities, rights, is part of any outdoor program. Strict observance of rules decided upon and accepted as fair should be required. A camper who sees his favorite counselor go up to a farmhouse and ask permission before he crosses a field, or who sticks the paper from his piece of gum into his pocket instead of tossing it away will very likely do the same.

Picking things—flowers, plants, berries, fruits—in fields and woods is a very natural thing to do. Youngsters (adults, too!) don't realize that woods and meadows all belong to *somebody* —to private owners, industry, light and power companies, States —even to the United States. Making collections, too, sometimes blinds campers to ownership rights. It's a good idea to say— truthfully, of course: "Mr. So-and-So (or the Park Department, or whoever) said we could pick leaves to take back to look up in our tree book, if we didn't break any branches." Or "I'm sure Mr. Brown won't mind if we collect insects in his woods. Let's go ask him." Or "I brought along a copy of the rules of the Park Department so that we won't break any laws." Or, "It's been so dry all week that we'd better call (or run over to see) the Fire Warden before we have our cook-out." Attitudes of adults, especially adults they *like*, rub off on children.

As a reminder, here are some Good Conduct rules:

- *Get permission* before going on private property. The fact that you don't see a house is no reason to trespass. *Somebody* owns that land if you don't.
- *Never cut across* anyone's yard, garden, or crop land.
- *Always close* any gate or fence that you opened.
- *Never pick* fruit, berries, flowers, et cetera on anybody's land except your own without permission.
- *Never carve on,* or strip bark from, any living tree.

- *Never leave* any litter, even little things like gum wrappers and facial tissue. If you brought it in, take it out!
- *Never thumb* a ride. In most states it's illegal; in all states it's dangerous.
- *Never build* a fire, hunt, or fish on land or water that isn't yours, without permission from the owner, and without the required legal permit or license.
- *Walk on the left side* of any public highway, facing oncoming traffic.
- *Walk in single file* when traffic is heavy, and in small lines of two or three abreast when light. On a sidewalk, don't spread out and make people walk around you.
- *Wait* and cross a road as a group. Don't straggle across.
- *Obey* all traffic, road, or trail signals and symbols. Never remove, change, or deface a trail marker.

## Ten Rules for Good Outdoor Conduct

The Outdoor Conduct Committee of the Isaak Walton League of America has compiled the following tentative set of Ten Rules for Good Outdoor Conduct. All counselors should know and observe such rules, and make them part of their program with young campers. (Anyone with suggestions is invited to write to the chairman of the Committee, Mr. Ralph W. Stark, 122 South Lebanon Street, Lebanon, Indiana.)

- Wherever you go, wherever you are—in the fields, in the forests, on the waters; whether it be hunting, fishing, hiking, camping, boating, swimming, water skiing, or mountain climbing—be courteous to all others with whom you come in contact.
- When you go outdoors for the enjoyment of any one of the many and various recreations, most likely you are to be on another person's premises. Secure his permission; otherwise, you are a trespasser. Respect his right of ownership and treat his possessions with estimable consideration.
- Familiarize yourself with all safety rules for going outdoors in general, and the recreation in particular you are engaging in. Be careful, be cautious, be safe. Don't take chances endangering yourself and the safety of others.
- Help Mother Nature with her outdoor housekeeping. Clean up your picnicking place or your camping ground when your outing is over. Refrain from scattering trash and debris anytime, anywhere. Don't be a "litterbug." Do your part in keeping your State and your America clean and beautiful.

- Be careful with fire. Be sure your picnic and campfires are extinguished when leaving, your cigarette and cigar stubs, and your pipe embers are out when discarded. Don't let one thoughtless, careless act stigmatize you as an arsonist.
- Know the hunting and fishing laws and all other outdoor regulations—federal and provincial, and of your state and of the state or country in which you may be a visitor. Abide by them and obey them.
- Don't wantonly and without reason kill or destroy wildlife or vegetation or otherwise mar and deface the beauty of the outdoors. Don't be a vandal.
- Learn the fundamental principles of conservation as they apply to soil, woods, waters, and wildlife, and practice them wherever you are, wherever you go, that our heritage of these precious natural resources may be conserved and, in some measure, restored.
- Teach and instruct others, particularly our young people, the principles of conservation and the value of adherence to these Ten Rules of Good Outdoor Conduct that they may find more pleasure and keener enjoyment in the outdoors and the many health-building, soul-refreshing recreations it affords.
- Memorize and adopt as your personal creed the Conservation Pledge: "I give my pledge as an American to save and faithfully defend from waste the natural resources of my Country—its soil and minerals, its forests, waters, and wildlife."

---

**Who picnics by these roaring waves
And all the bank with litter paves
May indigestion rack his chest
And ants invade his pants and vest.**
*Sign in Great Smokey Mts. National Park.*

CHAPTER **12:**

# CAMP
# EMERGENCIES

Emergencies of one sort or another are bound to come up in any program with groups of children. Whether simple or drastic, emergencies can alarm parents, and frighten or confuse children and counselors. Forethought may prevent regret. A basic part of leadership training should include a very thorough discussion of types of emergencies, possible ways of meeting them, and camp policy in handling certain types. Such training should include *practice* as well as discussion.

Some simple emergencies can be anticipated, and parents notified of the camp policy ahead of time. Delay in morning pick-up or afternoon return trip is an example, as is any policy regarding the cancelling of the camp program on a rainy day. These will be discussed more fully in Section IV.

Forethought is also highly important in the prevention of certain types of emergencies *before they have a chance to happen.* A day camp site, for example, can be rid of poison ivy before the day camp season opens. It can be grubbed out, or sprayed with any one of a number of selective weed killers. Mosquitoes can be controlled by special sprays, also.

Other hazards, like dead trees, rotten limbs, holes in the ground, and loose rocks, can be eliminated—not to change the camp environment to any extent, but to make for a safer site for use by children.

Safety equipment of one sort or another can be ready, and installed where needed—ropes, life preservers, ladders, board-walks at the swimming area; First Aid kit well selected and in easy access, along with a First Aid Manual of Instruction; a place for an emergency "infirmary" selected; fire extinguishers, hose, water and sand buckets, broom and shovel for possible fire-fighting provided; toilet, food, and water facilities tested for health and safety; some sort of signal system rigged up that can alert and call all campers together in emergency; method devised of notifying parents and returning child to home when necessary.

Trained personnel can be selected ahead of time. The Day Camp Standards of the American Camping Association require that "a registered nurse, licensed physician or person holding a current American Red Cross certificate in Advanced First Aid should be on the camp staff." They also require that every leader or counselor in camp have passed a thorough physical examination a month before camp opens. (This is required of campers also.)

Preparedness, common sense, good judgment, and a sense of humor, all go far in meeting minor and major emergencies.

### Accidents

No matter how well-prepared the staff, or well-planned the site, some accidents—hopefully minor—will happen. A bee will sting Billie. Sue will scrape her knee. Sam will get sunburned.

David will get car sick. A stubbed toe will make Ed cry. Betty will burn her finger at the campfire. Jon will get a blister on his heel.

Any competent nurse, doctor, or First-Aider can handle such small emergencies with "no sweat" as the military say—*if* supplies and equipment are at hand, and the youngsters are trained to report *all* accidents, even little ones, at once.

More serious accidents *can* occur. A child can slip on a mossy or slimy rock and sprain an ankle. An arm or leg can be broken. A child may require mouth-to-mouth breathing treatment if he has to be rescued from the pool or lake. A child may be bitten by a small animal he has cornered.

Such cases require trained treatment, delivery of child to home or hospital, report to parents, and reassurance of the other youngsters. Here again, however, campers—even very young ones —should be taught not to touch and not to move the hurt child, and to run to the camp nurse for help.

Much of the material in this chapter may not be regarded strictly as activity program. Keeping well, safe, and happy are dependent on campcraft skills; and learning what to do in accidents and other emergencies is *good* activity for day campers. Knowledge helps to reduce fears. Day campers can learn First Aid the *real* way, not out of a book, but by watching, asking questions, and practicing. They also learn the values of *prevention*—a most useful lesson to learn early.

*Heat* may cause one of several possible emergencies that can be classified under accidents. If common sense is used in selecting and conducting activities on very hot days, there will be little chance of such occurrences. As a matter of fact, adults are more likely to suffer a heat reaction than are children. Several types of heat reaction are possible. They are all serious and should be recognized by counselors and campers.

*Heat exhaustion* is a form of shock. The skin will be pale and clammy, the pulse rapid and weak. Dizziness and muscular cramps may be present. The patient should be stretched out in a shady place, feet higher than head, and body covered with a blanket. Sweet hot tea, coffee, or cocoa will help.

Heat cramps in the legs, arms, and abdomen are a sign that the body is losing more salt, through perspiration, than it is taking in. Prevention and cure is to add liquid and salt. This can be done by drinking salted water (1 teaspoon per gallon) or adding salt to food or drink. Tomato juice and grapefruit juice can take quite a lot of salt without tasting of it. So can sliced tomatoes. A bit of salt in cocoa adds to its flavor.

*Sunstroke* seldom occurs, but is serious. If the patient has a flushed face along with a headache, a pounding pulse, and *dry, hot* skin, *call a doctor.* Move the patient to the nearest shady and cool place, and try to cool him off. Take off most of his clothes, and sprinkle cold water on him. Put cold compresses on his head, using ice if possible. Keep sponging with cold water. The important thing is to reduce his temperature.

*Don't confuse heat exhaustion with sunstroke.* They are almost opposite in symptoms and in treatment. Both are serious, and sunstroke can be fatal if not treated promptly.

## Thunderstorms

If a sudden thunderstorm catches the campers away from shelter, stay away from tall trees, or trees or barns standing alone in an open area. Stay away from the tops of hills or mountains, or any high, exposed area. Put down any metal tool or object like a golf club or a rake.

Campers should leave any type of water or water facility—beach, pool, boat, canoe—at the first sign of storm. They should get into dry, warm clothing, under shelter.

If the storm comes up during the bus trip, the driver should keep an even, slow speed, so that the car behind won't run into the bus after a severe and blinding bolt. He should not drive off the road to stop under an isolated tree, telephone pole, power pole, or wire fence.

The chance of being hit by lightning is very slight, but precautions should be kept. It is important, however, that these precautions be done matter-of-factly, so that they do not alarm or frighten the youngsters.

Any kind of physical action is an antidote to fear. Sing, dance, play a game that involves clapping, or whistling, or quick movements if the youngsters seem apprehensive. Encourage them to *watch* the storm and enjoy its beauty if they are not frightened. Which direction is the wind? How hard is it blowing? How long will the storm last? Has the temperature dropped? Will there be a rainbow? What *is* a rainbow? Did the camp weather bureau predict the storm?

## Fire

A forest fire, whether started by carelessness in the day camp or on a course to endanger the day camp site, is usually not a problem as far as child safety is concerned. In the first place, help is fast in coming, as is warning. Fire travels fairly slowly, too, although it's hard to believe. It seldom goes more than 10 miles per hour, so that the camp bus or cars can easily outdistance it. There should be no delay. Get the youngsters out, *then* come back and help fight the fire.

In the far West, where there are many beautiful but narrow

canyons, a site should not be selected for a day camp *unless* it has two ways of getting out.

Occasionally a tent catches fire. If this happens, the best thing to do is to collapse it as fast as possible, *then* fight the fire.

Every day camper should learn and *practice* safety in using fire. (This is covered in Chapter 4, "Firemaking and Cooking.")

**Flood**

Floods, like fires, usually give ample warning. An exception is in dry sections of the country, where river or stream beds that are usually dry can be filled with a dangerous torrent by a flash flood some distance away. Experienced campers are careful when crossing such stream beds, and they never camp or pitch tents too close to them.

Big floods have been experienced in many parts of the country in recent years, usually as aftermaths of hurricanes. Hurricane warnings are sent out well in advance, and day campers should not be affected.

A heavy rainstorm can flood an improperly ditched tent. It can also wet clothing, wet food, put out fires, and upset tempers. If adequate shelter is not available, go home!

**Windstorm**

A sudden high windstorm can be dangerous because it can come up unexpectedly. It can create a fire hazard by blowing embers from any open fire. It can knock down tents, send branches or dead trees whirling down, and it can make a child fall or bang into a tree or wall or other object.

It is best to put out any fires, collapse any improvised shelters like pup tents, and weight down anything that might blow away, like outdoor furniture.

Youngsters should be inside any safe shelter and, if necessary, kept away from windows in case of breaking glass. Sometimes the camp bus is a safe place to be until the storm blows over. If a group is caught outdoors, without shelter, it should keep away from trees, and lie flat on the ground, close together, with arms over head.

**Tornado**

The windstorm above does not include the *tornado*—which is in a class of its own! Today, radio warnings of tornado activity are very helpful, and such warnings, even if vague, should be heeded. If there's time, the children should be taken at once to the nearest place of shelter, such as a farmhouse cellar, a hospital or church basement.

If by any chance there's no warning, and a tornado is seen, the youngsters crouch, hands over heads, against the cellar wall that's in the direction of the tornado. If there's no cellar, then against the ground-floor wall. Windows on the far side of the shelter should be raised slightly so as not to make a vacuum when the tornado hits.

### Wild Animals

The wild animals in most day camps will be squirrels and birds in the trees, rabbits in the bush, ants, turtles, bees, fish, and other harmless and interesting creatures.

In the West, and in some forest areas, porcupines may be a nuisance to camp gear, but not dangerous unless cornered or in too close range.

Occasionally skunks can be found, but they prefer dusk or evening; and they are harmless if not threatened.

In some places tame bear and deer, used to campers, can be a real menace and should NOT be fed.

**Poisonous Animals**

The United States has only four poisonous snakes, the rattlesnake (which doesn't always rattle!), the moccasin, the water or cotton-mouth moccasin, and the coral snake, which is found only in the South and Southwest. The chances of any of these being found at a day camp site are not very likely. Hiking skills, however, should include safety measures, such as these:

- Step over, not on, fallen logs, rocks, and other possible hiding places.

- Don't move such objects with the hands. A snake may have taken refuge there.
- Never put the hand or arm into the hole in a hollow tree or wall, or in the ground, or on a rock ledge above the head when climbing a hill or mountain.

Anyone bitten by a snake should be taken to a hospital or doctor at once, after a tourniquet has been applied between the bite and the heart. (Always loosen a tourniquet every 15 minutes.) Snake bite kits are useful in wilderness camping, but are not likely to be needed at day camp. They should never be used by anyone unfamiliar with them.

A few scorpions, the gila monster, and the black widow spider are the only other poisonous creatures. They are limited in range and are unlikely to be found or seen. If they are known in that section of the country, however, counselors and campers should be able to recognize them, know their habits, and give them a wide berth.

Mosquitoes, wasps, yellow jackets, hornets, midges, "chiggers," and their kin are nuisances and pests, and can cause minor discomfort. The most dangerous of this type is the tick, which can transmit Rocky Mountain fever, relapsing fever, and Q fever. It should never be pulled out of the skin because the head will stay imbedded and may cause infection. A drop of oil or alcohol, tweezers, or a drop of hot water can be used to make the tick drop off. *Never* handle ticks with the bare hands, whether removing them from humans or animals. Always use tweezers.

## Poisonous Plants

Of the three plants representing the greatest hazard to day campers, *poison ivy*, found everywhere in the United States except the Southwest, is by far the most prevalent. It can even be found sometimes under hedges on city streets! It climbs up trees, over fences and walls, or along the ground and the roadside. Its shiny green leaves that turn a lovely red in early fall are a great temptation to the unwary.

It is hard to eradicate permanently because its berries are

relished by birds whose droppings often start new patches. Every part of it is poisonous to most people—the leaves, stems, roots—and, if burned, the smoke can carry the toxic phenolic compound that causes the trouble. No one should take immunity for granted, because immunity to it often changes.

One of the very first lessons at day camp should be:

### LEAVES THREE—LET IT BE

Campers can do more than just find and identify a patch. When found, it should be staked off, so that no one goes through it accidentally.

Washing bare hands, arms, legs, or feet carefully with yellow soap as soon as possible after contact will prevent its effect—but it has to be soon and thorough. Calamine lotion is an old standby to dry the blisters and relieve the itching. Many new products are also on the market, and every First Aid kit should have some effective remedy.

Poison ivy should not be confused with woodbine or Virginia creeper, which is also a vine, and turns red in the fall. Woodbine has *five*, not three, leaves.

*Poison oak* looks and acts much like poison ivy. It is usually a low shrub, but it can resemble a vine. Its range is much more limited, however. It is found all down the Western coast, throughout the South, and up the East Coast almost to New England.

*Poison sumac* is seldom found except in swampy areas, and mostly in the South, East Coast, and around the Great Lakes. It does not look like the other types of sumac, because its leaves are glossy and broader, and its berries are white, not red. Day campers are not likely to find it, but again they should be able to recognize it, for it produces even more disagreeable and longer-lasting effects than poison ivy.

The berries of all three of these poisonous plants are relished by birds, and so they have a place in nature's plan. They should not be allowed to grow in a day camp site, however, unless isolated and kept for identification.

Some other plants, both wild and cultivated, are poisonous if eaten. The bean from the decorative castor oil plant, for example, is very poisonous. Aconite is poisonous, as is the root of the swamp iris and of the mandrake or May apple. The beautiful Amanita mushroom is rightly called the Angel of Death.

The identification of edible and of poisonous plants (including leaves, flowers, seeds, roots) can be one of the most interesting activities in day camp—but it must have an expert leader. Otherwise, it is good practice to eat nothing that is not familiar.

## Survival

The ability to put knowledge to practical use is something that can be encouraged in the day camp. Activities that are fun are also activities that might be a matter of life or death in an emergency. The fire that is only part of a council ring program today is the same fire that might keep the group warm and dry, might beckon a rescue party, might cook the food that has been caught or trapped—and might completely destroy the camp site.

The water that runs in the little brook that can be waded, the water that's fun to swim in, the water that comes out of the tap so easily, is the same water that can rise in a flood and that can be a hazard to life and property.

It is not the duty of a day camp leader to alarm young campers, or to add fears. Drawing comparisons, and using examples, however, are ways that help to lift an activity out of its play role into practical use.

"During that hurricane last year, all the electric power went off and stayed off for several days. We had to cook over the fire, just as we're doing now."

"If we were caught in a flood, and wanted to make a raft, we could lash logs together like this."

*Anticipating* emergencies—thinking about them, talking about them, and planning for them—are ways of meeting them without fear and panic. With young children, simple creative dramatic techniques can be used. "Let's 'play like' we're lost. What should we do?" Out of such a simple question can come a discussion of all that is involved—signaling for help, how to use compass, stars, wind, trees in locating directions; what to do about food and water, shelter and fire; what animals we might see; and what hazards to look out for.

Campers beyond the "play like" stage are ready for the "what would we do if"—type of discussion. "Suppose we were lost, and it was getting dark. What would we do?" "What would we do if it rained, and we wanted to build a fire?" "If all the gas and electricity went off, and stayed off for a week, how could our families keep warm, dry, and fed?" "The water is pumped in by electricity—how could you get along without drinking water for a while?" "If you were hungry, and the lake was full of fish but you didn't have a rod or a fish hook, what would you do?" "Suppose we were marooned somewhere and ate up all our provisions. What could we find to eat?" A discussion of edible fruits and plants, followed by collecting them and tasting them could follow. Also, of course, a warning about what *not* to touch or eat.

If the youngsters don't know the story of Robinson Crusoe, or have forgotten it, it's a good time to reread it.

Survival means the ability to improvise, to adapt one's self to unusual circumstances without panic. Simple basic skills that can be learned in camp, plus courage, plus physical stamina may be factors some day in personal survival. And even if emergencies never arise, learning how to meet them is basic in camping skills.

Some of the youngsters may bring up the question of bomb shelters, blast, fallout, and other problems of the nuclear age. It is best not to avoid such questions, if or when they arise. Discuss them as simply and factually as possible. The more the youngsters express their fears, the easier they are to recognize and overcome. Be matter-of-fact, optimistic, and emphasize healthy attitudes of readiness, of working together, and of willingness to share. Fitness to meet emergencies must include mental and emotional fitness just as much as physical fitness.

### Final Caution

The wise day camp director, as mentioned at the beginning of this chapter, tries to avoid emergencies by preventing them ahead of time, and by practice in advance, especially as a part of staff training. Activities that train the day campers in ways of meeting emergencies are an important part of the program.

A few basic, absolute rules should be set up, explained, and required. They should apply to counselor and camper alike.

- *Some sort of signal should be set up, which, when sounded, will bring everyone at once to a specific, central meeting place.*

    There should be no "fooling" about this. Wherever they are, whatever they are doing, all persons in camp should drop everything and run to that meeting place. Needless to say, this special signal is used only for a real emergency, but at least one practice "drill" will help.

- *Some system of camper counting should be set up, so that everyone* can be accounted for and *fast.*

- *A plan for leaving* should be drawn up, and known in advance by all counselors. This plan involves *special duties* for each, such as one counselor to get youngsters onto the bus; another to check and put out fires; another to be in charge of emergency food and water supplies; still another to be in charge of a First Aid Kit; et cetera.

A mass evacuation is very seldom necessary, but when it is, *time* will be very important. Emergencies never happen at convenient times. A smooth, efficient, "team" approach, with everyone doing his part quickly and without panic is the key to a quick, safe evacuation.

Action, as said before, is a good antidote to fear. Undirected action, however, can result in panic, which is sometimes more dangerous than the emergency. Have a plan. Learn it. Rehearse it. Use it—if it should become necessary.

# Related Program Activities

There was a child went forth every day;
   And the first object he looked upon,
   that object he became;
And that object became part of him for
   the day, or a certain part of the day,
   or for many years, or stretching cycles of years.

—WALT WHITMAN
*There Was a Child Went Forth*

CHAPTER **13:**

# ARTS
# AND
# CRAFTS

A look at the arts and crafts projects of a day camp is often a give-away of the extent of the real camping practices of the camp. Projects in a day camp that provides camping experiences will emphasize campcraft skills. Many projects described in Section II are technically craft projects, such as the construction of a sundial, the tying of knots.

As in the general day camp program, as opposed to other types of summer programs, camp activities including arts and crafts should, as far as possible, be related

- to the day camp setting
- to camping skills
- to other phases of the day camp program
- to camping objectives

In the case of arts and crafts, other criteria should be added:

- to make use of natural material whenever possible, but with discretion and thought of conservation.
- to use such materials honestly.
- to develop projects that are helpful and useful in the daily camp program.
- to develop projects that offer campers a creative opportunity and the opportunity of choice.

The suggested projects in this chapter are included primarily to *strengthen* the activities basic to camping, and to *enrich* related activities in music, drama, and dancing. They are selected also because they are relaxed, informal projects that have a purpose. They are not just busy work.

Hundreds of other projects might have been included. Day camps with well-equipped craft shops and adequate budgets for craft equipment and supplies can go much more intensively

167

into this phase of the program. Day camps with nature museums adequately equipped and with trained leadership can go much more intensively into activities involving the ecology of the site.

Any leader in any day camp, however, whether specialized or not, can use the projects here. They are not technical. They do not require specialized tools or supplies. Many, as a matter of fact, make use of supplies that any youngster can bring from home. Most, it is hoped, have a definite carry-over value, or are interest arousers. None of them requires a kit, or a pattern, or an exact design. The idea in each must be explored by the child, using his own imagination and creative ability.

## ART

Painting, sketching, photography, sculpture, ceramics, woodcarving, and other forms of art are types that depend very definitely on specialized leadership. Such leadership should be chosen not only for the skills involved, but also for the understanding of age characteristics and needs of children.

In the day camp, the art program should lean heavily upon the setting. It should be relaxed and informal. It should offer a wide variety of *choice,* and many opportunities to experiment with different media. Oils, pastels, watercolors, tempera, finger-paints, crayons, charcoal, pencil—all have their advantages and disadvantages. Local, native clay, plastic modeling clay, regular clay, self-hardening clay—all are plastic media worth exploring. Woodcarving can be practiced in soft balsa and pine, no more dangerous than making a model plane. Photography can become more than "snapping a picture."

Art programs depend upon the development of an eye that sees forms and colors, and the instinct to translate these things into a creative, personal interpretation. Both can be developed, and the day camp is an excellent place to start.

## CRAFTS

Crafts can be as highly specialized as art, but, for children in a day camp setting, the emphasis should be on indigenous projects. These include not only the use of natural materials (with conservation always in mind): they also include projects that will be helpful in other camp activities, or will increase the enjoyment of other activities. The projects in this section are primarily of these two types.

Many other craft projects have been described in Section II, since they are so completely environmental. Those, plus these which follow, will provide an exciting and interesting program, with ample opportunity for personal choice, experimentation, and decision making. They are grouped loosely under six classifications which frequently overlap:

> For All-Camp Use
> Nature and Science Tie-Ins
> Decorative Crafts
> Playthings
> For Personal Use
> Drama and Music Tie-Ins

## For All-Camp Use

ANT HOUSE

An Ant House can be made out of a shallow wooden box about 12 x 14 x 3 inches, with two rooms 4 x 4 inches, in the center of the box, approximately one-fourth inch deep and with one external opening (see diagram). Two pieces of glass should be provided, one to cover the entire box and one to cover the two rooms. The glass covering the rooms should be glued in place. The glass covering the box should be ant-tight and kept in place with adhesive tape which may be removed when necessary. A piece of cardboard or three-ply wood the size of the rooms should be prepared. It should be attached to a three-eighths inch piece of dowel wood about a foot long. The dowel should fit freely into a hole drilled in the side of the box. Through the use of this device the cardboard may be kept on the rooms except when you wish to observe the ants, when the cardboard may be removed by pulling the dowel without opening the ant house. Ants will perform normal nest functions only in the dark. It is said, however, that orange or red glass will give the same effect as darkness.

Several openings on the sides of the box, covered with fine carburetor screen, should be provided for ventilation. A piece of sponge tacked in the corner of the ant house and kept moist will prevent the air from becoming too dry.

Bits of meat, sweets, banana, and other food should be placed in the box. Holes drilled in the box and fitted with plugs can be opened for the placing of food and water within the ant house, so that ants will not be lost in opening the lid.

Occupants for the house should be collected with a small amount of dirt and dumped into the tray outside the rooms. The covers, cardboard, and glass should be placed on at once. The ants will find the dark cells and carry the immature ants into them. Ground-nesting ants, larvae, pupae, eggs, and a queen ant (if possible) should be collected. The dirt may be removed after the ants have set up housekeeping.

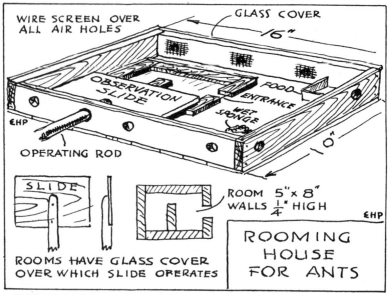

ROOMING HOUSE FOR ANTS

CARVING BOARD

The instinct to carve words, symbols, or initials on tree trunks, benches, or walls seems to be in every child. Recognize it—and provide a legitimate outlet. Provide a soft-wood board, or several. Work out with the campers a border, name, or decoration—then give each the opportunity to carve something on it—his initials, a heart, a ship—whatever he likes.

### FLOWER BOARD, LEAF BOARD, AND SEED BOARD

A *flower board* can be an attractive and useful tool in arousing and satisfying interest in wildflowers. It can also be used to good advantage along a nature trail. Finding specimens, and writing up cards for each, are good nature activities.

The sketch gives an idea of how a flower board is made, but each camp can adapt it for its own use. It is merely a square or rectangle of wood with an overhanging roof to protect its face. Make a double roof and use *both* sides if desired.

A test tube or small bottle is attached to the board with wire. A 3″ x 5″ or a 4″ x 6″ card is tacked on. A flower is placed in water in the test tube every day, and the card tells something interesting about it, or asks a question. "Why am I called Dandelion? Pull out one of my yellow petals. The French think it looks like a lion's tooth." Or "When I go to seed, touch my seedpod and you'll find out why I'm called Touch-Me-Not."

*Leaf Board.* Like the flower board, but using leaves instead of flowers.

*Seed Board.* Ditto, but uses different kinds of burrs, cones, seedpods, and the like.

### MODEL GARDEN

Little girls will enjoy making these. Each draws, paints, or crayons, and cuts out, a *large* flower head of her choice—tulip, zinnia, sunflower, daisy, or whatever. These are tacked to the end of long stakes, and then set up in the day camp area. (They make *very* pretty dividers for special areas, too.)

A MODEL ZOO

A model zoo is a group project that can be used later in a day camp carnival or circus. Collect boxes and paper bags in as wide a variety of sizes and shapes as possible. Let the youngsters staple them together, cover with paper, add appendages as needed, and paint.

Chicken wire bent into various shapes and covered over with strips of brown paper or newspaper pasted to each other to form a thin shell makes interesting animals, too. After the "skin" dries out thoroughly, it can be painted, and any needed decorations added.

SHARING BOARD

Campers set up and decorate a board of heavy cardboard, or wood, or even a four-dimensional board made by hanging a decorated box from a tree limb. Wire, string, tape, and thumbtacks can be used to attach the objects. A card can be filled out, to add interest and give credit. "Bill found this in the brook." "May's father brought this wooden shoe to her from Holland."

TOUCH BOX

A hatbox, or a cardboard carton, makes a good touch box. A cover that can be taken off when contents are changed is helpful, but when the box is in use, the cover should be tied or taped down. A hole big enough to allow a child's hand and wrist to get in, but not large enough to show the contents, should be cut in the top or one of the sides. Leave a flap, if you like. Decorating and labeling the box is part of the craft project.

Inside, the box should contain a number of different objects, some attached to the sides, some loose on the floor of the box. Each child gets a one-minute feel and then makes a list of what he thinks the box contains.

The contents should be changed often. At one time, the box

may have items of different *textures*. Another time, it might be natural objects like a stone, bit of moss, bird's nest, mushroom. Guessing can be for identification, or for descriptive adjectives —"something slippery, cold, fuzzy, feathery."

Campers should be asked to bring in items for the touch box and give them to the counselor, or to a special group in charge of changing the contents. Never put living animals, or sharp items in the touch box.

## Nature and Science Tie-Ins

### BIRD CALLERS

Bird callers are amazing things—and they work! Each young-ster can make his own. Each caller requires a piece of hard wood, like rock maple or mountain ash, about 2 inches long and 1 inch square. A piece of hammer handle will do. Buy a screw-eye. Drill a hole in one end of the wood slightly *smaller* than the threads of the screw-eye. Turn the screw-eye into the wood, take it out, and put some powdered resin in the hole.

When the screw-eye is turned back and forth, it will make a squeaky sound that attracts birds. (They won't come *to* the owner, but they'll come nearer, particularly in the late spring and early summer when they're raising their young.)

### BIRD FEEDERS

Bird feeders for camp or home are fine craft projects. Feeders to attract birds that live on insects and grubs should be built to hold suet and peanut butter mix-tures.

A short board, to which a piece of hardware cloth or wide metal screening is nailed in such a way that it flares out at the top for filling, but is closed at the bottom, makes an excellent suet holder. In squirrel or crow country, add a piece of the wire mesh to make a top that can be wired down.

If a saw is available, very attractive suet and peanut butter holders can be made out of gourds and coconuts. Just cut out a side, leaving a good-size "cup," and drill two holes in the top, through which a wire can be run so as to hang the feeder to a tree limb. Scrape out the inside of the coconut, of course—as if the youngsters won't! (Or leave it in for the downy woodpeckers, nut hatches, and chickadees to enjoy while it lasts.)

Some birds prefer *seeds*. Cut off the top and bottom of a waxed milk container, and cut a small triangle about an inch high, out of each side of the bottom. (The seeds will feed out through these holes.) Bore a hole in the center of each of two pie tins. Straighten out a metal coat hanger, leaving the hook. Run the coat hanger through the inverted top pie tin, and milk container, and the bottom pie tin (right side up) and hold the wire in place by running the bottom end through a washer and cork, bending the wire so that it won't come out. Fill the carton with wildbird seed, or with fine baby chick feed by raising the top pie tin.

Another, and even simpler, feeder can be made from the outside of half a grapefruit. Each camper can bring one from home. It should be scraped out carefully, then allowed to dry thoroughly, leaving a hard shell. Drill or poke a hole near the top of each side, being careful not to crack or break the shell, and hang it from short strings tied through these holes.

INSECT CAGE

Glass jars are bulky, slippery, and dangerous for youngsters to carry around. This kind of cage is simple and safe.

Cut a rectangle of screen, about 6″ x 12″, and roll it into a cylinder. Fit it into a peanut butter or jam jar lid which serves as bottom, sew the seam of the

Insect Cage

screen with a bit of wire, and cap the screening with another jar lid. Use it to *catch* as well as to carry insects back to day camps to look at carefully, look up, identify—and then let go!

INSECT NET

Insect nets can be improvised from wire coat hangers. Straighten out the hook, then bend the hanger into a ring. A length of broomstick or dowel or other stick can be used for a handle, drilled to hold the wire, or the wire lashed to it. The net should be made of mosquito netting or unbleached muslin, conical in shape, and deep enough to hold the insect securely, until it can be put in the insect cage. Insects can be brought to the camp site for study and identification, but should be released. They are hard to keep alive without specialized knowledge.

KILLING JAR

Killing jars are too dangerous for use by small children, by those who have not been given specific training in their use, or by youngsters unless closely supervised. A few older children with previous experience and interest in collecting, or a counselor himself, may wish to make and use a killing jar. It is simple to prepare.

All that is needed is a pint jar with a tight-fitting lid. Place a layer of absorbent cotton on the bottom of the jar and moisten it with ethyl acetate or Carbona cleaning fluid. Fit a round of blotting paper over the cotton so that the insect will not be in direct contact with the fluid. Leave the insect in for an hour, and use tweezers to remove it gently for mounting.

In general, and for most campers, it is wisest to stress the *living* insect and its place in nature. Collecting for killing and mounting should be done only by those with a real purpose and scientific interest.

SKYSCOPE

Day campers do not have the opportunity to study the night skies and learn to recognize any of the constellations. A skyscope made in day camp can be a way to introduce them to the stars.

Each youngster brings a shoebox, so that he can make a skyscope for himself. To make it is simple.

Cut an opening out of one end of the box and cover it with

white tissue paper, very tight and smooth. Cut a slit on both sides of the box about one-half inch from this end. Make the edges of these slits nice and smooth, because slides will go through them.

At the other end of the box make a small peephole in the exact center by pushing a pencil point through it. The skyscope is ready! The next step is to make the stars.

Youngsters will have to study and talk about some of the most familiar of the constellations, and decide which to use. The slides are made of black construction paper. The camper outlines the constellation he chooses, and then pricks out, with a needle, the stars in it. The bigger the star, the bigger the hole prick.

When the constellation is ready, slide the black paper through the slits so that the constellation is centered. Then face the box to the light, and look through the peephole. It will be like looking up at the summer sky!

Good constellations to use are Draco, Big Dipper, Little Dipper, and Cassiopea, but use the ones that will be seen at night in your section of the country at that season.

The Indians and the Greeks had fascinating legends about the stars. Use them for storytelling while making the skyscopes.

SPIDER WEB PRINT

A spider web print requires two persons. One stands behind the web, holding a large sheet of dark paper against the web, and as steadily as possible. The other sprays the web with lacquer or plastic spray, so that it is imprinted permanently against the paper. Let the print dry thoroughly and then mount it and use it for wall decoration, or use it for a visual aid in nature study.

This should be a *group* project. One web may be used for study, but dozens of webs should not be destroyed. One web print can be a permanent record, but daily observation of webs in action will be much more interesting.

## Decorative Crafts

### DRIFTWOOD

Driftwood includes not only the scarred, gray wood cast up on beaches, but similar pieces found along lake fronts, or twisted roots and limbs found in the woods and in dredged or bulldozed areas. Finding and selecting a piece that has decorative possibilities is in itself a creative activity, using observation and imagination.

Most pieces will need a thorough cleaning. They should be soaked, and scrubbed with a stiff brush to remove all sand, soil, loose bark, or bits of decayed wood. The pieces should be allowed to dry out.

They are then ready for careful planning. Each piece should be scraped thoroughly to remove all soft places. It should be "tested" then. Does it sit steadily? Which side is the most interesting? Is any part too long? Does it make an interesting shadow? Would it look better sitting or hanging freely, or against a wall? Does one part need accenting?

When the basic form is decided, then comes the real work—sandpapering until the wood is smooth and shows its grain, then sanding and waxing, until the piece has a lovely smooth finish that looks natural. No gilt or colored paint is needed or should be used on a fine piece of natural driftwood.

Sometimes a piece of root or driftwood will resemble a bird, animal, or prehistoric beast. Youngsters enjoy painting and decorating such pieces to bring out the resemblance. Beads, feathers, felt, shells, cones, can be added to such pieces to make amusing and interesting objects.

Sometimes stones can be used in similar fashion—flat, round ones at the beach may suggest the body of a turtle—and a camper prepares a gift for Dad's desk. By and large, however, nature objects are loveliest when kept natural.

### FISH PRINTS

Fish prints are delightfully messy. They are also an old Japanese art form! They may be made to record a child's catch—or as an interesting type of print. The result can be a very lovely, delicate print, worth framing.

Brush liquid tempera over the entire surface of one side of the fish. Run a dry roller over it to remove all brush marks. Place the fish carefully on a clean sheet of paper, and spread the fins and tail. Quickly, before the paint dries, place a piece of tissue paper over the painted fish, pressing it gently over the surface of the entire fish, paying special attention to the fins and tail. Remove the tissue paper, lifting it from the head first. Then mount the tissue paper on heavier paper.

Experiment with different shades of tempera and different colors of tissue paper. If the prints are successful, try making them with thin, lovely Japanese paper.

If fishing doesn't supply a fish for printing, buy a few smelts from the fish market. They're inexpensive, and small enough to handle easily.

FOIL PRINTS

Foil prints are simple. Every child has rubbed foil over a coin to get the impression, or done the same thing by rubbing a soft pencil or crayon over tissue paper covering a coin or other embossed object.

In this project, campers find and select one or more fully grown leaves that they think are interesting in shape. Place the dull side of heavy aluminum foil over the vein side of the leaf and rub it gently with the finger tips until the print stands out

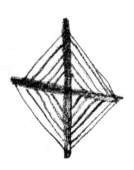

in detail. Poster paint brushed lightly over the print will give it an interesting and unusual effect. Mount the foil on heavy cardboard, and write the name of the leaf in the lower righthand corner. An exhibit of these prints can be very interesting. They also make very nice decorations for the camp, or to take home.

## MEXICAN GOD'S EYES

Mexican god's eyes are projects that offer a creative use of design and color. They make very effective wall or hanging ornaments for a patio or sunporch. Cross two dowel sticks by lashing them with wool yarn. Then work out a design by running the wool between the arms, circling each arm. Vary the design by using different colors and by leaving open spaces. Hang by a point. It's supposed to bring good luck.

Try making different types: light, fragile ones using small sticks and fine yarn or thread; big, spectacular ones by using larger sticks and heavy, colored cord.

## SPATTER PRINTING

This is an old favorite, but often not used to its fullest possibilities. Spatter prints, like any art form, must have good design.

Collecting grasses, leaves, flowers, slender tendrils of vines is the first step. Combining them into a pleasing arrangement, using the elements of design, is the next and very important step. The nature materials will show up best against a pale green, blue or gray background, but the selection of the background color can be varied, depending upon the materials used, and what sort of use the print will receive.

Spatter prints are really silhouettes. Tempera or poster paint is flicked across the design by rubbing a stiff, small brush (an old toothbrush is often used) across a small piece of screening held several inches above the paper. The material can be held in place by pins, but they should be placed straight up so that they do not make a silhouette on the design. The paint should not be too heavy, or cover the background too closely. With practice, a *shading* of the paint can be made. The final spatter print should be a graceful, identifiable object making in design an attractive picture of a nature silhouette.

## STONE JEWELRY

Stone jewelry is interesting to make because it involves finding just the right-size pebble or stone, in stream beds, on beaches, in driveways, or on hikes. All that's needed is an odd-shaped stone and some copper wire. (Also ear screws, if the camper wants to make earrings as well as a pendant.)

A pendant will need from 8 to 14 inches of 16-gauge copper wire, or 14-gauge silver wire. Wrap the wire around the stone, following its contours, and keeping the wire tight by slipping the wire over itself once in a while. Leave an inch at the top, and finally bring the wire back over the stone, twist it around the starting end, and twist a secure loop for a chain or ribbon. Use as little wire as possible, so as not to hide the stone. For earrings, use smaller stones and 18 or 20-gauge copper wire. Hook the wire finally to the earscrews.

Flat stones can be mounted easily by cutting out a "backing" of copper the shape of the stone, leaving three or four prongs to bend over it, so as to hold it securely in place. A top prong is rolled securely so that a chain or ribbon can be slipped through it.

### WIND HARPS

Wind harps have a pleasant, outdoor sound, and have come to us from the Orient where they have been enjoyed for centuries. Simple wooden wind harps are easy to make and create a gift that can bring pleasure to a family.

Like most good craft projects, they permit a wide variation in size, shape, and number of "dangles." The fundamental shape includes a ring, or circle of wire or wood, to which a number of lengths of wood or bamboo are attached in such a way, and at such distances apart, as to make them touch when blown by the wind. Unlike the glass ones found in many oriental shops, the wood or bamboo wind harps are natural in color and have a pleasant woodwind sound rather than a glassy tinkle.

Six lengths will make a good wind harp. They may range in length from two to eight inches, depending upon the size of the hoop and the design of placement.

Bamboo can be cut into the proper lengths. Each piece must be drilled so that a knotted cord will hold it to the hoop. These rounds may be hung with different lengths of cord, but must be within touch of the others so that they will make a pleasant sound when the wind moves them.

A hoop can be made from heavy wire (coat hanger wire is good), or from a wooden embroidery hoop. Four cords spaced evenly on the hoop and fastened to a metal ring or hook, are used to hang the harp from the edge of a porch, or a tree limb. Place the wind harp so that it can catch the breezes.

More elaborate wind harps can be made, using two or more levels of wood rounds. Dowels can be used instead of bamboo. The rounds may be waxed or shellacked, but should be kept the natural color. They are meant to blend, not to contrast with, the out-of-doors.

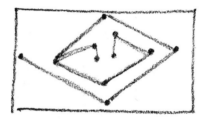

WIRE JEWELRY

Copper, brass, stainless steel, aluminum, or silver wire can be made into attractive bracelets, earrings, and dress ornaments. The use of nature designs from flowers, leaves, animals, fruits, butterflies, fish, or insects, makes such projects suitable for camp and stimulates creativity.

Wire of 18-gauge is best for such jewelry. Use 20-gauge wire if the project will require twisted wire. For extra weight, 16-gauge wire can be used.

Tools and supplies for such projects are simple. A block of wood, a hammer, finishing nails with heads clipped off, steel wool, lacquer, and pencil and paper to work out a design are all that are needed.

*Procedure* is simple. Work out a design on paper, using straight or curved lines, depending upon the model. Transfer the design to the block of wood. Place nails on the design wherever there will be an angle or corner. (The nail tops must be smooth so that the wire design will slip over them easily when the design is taken off the board.)

Begin in the center of the design, and outline it with the wire, looping the wire around each nail. On the last one, make a double loop to hold it in place.

Remove the design carefully by slipping it up and over the nails. Then place it on a piece of steel, very hard wood, or other smooth, hard surface that can be pounded. Flatten the design by pounding it carefully with the hammer. Smooth any sharp or rough edges with steel wool. Mount the design on "findings" for jewelry (those cuff links, earring backings, clasps, etc.). Spray with lacquer to prevent tarnishing.

### For Personal Use

#### LITTERBAGS

Litterbags can be made by decorating paper bags, adding masking tape to strengthen the tops, and decorating them with gay drawings, or phrases like

Don't Be a Pignic

Be a Neatnic

Let's Litter Less

A slit cut near the top of the bag and outlined with masking tape will let the bag be placed over the window or door handle of the family car.

#### NAME PLATE

Name plates are popular with small children. The simplest can be made from the round, metal-rimmed tags that can be bought in various colors in most stationery stores. Each child prints his name on one. Run a short string through it, and fasten with a safety pin.

Different colors can be supplied for different age groups: green for the 5 to 6 year-olds, red for the 7 to 9's, yellow for the 10 to 12's.

SALT AND PEPPER HOLDER

A craft to use for picnics or presents. Each holder requires a piece of bamboo, cut so that the joint forms the middle wall that separates the salt from the pepper. Bamboo splits, so it must be sawed carefully, and the edges smoothed. Fit a cork in each end after filling and mark each end to indicate contents. Colored nail polish can be used, or for a more rustic look, brand the ends with an S and a P.

VARIATIONS: Lengths of bamboo can be used for many camp and picnic purposes, depending upon the diameter of the bamboo. Matches, plastic or wooden spoons, paper napkins can be carried in the larger bamboos, and they will not require the middle joint. They *will* need corks or other covering for one or both of the ends.

WATERPROOF MATCHES

This project is useful for picnics and camping trips, and makes a fine gift for hunters and fishermen. Each match must be waterproofed separately.

One way to do this is to cover each matchhead with clear nail polish. It dries rapidly, so that waterproofing an entire box of kitchen matches will not take too long a time.

Another method is to dip the head of the match in melted paraffin. Paraffin, or other kinds of wax, should be heated in a double boiler, never over the fire, because it catches fire easily.

After the matches are waterproofed, they can be carried in a bottle, plastic box or bag, or in a bamboo carrier corked at both ends if a joint is not used.

WRIST BANDS

Wrist bands of felt, leather, leatherette, or plastic can also be used to indicate age groups. Staple, cement, or sew them the right size for each youngster.

## Playthings

CORN HUSKS

Corn husks are easy to get and fun to use. (Save the husks and the silk of the corn used in a cook-out, or let youngsters bring a supply from home.) When the husks are dried out they can be saved for just the right day. Husks must be dampened while using them, however. Otherwise, they'll break and tear.

A corn husk *whisk broom* will find many uses at camp. To make, braid three husks, fold the ends together and tie. This makes a looped handle. Then put two husks, tips up, through the handle loop and turn upside down. Put in two from the other side, inside the fold of the first two. Tie very tightly with bright yarn. Trim the ends and slash them to form a brush. (Corn husks can be dyed and take very pretty colors.)

In pioneer days, when dolls were few and very expensive, many little girls had to "make do" with corn husk dolls. Making such dolls in day camps is a good craft project, fitting nicely into such day camp themes as Pioneer Days, Western Days, Colonial Days.

The little girls at day camp will enjoy these dolls as playthings. Little boys who scorn playing with dolls can make pioneer or Indian families, to be the inhabitants of model villages.

Cut one husk four inches long, and fold it in half. Tie a string or cord about a half-inch from the top to form the head. Cut another husk two inches long, and put it between the first husk to form arms. Tie a cord around the first husk to form a waist. If it is a girl doll, the husk forms a long skirt. If it is to be a boy doll, divide the husk to form legs. Tie at wrists and ankles.

These are tiny, miniature dolls. Larger ones using the full-length husks make sturdier ones. To make:

Tie several husks together, turn the knot inside, tie a string or cord around this top to form the head. Use three husks to form arms. Braid them, tie them at the ends for wrists, put through the body, and tie a waist. For a boy doll, divide the legs below the waist, braid the legs, and tie at ankles. For girls, husks form skirts. Add a short husk for an apron, or make an apron out of a bit of calico or crepe paper. Eyes, nose, and mouth can be inked or painted on. Make pigtails for a girl, and a sunbonnet or colonial cap. Make a little hat for the boy. Use corn silk for hair, or fine yarn if preferred.

MINIATURE INDIAN PROJECTS

These fit nicely into day camp with an Indian theme, or into storytelling and dramatizations. Little girls can make a *papoose-in-a-cradleboard*. Each will need a bit of cardboard for the cradle that mother Indian carries on her back, a tiny doll made out of cloth or felt scraps, a strip of cloth to bind the doll to the board, tied with string and knotted in front. Decorate with crayon designs.

Little boys can make *tepees* out of a circle of brown wrapping paper cut in half, folded into a cone shape, and pasted or stapled. Decorate the cones with Indian designs before stapling. Cut a slit and fold back to form a door. Punch twigs or lollipop sticks through the tips for the tepee poles.

*Totem poles* for the miniature Indian encampment can be made out of spools, cone-shaped paper cups, mailing tubes, matchboxes, plus bits of aluminum foil, and other odds and ends. Just provide paste, poster paints, scissors, and glue. Plant the totem poles around the miniature village.

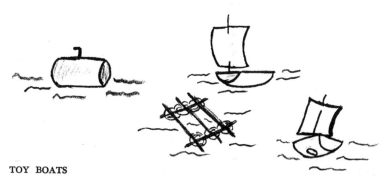

TOY BOATS

Given any supply of water from bathtub to beach, youngsters will improvise floating objects that immediately become "boats." The very simplest are such things as a leaf on which an ant is the bewildered captain, a twig, piece of bark, acorn cup, or walnut shell, or a block of wood. The very youngest and, at first, the slightly olders will be satisfied with these. When the novelty of floating wears off, the imagination takes over, and youngsters add other things to basic floating objects for both ornament and increased efficiency in the water.

The walnut shell can get a toothpick mast, to which a paper sail has been glued.

The twig glued to the block of wood becomes a ship's bridge; the acorn cup on top of it becomes the pilot house.

The day camp should provide a supply of pieces of wood in various sizes and shapes; cement; odds and ends like paper, string, thumbtacks, crayons; hammers, shellack, corks of various sizes and shapes, bits of cloth for sails and flags. Campers can choose their own supplies, and make their own boat to enter in a regatta. They may make simple or multiple sailboats, destroyers, tugboats, barges, submarines, proas, rafts, houseboats—but make them all by themselves. Counselors may have to give some suggestions and advice. Simple types of boats might include such as the following:

*Walnut Raft.* Six half-shells, three each cemented to two ice cream sticks. Then cement three more sticks to these, to form the flooring of the raft. Shellack the raft to make it waterproof. How much of a load will it carry? Try and see. Add a sail. Where does it balance best?

*Cork Boats.* Corks of all sizes and shapes can be used. The flat ones inside bottle caps make fine rafts or outriggers. Bottle corks should be cut in half lengthwise, so as to provide a flat deck surface for boats, or a flat floating surface for a submarine, or to cement to other parts to make superstructures.

Cork boats with rounded bottoms capsize easily. Give them more stability by sticking a thumbtack in the rounded side to provide balance. Matchsticks or toothpicks make fine masts.

Stick a bit of wire or a toothpick into a cork that has not been halved, to make a periscope for a *submarine.* The bottom of the submarine will need weighting with several tacks to keep it topside. A small conning tower can be added, too.

*Jar Lid Boats* are a step away from the simple cork boats. Stick a paper sail onto a toothpick mast. Stick the mast into a cork.

Cement the cork to a jar lid, next to the rim. Make a whole navy and race them.

A *Space Capsule* waiting to be picked up by a destroyer can be made out of a rubber jar ring inside of which a Ping-pong ball is attached. Use waterproof cement to attach with straws, tiny cloth strip, adhesive tape, or whatever method the camper can devise.

A *Motorboat* that will move in the water can be improvised by sticking a sliver of soap in a slit at one end of a piece of thin wood or cardboard cut in a boat shape.

*Destroyer.* Older, or more skilled, campers may wish to make a ship that will require a bit of sawing, drilling, and painting. They'll enjoy making and sailing the *destroyer* as youngsters in Baltimore made it. Dimensions and material can be changed, but the following is one way to do it:

Needed: ¾-inch lumber. Four small spools for smokestacks. ¼-inch dowels. Tacks. Paint. Glue. The following sketch gives dimensions.

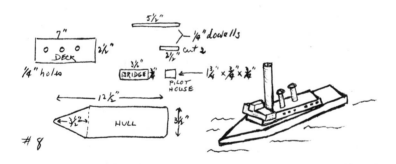

Saw wood as indicated. Drill three holes ½ inch deep in the deck.

File one end off two of the spools and both ends off the other two spools. Glue each spool with one end uncut to a spool with both ends cut. These will make the tops of the smokestacks. Sand all the pieces.

Glue, then nail the pilot house to the deck ¼ inch from the front. Glue, then nail the bridge to the pilot house. Glue the long dowel into the first hole in the deck, and the two shorter dowels into the other holes.

Glue the smokestacks to the two short dowels. Paint and let dry. Then add any other colors or decorations. Use tacks in the sides for portholes—or paint them in.

See Chapter 18, "Water Play," for activities *using* toy watercraft.

## Drama and Music Tie-Ins

### CAVEMAN WEAPONS

Caveman weapons are good craft projects and fit nicely into themes or dramatizations. They are excellent ways to put knotting and lashing to play use.

A *stone hammer* can be made by lashing just the right stone to just the right-shaped stick.

A *stone spear* needs a stone that is pointed, lashed to a long stick.

A *stone knife* requires finding a narrow, flintlike stone, and lashing it securely to a stick.

Finding and selecting just the right stones, then trying to find just the right sticks and the right method to lash them makes this project a real challenge.

### MASKS

Masks can be made out of paper bags that fit over the head, and have openings for the eyes, nose, and mouth. Paint them. Tie corners for ears, or make ears and staple them on. Add rope or yarn or paper hair.

*Half-Masks* can be made out of cardboard, painted and decorated to look like cats, lions, birds, or whatever. Staple one side to a stick. Child holds the mask against the upper part of his face. Cut out eye holes so that he can see.

PINATA

Breaking a piñata is the high point in Mexican parties and can be great fun for a day camp special event, surprise, or party at the close of camp. Making it can be a fine craft project.

A piñata is simply a large container that is filled with candies, small gifts, and other goodies, and hung by a rope over a tree limb. Blindfolded youngsters take turns trying to *break* the piñata by hitting it with a long stick. (Sometimes a parent or leader raises or lowers the piñata just to prolong the suspense.) When it breaks, everyone dives in to pick up the goodies.

A piñata is often made in the form of a bird, animal, or person, and is always painted in bright, gay colors. It is made by glueing strips of brown paper or newspaper to a light framework of some sort—a cardboard box with sides cut out, leaving just a framework, can be used. Arms, legs, tails, wings can be made by attaching stuffed paper bags, light cardboard boxes, and the like. The "creature," whatever it is decided to make, must be strong enough and big enough to hold a supply of candies sufficient for everyone, fragile enough to break eventually—but not too soon.

RHYTHM INSTRUMENTS

Basic to music and to dancing is rhythm. Making rhythm instruments is a project that unites these arts with the craft program. Make them—and use them.

*Maracas* are gay soundmakers. Variations of them are made and used in almost every country. In the West Indies they are made from gourds that are rattle-shaped.

The gourds must be dried thoroughly. Then a piece is cut off each end, and the inside is scraped out by using a wire, a long-handled spoon, or other tool. When dried, the plugs are replaced. The seeds are left inside. Sometimes a wooden handle is put into the gourd. Sometimes the natural handle is kept. The outside of the gourd must be scraped smooth. Then it can be carved, or shellacked, or enameled.

They are used in pairs. They should not be just shaken, but should be moved quickly so that all the seeds hit one side, then the other side of the gourd.

Gourds are not always easy to come by, and often are not ripe for picking until after the day camp season. Luckily maracas can be improvised easily. One method is to roll cardboard into a cylinder about six inches long and glue it into the end of a worn-out electric light bulb. This gives a rattle shape. Then the bulb and handle are covered with small squares of newspaper dipped into paste, or gummed, narrow strips of paper, or newsprint "mash" that can be modeled over the form. When enough layers have been made to provide a hard, tough surface, the maracas must dry out thoroughly. It may take several days, depending upon the thickness of the *papier-mâché*. Once dry, a sharp tap will break the bulb inside, and the pieces will make a fine, silky sound. The maracas should be sanded until smooth, and can then be painted in gay colors.

*Bells* are perhaps one of the most familiar sounds to children. They hear church bells and school bells. Some have seen and  heard cowbells. All have heard sleigh bells, telephone bells, and doorbells. Some have seen and heard gongs that are bells without clappers and must be struck instead of rung. Many have seen and heard the pretty, delicate little glass or china bells used at the dinner table, or by the sickbed.

Some day campers can bring in different bells from home—perhaps a Sarna bell from India, a cowbell, or other kinds.

If a local church has a belltower that can be visited, take the youngsters to visit it at a time when the sound will almost sweep them off their feet. See if the local telephone company can let them visit and find out how telephones are rung. How does a fire alarm work? A counselor with a bit of electrical training can show how batteries can be hooked up to ring bells.

A cowbell is often used in a rhythm band. It can be held in the hand and struck with a small mallet or drumstick for a muted sound. For a resonant, "clanky" sound, hold the bell by a string or piece of leather.

*Rhythm sticks* make a nice "click" when tapped together. Each camper can make his own, decorating each pair according to individual preferences. They are merely two straight sticks—dowels, broomsticks, or other round, wooden sticks about a foot long. They should be sanded until perfectly smooth, then shellacked or enameled in gay, bright colors and designs.

They are tapped together to make a nice, resonant sound, very fine with singing. Sometimes several sleighbells are tied together and fastened to the top and bottom of each stick to give an added jingle.

*Wood blocks* give somewhat the same sound. A wood block is just what the name says—a block of wood. It is not a *solid* block, however. The block is hollowed out across the center from side to side. When the block is tapped lightly with a wooden hammer or mallet this hollow makes the block give a very lovely, resonant sound.

*Sand blocks* make raspy sounds that fit into all sorts of rhythms and pantomime. They are a bit like *woodblocks*, except that they are solid, have a knob for holding, and their sound is made by rubbing them across each other instead of being tapped with a wooden stick or mallet. They are easy to make.

They are used in pairs. Each is a small block of wood 3" x 5" or 4" x 6", and about an inch thick. One flat side is covered with coarse sandpaper, securely fastened to the narrow sides with thumbtacks. The other flat side of each block should be nicely sanded, and can be painted or shellacked. A knob or bar of wood should be screwed into this flat side. A sand block is held in each hand by this knob.

The *guiro* (Spanish for gourd, and pronounced "gweerah") is also made from a gourd. The guiro is shaped like a curved cucumber. Again the gourd must dry out thoroughly. Then cut a piece from the narrow end and scrape out the inside, seeds and all. Leave the hole for a finger to fit into.

The outside of the guiro should be sanded and smoothed. It should then be scored with a knife or file, the ridges running across the *width* of the gourd.

To use a guiro, fit it securely on a finger of the left hand. Hold a piece of wire, a long nail, a fork, or other thin metal length in the right hand and stroke it against the ridges in the gourd.

To improvise, when gourds are not available or are not the right kind, use a block of wood. Thumbtack a piece of canvas or leather across one side, so that the left hand will fit through it, holding the board comfortably. Sand the other side until it is very smooth. Then using a steel-edged ruler as a guide, score lines across the board, making them deep enough, and close enough together to make a fine rasping sound when a thin-edged tongue depressor stick is stroked over it.

A *tambourine* is a combination of drum and rattle. Almost every country uses some type of tambourine. The very best known are probably those used by Spanish dancers, and the Salvation Army lasses!

Tambourines can be made in any number of ways. The campers can improvise their own. They'll need some sort of frame. This can be a wire coat hanger straightened out and then bent into a circle, the outside rim of a circular cheese box, the outside of a coffee can cut down to around two inches high, or an embroidery hoop that can be bought in any department store.

The outside frame must be covered with a tight drumhead of

heavy oiled paper, or leather, or rubber, or parchment (an old lampshade can be used). Small pieces of thin metal should be wired around the edges, so that when the tambourine is struck or shaken, the bits of metal will jingle. Bottle caps can be used for this. Gay, narrow ribbons are sometimes tied to a tambourine and look pretty when it is held over the head and shaken in a dance or song.

A *plate gong* is wonderful for oriental sound effects, because it is very dramatic and vibrant. It can be improvised by finding a copper, iron, aluminum, or other metal tray. Bore several holes in the top and run a strong cord or leather thong through the holes, so that the tray swings free. It is held by the thong in the left hand, and then hit with a padded mallet held in the right hand. A stick, the top of which is padded with cotton and then covered with leather, makes a good mallet.

Such a gong also can be held in the hand and hit, but the sound will be very different. Use both for different sound effects.

Striking such a gong is a dramatic way to open or close a program, introduce an act, emphasize an award, or make an important announcement.

*Bongo drums* are familiar to most youngsters who watch television. They are used in *pairs*. One drum should be slightly larger than the other, in both height and width. They are held side by side between the knees, so that the flat fingers of the right hand play one drum, those of the left hand the other drum. One drum should sound higher in tone than the other.

It is quite possible that some of the youngsters may have a pair of bongos. If so, encourage their bringing the drums to day camp, because well-built drums always sound better than improvised ones. They are no more fun to tap, however, so make bongos if they're not available.

They may be improvised by using oatmeal boxes cut down so that they aren't so deep, or any other round, sturdy box. The box top, if it fits very tightly, can be used as the drumhead. Otherwise, make the drumhead from parchment paper, thin leather, rubber, or other thin but strong material.

The *conga drum* is known in most countries throughout the world. It is usually associated with the West Indies and Africa. The conga is a tall drum, usually a bit wider at the top than at the bottom. It sits on the ground or floor, but is held between the knees, and is patted by the flat of the hand. In African songs or chants, the drumming starts with the left hand, and the last beat in any line is accented.

A pickle barrel, a barrel that smoked fish came packed in, a nail keg—any type of small keg or barrel can be made into a substitute conga drum. Its sides should be decorated with bright colors and symbols. Its drumhead must be smooth, tight, and strong.

*Other drums* can be improvised out of all sorts of boxes, bowls, buckets, and cans. These may be used with drumsticks to make all sorts of sounds and rhythms. Each should be made and *played*. Try all sorts of sizes—tall, short, wide, narrow—and see what sorts of sounds they make. Use them to beat our rhythms for walking, skipping, leaping, galloping, and other movements.

*Improvised instruments* combine the skill of making things with skill in using the finished product. Thinking up ingenious ways of using different sizes, shapes, and substances, and experimenting with the different tones that can be made is a creative activity, full of colorful uses in day camp.

Tin cans of various sizes, boxes of various sizes and shapes, small containers of glass, metal or plastic, peas, beans, marbles, pebbles, nails, pans, buckets, washboards, files, metal and wooden spoons, iron, tin, and copper tubing, a length of chain, saucepan covers—are only a few of the things that can be used to make rhythm band instruments and sounds.

Making reed whistles and pipes, blowing across a hollow reed or bottle, clapping two smooth stones together, making whistles out of self-hardening clay (primitive tribes often made them bird-shaped) are other ways of making sounds that can be used to accent beats. Devise other sound makers out of natural or manufactured materials. Both types are good to use because they prove that rhythm and sound are everywhere, not just outdoors, not just in ready-made instruments.

Twigs, grass, bamboo, bones, water, bark, hollow trunks and limbs of trees, feathers, coconut shells, gourds, reeds—all these and many other natural materials can be used to make sounds and rhythms for the day camper. The more he can find and devise for himself, the more aware he will become of the many and varied rhythms all around him—the beating of his own heart, the changing of day to night, summer to autumn, the hum of his city, the ticking of a clock, the strident, hot-sounding cicadas, and the fluttering of a butterfly's wing, all rhythmic, all beautiful in their own ways.

WALKING DOLLS

Walking dolls can be used in story dramatizations, circus, carnival, parade, and other settings. For a girl doll, use two large paper bags and one small one (5-pound size). Stuff the small one for the head, and paint the doll's face on it. Cut the bottom out of a big bag, and scallop it for the hem of the skirt. Insert the head in the other end and tie securely. Cut arms and legs from the other big bag and staple into place. Add yarn or paper hair. Decorate the dress.

The child holds the doll by a piece of string inserted in each side of the paper bag head, and "walks" it in front of her.

A boy doll is made the same way, but needs two extra bags to make trousered legs. Try making a pirate, clown, cowboy, Indian. Try making a favorite storybook character, then using it to tell the story.

Add a broom handle as a stake, and turn the doll into a *scarecrow*. Use for Wizard of Oz stories.

CHAPTER **14:**

# DRAMA AND STORYTELLING

Time spent at day camp is often too short, both by day and by season, for formalized drama in which lines must be memorized, costumes made, and rehearsals held. More important, youngsters of day camp age need dramatic activities that have a wider range and a more informal approach. The following are most appropriate:

- Creative dramatics, in which youngsters "act out" stories or situations, making up their own lines through improvisation.
- Story dramatization, a natural outgrowth of storytelling, in which youngsters prepare or improvise the lines.
- Informal dramatics, in which they play out camp, home, or other situations that they have discussed in advance.
- Games that require or provide a dramatic element.
- Dramatization of folk songs and ballads, in which music, drama, and sometimes dance are combined.
- Dramatic play that results from the creative use of play equipment and supplies, such as the sandpile or box, the treehouse, Indian tepee, toy boats, pirate ship. Such equipment, supplies, or projects are valuable not so much for themselves as for the outlet and stimulus they provide for creative dramatic play. Drama and storytelling combine naturally and inevitably with music and dancing. The day camp environment thus serves as a dramatic outlet.

**The Place**

Drama and storytelling in day camp should take place wherever the campers happen to be—on a lake or the beach, on the bus, in the brook. Often the place or event suggests some form of dramatic action.

196

There are times, however, when these spur-of-the-moment, informal types are supplemented by specifically scheduled programs, particularly if a storyteller comes out to day camp at special periods, or when a group or the entire camp wants to entertain the others or the parents.

A Magic Tree, or a Magic Carpet, can be selected or provided for small group storytelling and informal drama periods.

A sloping hillside can become a little outdoor theater. So can a clearing, where a thicket, or woods, or a rocky ledge can serve as a backdrop. A council ring can become a theater-in-the-round.

Such sites, and their seating, should be kept compact. Children's voices do not carry well. It is a good idea not to separate players from audience by water, even though it *looks* pretty, because the water will further muffle the voices.

Stunts, skits, playlets, puppet shows, and other dramatic special events should be based upon pantomime as far as possible, perhaps using a narrator with a strong voice, or providing a loudspeaker system through the use of mobile equipment. Voices carry better indoors—but who wants to go indoors at day camp?

## Mobile Units

The provision of puppet shows and show wagons through the use of mobile units is gaining favor. Public recreation departments in many cities provide such units, and the possibility of getting the day camp put on their schedule should be explored. In this way, children's plays or puppet shows can be prepared elsewhere, and brought to the day camp site as special entertainment. Such shows, however, should supplement, not usurp, the day camp drama program.

## Costumes and Set

Costumes and sets are seldom necessary, because children's imagination makes a Prince out of Eddie, or a Wicked Witch out of Susie. A *suggestion* of a costume can provide added glamour, and add a touch of prestige. A bit of gold paper on a stick makes a magic wand; a bit of tinsel gives sparkle to a Fairy Queen; cardboard horns identify Ferdinand the Bull. The selection and production of costume symbols can be left to the youngsters.

Sets, too are seldom necessary. A box covered with a tarpaulin makes a big rock or a mountain. A blanket, a sheet—even just a rope—can become a curtain for the stage. Finding the right props and improvising any necessary stage sets or backdrops are all part of the fun of informal drama and of the creative process.

### Storytelling

Storytelling is probably the easiest first step in the drama program for counselors without special training in children's dramatics. It is familiar to all, popular with youngsters, not difficult to prepare, and therefore a fine jumping-off point.

.In day camp, whenever possible, the stories used should fit into or supplement other parts of the program. They should serve as opportunities for as many types of creative self-expression as possible. These may include various art and craft projects, rhythm, music, drama, poetry, and games.

There are a few, general, basic rules that a storyteller, to be successful, should follow:

- Never tell a story not personally enjoyed.
- Select stories that have *action*. Descriptions and character-development should be at a minimum.
- Make sure that the group is comfortable; that everyone can see and hear; and that no one has the sun in his eyes.
- Catch the eyes of the children as the story is told. It helps to hold their interest.
- Don't be afraid to use gestures, but use them only when they help the story along.
- Keep your voice lively and sparkling. A monotone takes the fun out of listening.
- *Seize the moment.* Coming across a wild apple tree in the

woods would be a perfect time to tell the story of Johnny Appleseed. When the youngsters are examining the parachute of the dandelion, is the best time to tell the Indian legend about it.

- Encourage the *campers* to tell stories—not only ones they have read, but stories of what they did on vacation, how they caught their first fish, what they saw at the movies. Learning to communicate and to share experiences is an important part of growing up.
- Make stories, drama, games—*anything* at camp—*fun*. Keep it relaxed and informal.

## Poetry

The reading and the writing of poetry are activities that correlate with the music, drama, and storytelling program. Many ballads, as mentioned in Chapter 15, "Music and Dancing," lend themselves not only to singing but to dramatizing.

Many poems, like those of Carl Sandburg, Vachel Lindsay, and Alfred Noyes, have strong rhythmic beats that can lead to chanting, or to the use of sound effects with or without instruments.

Other poems, such as Emily Dickinson's, say in a few lines what would 'take most people pages to say. Such poetry crystallizes beauty; holds up an ordinary object and points out unseen loveliness; expresses in words what everyone can feel, but few can say.

The very young day camper often is unself-conscious, and puts his ideas and thoughts freely into words that become poetic. His writing skill is not equal to his ideas, so the counselor who is encouraging him to express his feelings in words should be ready to "write it down" for him.

Poetry writing may develop as day campers become aware of

how exciting and interesting it can be to use their five senses. Finding words to describe the things they see, hear, feel, smell, and taste increases their perception and sensitivity.

Writing poetry requires an atmosphere of harmony and encouragement. It is very different from developing jingles or doggerel for a stunt or skit. It cannot be forced. It must come from within.

## Legends, Myths, and Fables

Throughout the ages, the wonders of nature have puzzled and fascinated man. In the early, nomadic or agricultural societies, man tried to explain mysterious things like Fire, Thunder, and Lightning. He tried to account for the arrangements of stars in the skies, for the passing of the seasons, and for the flowers, birds, and animals around him.

Many of man's early beliefs have come down to us as *legends*. Since so often they deal with the world of nature, they are particularly suitable for storytelling and creative dramatics. Bullfinch's famous *Age of Fables,* found in most libraries, covers Greek and Roman legends.

Particularly suitable for day camp programs, however, are many of the charming legends of the American Indians. Since they often deal with familiar objects found in outdoor settings, they tie in nicely with the nature experiences of campers. The two following outlines, one explaining the change in the dandelion, the other explaining why the thistle is so prickly, are examples of such legends.

### THE DANDELION

Every youngster knows the gay, bright yellow, little dandelion. Every youngster has picked it when it has gone to seed, and blown the little white parachutes into the air.

Behind this legend is one of the many variations on the theme of the coming of winter and the return of spring. Contrast this Indian legend with the Greek legend of Persephone carried away by Hades to be his bride in the underworld, and her return, bringing spring to the earth each year.

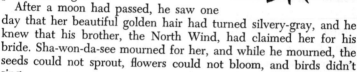

The South Wind, Sha-won-da-see, was a very lazy manitou. He spent most of his time lying in the sun near a grassy meadow, watching the clouds and listening to the birds. One day he looked across the meadow and saw a strange and beautiful, golden-haired maiden walking there. He wanted to go to her, and talk with her; but the sun was warm, the birds sang, and he was too lazy to move. So each day he watched her from afar, and put off wooing her.

After a moon had passed, he saw one day that her beautiful golden hair had turned silvery-gray, and he knew that his brother, the North Wind, had claimed her for his bride. Sha-won-da-see mourned for her, and while he mourned, the seeds could not sprout, flowers could not bloom, and birds didn't sing.

Finally, the Great Spirit took pity on him, and turned the maiden into a dandelion. Now every spring she walks in the meadow and her golden hair shines in the sun as Sha-won-da-see watches her. She lingers a month, until it is time for her to fly away again with the North Wind. And while she lingers, spring returns to the earth, the flowers bloom again, the sun's warm, and birds sing. Sha-won-da-see, the South Wind, is happy again.

**THE THISTLE**

Many youngsters have been tempted to pick the big, purple flower heads of the thistle, and given up because of the prickly leaves and stem. The Indians had a story about those prickles.

Once there lived a beautiful Indian maiden, so beautiful that many young braves tried to woo her. This maiden's tongue was sharp as a hunting arrow, and, one by one, the young braves withheld their wooing and sought out gentler maidens.

Finally a spirit man saw her, and admired her beauty. He sought her out, and offered to make her his bride if she would speak only sweet and kindly words as a lovely maiden should.

She agreed, but the wedding was scarcely over when she started to berate and scold her new husband. In sorrow he reminded her of her promise, and changed her into a thistle—beautiful to look at, but shunned by everyone because it is so prickly.

These two story outlines are typical of legends. They are short, easy to remember, and can be told not only at story hour but as the campers encounter either dandelions or thistles. They will make good subjects for a group mural. They can be dramatized by making up dialogue, or they may be pantomimed while someone reads the story. Each could be made into a creative dance. Each could be used as a theme for a puppet show. Other Indian legends, and legends of other countries, are equally adaptable.

Longfellow's *Hiawatha* changes many Indian legends into poetry. Read some of them aloud as a change from storytelling.

Aesop's *Fables* are excellent camp material. They have a modern punch line that youngsters enjoy—and campers get the point.

The old Greek myths also fit into camping experiences. For example, the name of the spider family, Arachnida, comes from the story of a girl, Arachne, who was such a wonderful spinner and weaver that she dared to compete with Athena, the goddess of spinning and weaving. Athena was so angry with her and so jealous of her skill, that she changed the poor girl into a spider—and that's why the spider spins and weaves such lovely webs.

The story of Arachne should lead to another story of a spider that saved the Scottish hero, Bruce, from capture by his enemies. He hid in a cave. When the enemy came past, they started to go into the cave. One of them noticed a spider's web across the entrance. Reasoning that Bruce couldn't have gone in without breaking the web, the enemy went on. And so a spider saved the life of a king.

### Animal stories

Many myths, legends, and fables are animal stories whose origins are lost in time. Many others, however, have been written by famous authors and have become classics. Some, like Babar the Elephant, and Ferdinand the Bull, have become modern classics.

Storytelling that builds on itself can be a fascinating activity. One topic—for example, the *rabbit*—can take a storyteller into a wide variety of tales, from the beloved *Peter Rabbit* to the Rabbit in *Alice in Wonderland;* from *B'rer Rabbit* of Uncle Remus fame to *Raggylug*, in Ernest Thompson Seton's classic *Wild Animals I Have Known.*

Kipling's *Just So Stories* are gems. There's no youngster alive who won't be spellbound by them.

Carl Sandburg's *Rootabaga Stories* are as modern as youth. Today's children will love hearing about the skyscraper that had a baby, and giggle over the idea of popcorn exploding in the heat and coming down like snow. These tales have a sly humor that builds up to hilarity.

Kenneth Grahame's *The Wind in the Willows,* telling the exciting adventures of Rat and Toad, is a storytelling or reading must. Each camper understands perfectly the joy of Rat's "just messing around."

## Storytelling Variations

In addition to a regular story hour, where stories are told or read, storytelling can be kept flexible by using different techniques. Those which follow have a participation, humor, or suspense element that youngsters enjoy and will demand over and over again. Make up new variations for them.

### MAKE-A-NOISE STORIES

Make-a-noise stories are fine because every youngster gets personally involved. The various characters in such stories all require identifying sounds. These sounds should be rehearsed before the leader tells the story. Then *each time a character is mentioned, one child or a group of them, must make the proper sound.*

#### THE LITTLE OLD LADY

| | |
|---|---|
| Cow—Moo-o-o | Chicks—Peep-peep |
| Dog—Bow-wow | Pig—Oink-oink |
| Cat—Miaow | Car—Honk-honk |
| Duck—Quack-quack | Big boy—Loud whistle |
| Hen—Cluck-cluck | Little boy—Little whistle |
| Rooster—Cockle-doo-doo | |

There was once an old woman who lived in the noisy city. She had lived there all her life. Trucks, buses, taxis, newsboys, and lots of people passed her house all day long, every day. One day the little old woman got a letter in the mail telling her that

she had been left a fine farm in the country. So she sold her house and moved to the nice peaceful farm. The farm was green and pretty. The farmhouse was clean and comfortable—BUT she couldn't rest because it was SO QUIET. . . . When she told her neighbor about this, the neighbor said, "Get some animals." "By all means—some animals with some voices to them," said the little old woman, so she hurried away and bought a cow _____ (cow moos). The little woman thought that was a fine noise, but one noise was not enough, so she bought a dog _____ (dog barks). She liked this new noise, for all day long she could hear _____ (cow and dog together). She still couldn't rest well, so she bought a cat _____ (cat miaows). However, she still wanted more, so she bought a duck _____ (duck quacks). Now she had more noise _____ (all four together). But still the big farm was too quiet, so she bought a hen and a rooster _____ (hen clucks, rooster crows). The hen laid some eggs and sat on them, so there soon were some little chicks _____ (chicks peep-peep). So most of the day the farm sounded like this _____ (all noises). Still the little old lady had no peace of mind, so she bought a pig _____ (he grunts). It was grand on the farm with the pig _____ (all together). But she wanted even more noise, so she bought an old car with a good loud horn _____ (sound horn). Whenever it was too quiet, the old lady sat in her car and honked the horn _____ (all noises). One fine day she got in her little old car and drove to the big city. There she heard the most terrific noise. She stopped the car and listened. It was a lovely noise —just what she needed. She got out of her car and went in, and the place was filled with boys, and all of them were making a noise _____ (big boys give a loud whistle and little boys give a little whistle). "This noise is delicious," said the little old woman, so she took a big and a little boy home, and after that there was plenty of noise on the farm. It was never quiet any more _____ (all noises) and the little old lady was happy.

**MAKE-UP STORIES**

Make-up stories can be used just for storytelling or as plots for story acting. Make out lists of several different items and put them on a card. Give each group of youngsters a card, and tell them that in ten minutes (less for small or young groups) each group must be ready with a story that involves every item on the card. For example:

- A talking bird—a cave—a diamond ring—a flashlight—a submarine—a letter
- A tornado—a cellar—a pair of shoes—a paper bag—a car—a glass of milk
- A princess—a magic mirror—an umbrella—a flying horse—a poodle—a tree

### FILL-IN STORIES

Fill-in stories provide the type of humor that small children love. Take any story, or make up a story, and leave out most of the nouns. Then give each child several slips of paper, each of which has some word on it, like "Fish Eyes," "Old Grouch," "Three Ducks," "Chewing Gum," "Castor Oil," and so on. Read the story, and each child in turn fills in a blank by reading one of his slips. They make wonderful nonsense. The story might sound like this:

One fine spring day _____ was walking along the street with _____. They were talking about the good time they had had at a birthday party that _____ had given the day before. After playing the game of dropping _____ into a bottle and throwing _____ into a hat, they had thrown _____ at _____, which had been the most fun of all. For dinner they had eaten _____, _____, and _____ which was covered with chocolate sauce. The best present that was given to the birthday child was _____, and he played with it all day.

### FOLLOW-THE-LEADER STORIES

Follow-the-leader stories are first cousins to make-a-noise stories, and these can be combined. Leader and youngsters make a big circle. Leader tells the story, and the youngsters must imitate every movement he makes. Try this old favorite:

#### KING WITH A TERRIBLE TEMPER

Once upon a time there was a King who lived in a *great* big castle. (Action: describe tall building with hands.) Now this King who lived in the big castle (action) had a terrible temper. He would get angry at every little thing, and he would stamp his feet (action) and shake his fists at everyone (action). The King had three daughters; one was very short (all squat); one was very tall (all stand on tiptoes and stretch arms overhead); and one was very beautiful (all place palms together and lay hands under side of chin, head tilted). The three daughters spent their time playing the garden. They would skip in a circle (all join hands and skip in circle); then sometimes they would skip around the other way (reverse direction of skipping).

Well, one day, while the girls were playing in the garden, along came a handsome Prince riding on a beautiful white horse (gallop around circle). When he saw the three girls, he stopped his horse (whoa!). Immediately, he fell in love with one of the three daughters, not the short one (squat), not the tall one (stretch), but with the one who was beautiful (attitude of beauty). He decided that she would have to be his wife, so he rode his horse (gallop) up to the big castle (action) and went inside to ask the King with the terrible temper (action) for his daughter's hand in marriage; not the short one (squat), not the tall one (stretch), but the one who was beautiful (action).

The King with the terrible temper (action) told the Prince that before he could marry his daughter, the Prince would have to go out in the forest and kill a dragon. The Prince jumped up on his horse and rode fast (gallop in other direction around the circle) to the forest. There he saw the dragon (sway from side to side and make frightening noises). He was such a terrible dragon that all the trees and bushes trembled with fear (shake and tremble). The Prince was not afraid; he drew his sword and killed the dragon. (Action: draw sword and thrust into dragon). The dragon fell and died! (Action: all fall to floor). The Prince jumped on his horse and galloped (action) back to the big castle (describe). He went to the King with the terrible temper (action). The Prince told the King that he had gone to the forest and had killed the dragon with his sword (action). The King then gave his consent to the marriage. So the Prince married the daughter, not the short one (squat), not the tall one (stretch), but the one who was beautiful (attitude) and then the Prince joined the girls in the garden and they all lived happily ever after. (Join hands and skip around. Girls finish with curtsy and boys bow.)

### MAGIC GLASSES

Magic Glasses is a simple play-way to free a youngster's imagination and help him to overcome any self-consciousness. Decorate the frames of a pair of spectacles, making them very glittery, fantastic, and strange-looking. Each child gets a chance to put on the Magic Glasses—and to tell the others what magic things and people he sees in them.

## Informal Dramatic Activities

Story dramatization has been mentioned before, in connection with legends, myths, and fables. Mother Goose rhymes and folk or fairy tales are an unending source of material. Tell—and let the youngsters dramatize—the old favorites:

| | |
|---|---|
| The Gingerbread Man | Jack and the Beanstalk |
| Chicken Little | Cinderella |
| Three Billy Goats Gruff | Snow White |
| The Ugly Duckling | The Tin Soldier |
| Rumpelstiltskin | |

## Game Dramatization

Drama is an important element in almost any game. All too often, however, an inexperienced leader plays a game without emphasizing this dramatic element. Well-known games that lend themselves to dramatic emphasis for young children include the following:

| | |
|---|---|
| Squirrel in the Trees | Charlie Over the Water |
| Puss Wants a Corner | Crows and Cranes |
| Cat and Mouse | Huckle Buckle Beanstalk |

The following games, plus many in the chapters on "Games," "Rainy and Hot Day Activities," and others, have a high dramatic quality and will add color to the informal drama program.

ACTING RHYMES

FORMATION: Informal.

EQUIPMENT: None.

ACTION: One player starts off by pantomiming by facial expression, movement or sound, a simple, one-syllable word. He might pantomime "fat." The second player must pantomime another word that rhymes with "fat," such as "cat." The third player may take "mat," and so on. Anyone unable to add a new word gets a point against him. Suggested words to try first—*car, van, link, cry.*

THE BOILER BURST

FORMATION: Informal, around the leader. A goal line some distance away is marked.

EQUIPMENT: None.

ACTION: The leader improvises an exciting story, and when suspense is at its height, he ends it with "and the boiler burst!" All the youngsters must dash for the goal or goal line, and the last to reach it becomes the storyteller for the next round.

INDIAN PASS

FORMATION: Two lines of players, facing each other, a foot or two apart. Player at head of each line is the Chief of his tribe. Player at the end of each line is that tribe's Papoose. Players may stand, sit on ground, or at a table.

EQUIPMENT: Twenty-five (or less, if desired) grains of corn, or beans, or pebbles, or other small objects, placed in front of each Chief.

ACTION: In the right line, each player grasps his neighbor's right wrist with his left hand. In the left line, each person grasps his neighbor's left wrist with his right hand. Each person then has only one hand for passing.

The objects are placed in front of the Chiefs—on the floor if the group is standing, on the table if the group is seated. At the signal, each Chief picks up one object at a time, passes it to the person next to him, and so on, until the Papoose, who counts the objects as they arrive, has all twenty-five in front of him.

When the last one arrives, the Papoose gives a low war whoop and starts the objects back up this time, one at a time. The Chief who gets all the objects back in front of him first, gives a *loud* war whoop, and his tribe wins.

If an object is dropped, the whole line must hold in formation until it is picked up. The line may not be broken for any reason.

VARIATION: Add drama by supplying the Chiefs with an Indian headdress, the Papoose with a headband.

Require each player to say "How" as he passes each object to the next player.

Require the Chief to war dance around his tribe before he can give the final war whoop.

Use this game as a campfire game or ceremony, too.

**PROFESSIONS**

FORMATION: A circle, with players seated.

EQUIPMENT: Nothing but quick reactions!

ACTION: Each player chooses a trade or profession that he can demonstrate with pantomime while seated. Let everybody practice a while—and enjoy each other's pantomimes. Everyone keeps his own gestures throughout the game.

One player is "It," and stands in the middle of the circle. He then steps up in front of any player and starts the game by holding both thumbs to his temples and flapping his fingers. The player he faces must start pantomiming his profession. "It" changes his gestures at any time and copies the other player's action. When this happens, that player must quickly put his thumbs to his temple and flap his fingers.

The object of the game is not to be tricked into doing the same gestures that "It" is doing. When this happens, the player making the error becomes "It."

VARIATIONS: Can be played with sounds instead of gestures. And try it with just smiles and frowns!

A good game for developing quick reactions—and for melting everyone into laughter.

**SYMBOLS**

FORMATION: Players sit in a circle. Keep circles small—not more than eight or ten players.

EQUIPMENT: Nothing but a good memory and quick wit!

ACTION: Before the game starts, each player chooses his own symbol—winking one eye, waving one hand, pulling the ear lobe, rubbing the nose, or such. Give time to practice and to note one anothers' symbols.

The game starts by the leader using a four-part rhythm:

On Count 1—clap hands on knees.
    "      "    2—clap hands together.
    "      "    3—leader makes his own symbol.
    "      "    4—leader makes symbol of some other player.

That other player picks up the rhythm by repeating counts 1 and 2. On count 3, he makes his own symbol, and, on count 4, the symbol of some other player. The rhythm must continue without a break. Any player who breaks the rhythm stops the game, and gets a point scored against him.

The object of the game is to have *no* points scored against you.

This is a wonderful game for cabins, small groups, rainy days, or any time when laughing will clear the air. It can become a very fast game with practice, and is fun for developing co-ordination. Go slow at first, though, until players get used to it.

### THE TELEPHONE

FORMATION: Players sit in a circle.

EQUIPMENT: None.

ACTION: The leader starts a "telephone conversation" by whispering a word or phrase to the person on his right—such as "I met a dozen divers last night." No word can be repeated. The player on his right repeats the message the best he can to the player on *his* right—and so on around the circle. The last person repeats what he *thought* he heard.

### TRADES

FORMATION: Two informal groups, preparing their "trade" out of sight and hearing of each other.

EQUIPMENT: None.

ACTION: Each group selects some action or profession to pantomime for the other side to try to guess. Taking turns, the groups come face to face when ready. A dialogue sets the stage:

> Group 1—Here we come.
> Group 2—Where from?
> Group 1—New Orleans.
> Group 2—What's your trade?
> Group 1—Lemonade.
> Group 2—How's it made?

Group 1 pantomimes its chosen word and group 2 tries to guess. When played as a running game, group 1 races for safety if group 2 guesses correctly. Group 2 adds caught players to its side.

WHATSIT

FORMATION: Informal. Works well around a table, or other flat surface like a rock or the beach.

EQUIPMENT: Six or more irregular, odd shapes, cut from felt, paper, cardboard, or other material, of different colors. Imagination.

ACTION: The first player takes any one of the pieces, puts it down, and says "This is a _____" (anything the piece reminds him of). The second player selects another piece, lays it on or near the first, saying "This is a _____" (whatever the shape suggests) and relating it to the first. Each player takes his turn, until all the pieces have been used, and the "whatsit" completed and described. The final answer might be "This is a *bird* in the *sky* over the *tree* by the *house* with the *path* that leads to the *river*."

VARIATION: Every time this game is played, the shapes will have a different meaning for each person. If answers become repetitive, just add or make new shapes, and use new colors.

## Puppets

No dramatic, storytelling, or craft program is complete without some type of puppetry. The hard-to-dry papier-mâché head should be kept for indoor, winter programs. At day camp, puppets can be made out of what is at hand. A rubber ball makes a fine head. Cut a hole for the index finger to fit into. Paint or crayon a perky little face. Add wool, rope, or other material for hair. Cover the finger with a handkerchief, scarf, or other material, then stick it into the hole of the ball—and the puppet has a dress! Stick puppets can be paper cut-outs glued or stapled to a lollipop stick.

Spools, spoons, tin cans, boxes—almost anything can be improvised to make a puppet. Ready-made dolls and toy animals can be used "as is" for puppets and, when strings are added, as marionettes.

Puppets made to represent insects, or birds, or animals of the forest can be used to supplement nature and science programs, as well as dramatization of stories and songs.

Puppet stages can be as simple as the puppets. A blanket over a rope between two trees is one of the simplest. The players stand or sit behind the blanket, and the puppets act their roles on the top of the rope. Big cardboard boxes, an open suitcase, a porch railing, a doorway, an orange crate, all are useful as puppet stages.

PUPPET SHOWS

The following are useful techniques in putting on a puppet show of any kind:

- Exaggerate the actions.
- Use action! Let the puppets jump, clap, hit each other, fall down, bow.
- Every child who makes a puppet should operate it.
- A puppet that is talking should always *move*. When the other one replies, the first one should stay still.
- Involve the audience. The puppet should ask a question, or

tell the audience to clap, or make comments about the audience between acts.

- The child should speak *loud*. He is hidden from view, so his voice gets muffled.
- Each puppet should have a different-sounding voice.
- Add animal puppets. They are fun and any child, no matter how shy, can say "bow-wow!" or roar like a lion, or growl like a bear.
- Plan several short puppet shows to be produced as one program, so as to involve all or most of the youngsters.

# CHAPTER 15

## MUSIC AND DANCING

Music and dancing as camp activities are performing arts that can't help but include drama and storytelling. In children's day camp activities they should all be integrated as closely as possible. Games should be sung and played in a manner that brings out the music and emphasizes the dramatic story element. Songs can be dramatized. Action songs can provide exercise as well as humor. Rhythms can be created, making full use of simple instruments made in craft sessions. Simple dance mixers can make the boy-meets-girl problem much easier.

### MUSIC

Music is perhaps the most all-pervasive activity in the day camp program. It goes on hikes, on trips, on the bus; it flows through craft projects; it is a mainstay on rainy days; it is a necessity for dancing and singing.

 Everybody can take part in some form of music. The craft class can make musical instruments. Painting and drawing become free and more creative when they're done to music. Humming, whistling, clapping, tapping—they're all mixed in with music. Formal or informal, the time of day, the occasion, the group, the activity, all become richer, happier, and more creative when music is added.

The two main areas in music at day camp are in singing (in any of its many forms) and the use of musical instruments for music and dance accompaniment. Both should be kept simple and informal. Both should be used freely to supplement other activity areas.

For example, a Pirate Week or Day could use songs like "High Barbaree," "Captain Kidd," "The Pirates," "The Golden Vanity."

A Cowboy Rodeo can include "The Cowboy's Lament," "What Was Your Name in the States?." Pioneer Day will be the better for "Sourwood Mountain," "Sweet Betsy from Pike," "Skip to My Loo," and "The Erie Canal."

## Selection of Songs

Song selection in day camp is not quite so difficult as it is in resident camping. For one thing, the day campers are younger. For another, the time is more limited, both as to extent and occasion.

Counselors are always faced with two problems: how much of popular, current music to include, and how to supplement these "nonsense" songs that campers insist upon—and highly enjoy—singing. The answers are not difficult.

There is no reason why popular, current songs cannot be included, *if* they are in good taste, and suitable for the ages of the campers. Some of them are nonsense songs, full of the repetition that youngsters enjoy.

The usual camp songs of the "Itty Bitty Spider" variety are novel to young children. Counselors who have heard them sung too often at too many campfires tend to forget that children in day camp have *not* heard them, and find them hilarious. These songs appeal strongly to the simple, uncomplicated sense of humor that youngsters have at day camp age.

The chief thing, then, is not to censor and restrict, but to strengthen and enlarge the music repertory. No child under twelve will choose to sing a current, torrid torch song, or even a rock-and-roll, twist, or whatever the current song fad may be, if he has learned a rousing sea chanty with a rollicking chorus, or gets involved in an Indian chant, or tries to keep the movements straight in a fast action song.

Eminently suitable for day camps are songs of the following types:

| | |
|---|---|
| Singing Games | Work Songs |
| Action Songs | Marching Songs |
| Folk Songs | Patriotic Songs |
| Rounds | Spirituals |

### Records

Whether or not to use records is sometimes a difficult question. The answer depends upon one thing: Will records make the music and dance activities effective?

Records can supplement beautifully, but they cannot replace personal leadership. The "Selected Resource References" at the end of this book will give a few suggestions for useful, interesting records, and the addresses of record companies from whom catalogues may be collected will be found there under "Addresses of Publishers and Distributors."

### Leading a Song

A counselor need not be a music specialist to develop a "singing camp." He must be able to carry a tune—and he must know lots of tunes. If he can sing reasonably well, or whistle—or wonderful thought—play a guitar, accordion, harmonica, or other musical instrument, he has it made! He'll be the Pied Piper of Day Camp.

A few suggestions for making singing fun are these:

- Select songs and tunes with strong beats and rhythms.
- Encourage soft, sweet tones. Too often campers ruin their voices, the music, and the counselor's disposition by screaming, high pitched, strident singing.
- Encourage *action*. Sway, tap the foot, clap, whistle. They all provide extra outlets for youngsters bursting with enthusiasm.
- Include songs that ask and answer questions, that require a chorus, that need action, that require observation and specific timing (like rounds).
- Include songs with humor in them.
- Use the familiar songs before going into brand-new ones.
- Use songs that *augment* an activity—such as cowboy songs for a rodeo, pirate songs for a water carnival.

- Wherever it fits, dramatize a song.
- Encourage making up songs. Chants telling of adventures while hiking are creative experiences.
- Encourage individual songs. Young children become self-conscious as they grow up unless they learn early to feel free in sharing their songs, dances, and stories. Music is an important method of communication.
- Encourage learning songs of other lands. Excellent collections are now available.
- Make singing seem as natural and normal as breathing. It is! And show personal enjoyment. It's catching.

### ROUNDS

Rounds are good musical discipline. Youngsters must keep time, and chime in at just the right moment. Often actions can be added to them, making them even more interesting to sing, to act, and to see. "Three Blind Mice" and "Row, Row, Row Your Boat" are excellent examples. Everyone knows the tunes.

#### THREE BLIND MICE

In "Three Blind Mice" campers can add action:

1-2 Raise three fingers, cover eyes (Three blind mice, repeat).

3-4 Hand to shade eyes (See how they run, repeat).

5 Fingers move rapidly (They all ran after the farmer's wife).

6 Slicing motion with right hand (Who cut off their tails with a carving knife).

7 Hands to ears (Did you ever hear such a thing in your life?).

8 Raise three fingers, cover eyes (Three blind mice).

#### ROW, ROW, ROW YOUR BOAT

"Row, Row, Row Your Boat" can add these actions:

1 Arms moving in rowing action (Row, row, row your boat).

2 Fingers move gently, arms outstretched (Gently down the stream).

3   Merrily, merrily, merrily, merrily.
4   Hands to cheek in sleeping position (Life is but a dream).

### MAKE NEW FRIENDS

"Make New Friends" is a pretty, two-part round very suitable for early days at camp.

Make New Friends

"Make new friends and keep the old;
the first are silver, the others gold."

### THE FROGS

Another round that is very well-suited to camp and not too familiar to most children is "The Frogs."

### ACTION SONGS

Action Songs are well-known camp standbys. Many are old-timers. One of these was given new interest by its use as "The Children's March" in the movie "Inn of the Sixth Happiness." It is "This Old Man," and the youngsters will know the tune. The action goes like this:

### THIS OLD MAN

1. This old man, he played one
   He played knickknack on my thumb
   (Tap thumb with index finger.)
   Knickknack, paddywack, give your dog a bone
   This old man came rolling home.
2. This old man, he played two
   He played knickknack on my shoe
   (Tap shoe with knuckles.)
3. On my knee
   (Tap on knee.)
4. On the floor
   (Bend and beat time on floor.)
5. On my hive
   (Bend and brush bees away from ears.)
6. On my sticks
   (Tap knuckles.)
7. Up to Devon
   (Shakes fist.)
8. On my pate
   (Tap top of head.)
9. On my spine
   (Drum knuckles on backbone.)
10. Now and then
    (Hands shoulder high. Beat twice with closed fist, third
    time with open hands.)

An action song that can be played in a circle, or played by each child taking a turn, is like the one below:

### THE ANIMALS IN THE ZOO

*Tune:* Mulberry Bush
*Words and Action:*
*Chorus:*

Look at the animals in the Zoo,
In the Zoo, in the Zoo,
And all the funny things they do,
And we can do them too.

*Verses:*

1. The elephant walks and swings his trunk,
   Swings his trunk, swings his trunk.
   The elephant walks and swings his trunk,
   And we can do it too.
2. The eagle flaps his great big wings, etc.
3. See how the snake goes twisting about, etc.
4. The big hippopotamus winks and blinks, etc.
5. The tall giraffe can stretch his neck, etc.
6. The kangaroo goes jumping about, etc.
7. Camels can march like soldier men, etc.
8. Each little mouse can tiptoe away, etc.
   (Each child tiptoes back to place.)

### SINGING GAMES

Singing games, like rhythms, include music, movement, and drama. They should be played so as to bring out all those qualities. Many are old-time games that were originally based upon religious ceremonies. "London Bridge," for example, is based upon the barbaric custom of making a human sacrifice to the river god when building a bridge over the river. A counselor interested in tracing the history of some of the games now regarded as suitable only for very young children will be fascinated by their origins.

Some, like the old "Go in and out the Window," are leftovers from the guild system. It was used by the weavers' guild, and the movements represent weaving.

Some, like "Thorn Rosa," are fairy tales set to music and made into a little game.

Old favorites that every child should know, and that are found in most game books, include

| | |
|---|---|
| Looby Loo | London Bridge |
| Farmer in the Dell | Round and Round the Village |
| A-Hunting We Will Go | Itisket, Itasket |
| Roman Soldiers | Thorn Rosa |

### DRAMATIZING SINGING GAMES

Song dramatization can be conducted as a simple circle game, or become the action for a pantomimed plot. One group, for example, can provide the singing words, while the other acts out the plot. In the case of "The Sleeping Beauty," extra parts can be added to enlarge the cast, by using more guards, trees, cooks, and so on. It is a very good example of a musical story-play.

#### THE SLEEPING BEAUTY

*Tune:*

Sleeping Beauty

*Words:*

1. There was an ancient castle, a castle, a castle,
   There was an ancient castle, long ago.
2. The guards were on the portals, the portals, the portals, etc.
3. The king and queen they lived there, they lived there, they lived there, etc.
4. The cook was in the kitchen, the kitchen, the kitchen, etc.
5. There was a lovely princess, a princess, a princess, etc.
6. The princess she was spinning, was spinning, was spinning, etc.
7. She pricked her little finger, her finger, her finger, etc.
8. The wicked witch bewitched them, bewitched them, bewitched them, etc.
9. One hundred years they slept there, they slept there, they slept there, etc.
10. The bushes grew up slowly, up slowly, up slowly, etc.
11. A handsome prince came riding, came riding, came riding, etc.

12. He woke the lovely princess, the princess, the princess, etc.
13. They had a royal wedding, a wedding, a wedding, etc.
14. They all were very happy, were happy, were happy, etc.

Children take the parts of the guards, the King and Queen, the Cook, the Princess, the Wicked Witch, the bushes, and the Handsome Prince. They pantomime the actions. The guards can shoulder arms, march up and down, etc. The "bushes" start off flat on the ground, and grow tiptoe tall. The Prince has to ride, chop a path in the bushes. The household wakens, everyone stretches, and they form a big parade for the wedding.

A variation of this sort of music-play is to tell a story that requires repetition and have the youngsters *sing* the repeated lines wherever they occur. "The Gingerbread Boy" is a good example. The counselor reads or tells the story, and the youngsters sing the gingerbread boy's taunt:

Gingerbread Man

"Run, run, run, as fast as you can
You can't catch me, I'm a Gingerbread Man."

### BALLADS AND WORK SONGS

Ballads and work songs are usually rollicking, gay tunes. Many of them can be dramatized and pantomimed. "The Three Pirates" has a lovely swing to it, and is a question-and-answer song. Sing it back and forth, then act it out.

### THE THREE PIRATES

1. Three pirates came to London Town, yo ho, yo ho,
   To see the King put on his crown, yo ho, yo ho.

Three Pirates came to London Town to see the King put
on his crown,
Yo ho, ye lubbers, yo ho, ye lubbers, yo ho, yo ho, yo ho.

2. First they came to a wayside inn, yo ho, yo ho,
   And said, Good landlord, let us in, etc.

3. Oh, Landlord, have you bags of gold, yo ho, yo ho,
   Enough to fill the afterhold, etc.

4. Oh, yes sir, I have bags of gold, yo ho, yo ho,
   Enough to fill the afterhold, etc.

5. Oh, Landlord, have you a daughter fair, yo ho, yo ho,
   With laughing eyes and curly hair, etc.

6. Oh, yes sir, I have a daughter fair, yo ho, yo ho,
   With laughing eyes and curly hair, etc.

7. Oh, Landlord, will she marry me, yo ho, yo ho,
   And sail with me across the sea, etc.

8. Oh, yes sir, she will marry thee, yo ho, yo ho,
   And sail with thee across the sea, etc.

JUST-FOR-FUN SINGING

Musical quizzes provide good motivation for group singing,
and can be used with pleasure on rainy or hot days, while hiking, or anywhere when singing. They appeal particularly to the
older day campers. Such quizzes can be developed in several
ways:

- By alternate singing of a tune by two groups, one group singing, the other guessing.
- By listing as many answers as possible and then singing them; such as "How many songs can we think of that mention *animals?*"
- By the leader playing or humming the tune to the campers who are guessing the song.

Categories that tie in, no matter how slightly, with nature themes make such programs suitable for day camp. A few examples of categories and the songs are as follows:

*Animals*
    The Old Gray Mare
    The Bear Went Over the Mountain
    How Much Is That Doggie in the Window?
    Home on the Range (where the deer and the antelope play)
    Rudolph the Red-Nosed Reindeer

*Flowers*
    Daisy, Daisy
    Heather on the Hill
    When You Wore a Tulip
    My Wild Irish Rose

*Trees*
    Here We Go Round the Mulberry Bush
    Don't Sit Under the Apple Tree
    Willow, Tit Willow

*Birds*
    Woodpecker Song
    When the Red, Red Robin Comes Bob-Bob-Bobbing Along
    When the Swallows Come Back to Capistrano
    Bye, Bye Blackbird

Other categories that can be developed are these:

| | |
|---|---|
| Stars | Rain |
| Mountains | Spring |
| Colors | Girls' Names |
| Boys' Names | |

**TOGETHER SONGS**

"Together Songs" are fun. They're the songs that fit together. One group sings one song, another group sings another, and the two together make nice harmony. Sometimes three or four songs can be sung together. Try these:

> Sidewalks of New York
> Bicycle Built for Two
> In the Good Old Summertime

> Swanee River
> Put On Your Old Gray Bonnet
> Annie Laurie

> The Old Gray Mare
> London Bridge
> Frère Jacque

> Oh, Susanna
> Turkey in the Straw

> Take Me Out to the Ball Game
> In the Good Old Summertime

**ACTIVITY THEME SONGS**

Activity theme songs can be selected by campers. They can be kept all season or changed weekly, and be accepted as part of the camp program. For example, for Crafts, the campers might select "Whistle While You Work." For Music, perhaps "The Music Goes Round and Round," or "Sing Something Simple."

They might also enjoy selecting and using daily, a Song of the Week.

## DANCING

Dancing, in day camping, should be kept as informal and relaxed as possible. For small children, moving to music or rhythmic activity is the first step, combining music with imitative play and creative movement.

Campers should be encouraged to create their own dance movements through trying to express their emotions or through trying to tell a story or express an idea. For example, in observing bees, and finding out that they communicate through a sort of drama, the campers might attempt to work out a Dance of the Bees. They might dramatize through a dance the gathering of birds for migration, or the legend of the spider.

Folk dances that provide plenty of action, but little if any bodily contact, are useful for boys in that "I hate girls" age.

### Rhythms

Very closely allied to drama, rhythms require some type of music and movement, making them fit into the music and dance program. They are an excellent example of how closely correlated the performing arts are and should be.

Rhythms, in small children, take the form of imitative action. The small boy gallops like a horse, and identifies himself *with* a horse. The little girl dances and whirls—and *is* a fairy. The children at day camp may look like normal, healthy youngsters on the outside, but inside they're really Wyatt Earp, or Space Man, or Cinderella, or Robin Hood. This identification of self makes rhythms very easily motivated. With children, movements are easier and more meaningful than words. Such movements are called mimetics. Try these, and let the youngsters suggest others:

| *Animals* | *Occupations* |
|---|---|
| Bear walk | Chopping wood |
| Bird hop | Pumping a tire |
| Frog jump | Laying bricks |
| Elephant walk | Digging up a sidewalk |

| *Transportation* | *Sports* |
|---|---|
| Railroad train | Throwing snowballs |
| Aeroplane | Ice skating |
| Bicycle | Swimming |
| Horse and wagon | Horseback riding |

The musical instruments described in Chapter 13 on "Arts and Crafts" may be used for these rhythms, and for other activities with music and dance program.

These instruments may be used, too, to *motivate* the responses. Long, regular, slow beats slow the group down to a big-step march. A quick, accentuated beat, and they gallop around like ponies; an irregular beat, and they'll combine a hop and a step.

Use the rhythm instruments in the following song. The words are just syllables. The song gathers speed as the Indians ride faster. Clap the hands, click sticks, beat drums, in time to the music. Dramatize, using stick horses, too, for the younger campers.

### NAVAJO HAPPY SONG
(A Riding Song)

Rhythms can be made into games, too. Using the rhythm instruments, add drama to action:

1. The Drum says

| *Even beat* | *Uneven beat* |
|-------------|---------------|
| walk | gallop |
| run | skip |
| jump | slide |
| hop | |

2. The "Ing" game

| *Moving* | *Standing* |
|---|---|
| running | jumping |
| sliding | hopping |
| walking | clapping |
| galloping | nodding |
| pulling | bending |

3. Interpretation of Words

I'm a top spinning across the floor.
I'm a whirlpool swirling in the river.
I'm a dishrag flopping on the floor.
I'm a ragdoll, loose and limber.
I'm happy. I'm free.
I'm dancing.

## Simple Dances and Mixers

The next dance is lively, and everyone must duck at the right moment or get bopped!

### THE DUCK DANCE

*Music:* Any lively 2/4 rhythm, like "Nellie Bly," "Captain Jinks," "Rig-a-Jig, Jig."

*Formation:* Sets of five or six couples, boys in one line, girls in another, like the Virginia Reel.

*Action:* Head couple join hands and slide down to the front of the set, their hands joined over the heads of the girls' line (girls must duck). At the foot of the set, they turn, boy still on the inside, and slide back up over the heads of the boys (boys must duck). When the head couple is back in place, the girl turns right and marches down to the end of the line; the boy turns left and marches down to the end of the line. The lines follow their lead. At the foot of the set, the head couple join hands and the others go under that arch, back into place. The new head couple repeats the action, and so on until the original couple is back at the head of the line.

### LILI MARLENE

*Music:* The same. (Keep music lively.)

*Formation:* Couples facing counterclockwise, inside hands joined.

*Action:*

1. Walk forward four steps, face, join both hands, slide four slides, same direction.
2. Repeat in opposite direction.
3. Clap own hands, clap partner's right hand, clap own hands.
4. Clap partner's left hand, clap own hands, clap both hands of partner, clap own hands.
5. Link right elbows and turn halfway around; back with left elbow.
6. Repeat clapping. Boy moves ahead to the next girl.

MY NAME IS _____

*Music:* "Good Night Ladies"

*Formation:* Lines of three, in promenade position. (If girls outnumber boys, put a boy between two girls.)

*Action:*

1. Those on left side sing, "My name is . . . " (own name)
2. Those on right side sing, "My name is . . . " (own name)
3. Those in center sing, "My name is . . . " (own name)
4. Everyone together sings,
   "Let's go and meet the rest
   Merrily we roll along," etc.
5. On the fourth line the center people move ahead to the next line. Promenade during the chorus.

BOOMPSY DAISY

Teen-agers know that "Boompsy Daisy" is a good dance mixer. It's also an action song and dance that below-teens will enjoy.

*Music:* Any waltz.

*Formation:* All face a partner, informal groupings.

| Words | Action |
|---|---|
| 1. Knees, knees, knees | 1. Clap own knees three times. |
| 2. Hands, hands, hands | 2. Clap own hands three times. |

| | |
|---|---|
| 3. Right, right, right | 3. Clap right hands with partner. |
| 4. Left, left, left | 4. Clap left hands with partner. |
| 5. Knees, hands together | 5. Clap own knees once, clap own hands once, clap partner's hands once. |
| 6. Knees, hands together | 6. Repeat. |
| 7. Clap 1-2-3-4-5-6 | 7. Clap own hands together and very quickly turn to face another partner and start again. |

If the boys think that dancing is for girls only, give them *Indian* dances. Only the men were allowed to do most of them. The women just sat around and clapped. Here is a good one for day camp:

INDIAN CORN DANCE

*Music:* Tom-Tom. Beat of one-two-three-four. First four movements quite slow and deliberate, with strong accent on the first beat.

*Formation:* Braves in a single line. They dance to end of area and back twice. (Forward to make the furrow, turn around, and come back planting the seed; return to cover seed; turn and come back to firm the ground; return to bring the rain.)

1. *Digging the Furrows:* Take a long, lunging step forward with the left foot on the first beat. Drag the right foot, toes down, up to meet the left foot on beats 2, 3, 4. Shift weight and repeat to end of area.

2. *Planting the Seed:* On first beat, take long step forward with left foot, bring right foot to meet it, and raise right arm as high as possible. On beats 2, 3, 4, bend from waist and touch ground with right hand as though planting seed.

3. *Covering the Seeds:* On beat 1, take long step forward with left foot, turning body sideways. On beats 2, 3, 4, drag right foot up, as though covering seeds. Shift weight, turn body sideways, and step forward on right foot, dragging left foot up. Alternate to end of furrow.

4. *Stamping the Ground:* (This is tricky but very Indian. Beats

are faster, and the pivot will take practice.) Start with feet together, knees loose and slightly flexed. With the left foot stamp four beats forward, each stamp a few inches farther than the last. Then pivot the body, shifting weight to the left foot, and stamp the right foot forward four beats. The body makes a full half-turn, and each foot gives four short but hard stamps.

5. *The Rain:* Like (2), except that both arms are raised on count one, lowered with fingers moving to indicate rain on counts 2, 3, 4.

CHAPTER **16:**

# GAMES IN THE
# ACTIVITY PROGRAM

Games cut across almost every other activity in the day camp program. They show up in drama and music, on hikes, at lunch-time, at rest period, on the bus, indoors on rainy days, outdoors on good days.

There are games for every age group; games for boys, for girls, for boys and girls; games for sitting down, and standing up; for hot and rainy weather; for bus trips; games for one, two, or any number of players; games that require no equipment; games that need lots of space—and little space; games that develop the vocabulary; laugh-making games.

### Games—Their Values and Use

Games can tell a story, like the singing games, "Roman Soldiers" and "Thorn Rosa." Pantomimes and creative dramatics grow out from games like "Farmer in the Dell," "Trades," and "Looby Loo."

Games like "Captain Jenks," "Ach Ya," and "How Do You Do, My Partner" lead straight into folk and square dancing.

The line games, tag games, and relays are fine big-muscle activities that encourage hopping, skipping, running, and jumping. Catching, throwing, and kicking skills grow out of the many games involving balls. These are all important in developing physical fitness.

Tracking games, nature games, magic and mystery games, all train youngsters to *see,* not just look; to *think,* not just guess.

Children learn control of body and self-discipline from games requiring obedience and rapid response to directions in games like Simon Says, and Crows and Cranes.

The guessing games, puzzles, and quizzes encourage mental alertness.

The games in this chapter will serve to identify the types best suited for day camp use, and include those in which the major emphasis is the game itself.

Others, in which the major emphasis may be dramatics, or music, or nature, will be found in other chapters. Consult "Selected Resource References" at the rear for excellent books to supplement the games given in this book.

One of the indications of a trained, experienced counselor is his personal library of professional resources. And one of the characteristics of a well-planned and organized day camp is the provision of an adequate camp library for use by counselors and campers.

### Twelve Points for Game Leadership

- Make sure the game is suitable for the age-group.
- Know it thoroughly.
- Get the players into formation quickly and without confusion.
- Explain the game, but be brief.
- Demonstrate any difficult part, if necessary.
- Play along with the youngsters when the game is new to them, or when your presence makes it more fun—as it usually does. In some of the games with the older youngsters, you'll need to act as umpire, starter, referee, or in other official capacity.
- Select at least twice as many games as you'll probably use. It gives you a chance to pick and choose.
- Play as long as interest is high, but never let a game peter out. Don't be afraid to *repeat* a game if the children want it. It may be old to you—but remember that *everything* is new to a child. Emphasize the dramatic element that exists in all games.
- Teach good playing techniques, but do it unobtrusively. For example: "Jack, try holding your elbows like this. I think you'll make more speed."

- In a singing game, keep the music soft and sweet. Discourage screaming. Encourage singing.
- Insist on fair play. Keep the rules simple, but *rules.*
- Encourage laughing, having a good time, friendliness, and co-operation rather than intense competition.

### Game Formation

In many games, the players must get into a certain formation. Getting them into the proper formation without confusion and delay is a sign of skillful game leadership. An easy way to get youngsters into several teams is to have them all join hands and form a circle. Starting with one youngster, have them count off, using as many numbers as there should be teams. For example, for four teams for a relay race, the youngsters would count 1, 2, 3, 4, 1, 2, 3, 4, on and on, until each had a number. Then "All Number Ones line up behind Bill," "Number Twos line up behind Mary," and so it would go.

The major game formations used in low-organized games (as opposed to the high-organized, or team sports), are the file, the rank, the relay, single circle, double circle, zigzag, and informal, and they can be described thus:

*File:* Players are in a single line, one behind the other.

*Rank:* Players are in a single line, side by side.

*Relay:* A file, with the first player in place behind a starting line.

*Single Circle:* Players stand or sit in a ring. For various games they may face out, or face in, or face clockwise or counterclockwise, depending upon the direction they will move in the game.

*Double Circle:* Two rings, one inside the other.

*Zigzag:* Players are in two ranks, each player usually an arm's length away, in such a way that the players in any rank are not directly behind those in the rank before or behind them.

*Informal:* Players stand around the counselor or "It" in easy, informal grouping, usually fairly semicircular in shape. They are near enough to see, to hear, and usually to touch each other and the counselor. This information is often used in games involving the giving of instruction, or of question and answer prior to a chase or hunt.

```
   Leader & Group          Relay              Zig Zag

           X (leader)     V V V V        V  V  V  V  V
 V                V       V V V V         V  V  V  V  V
   V           V          V V V V
     V       V            V V V V            File
       V V                V V V V

                                             V
                                             V
           X                                 V
                            Rank             V
 V V V V V V V V                             V
                         V V V V V V         V
```

Single circle     Double circle

## Adapting Games

Interest is the major motivation in any game. If too many players are in it, and each player has to wait too long for his turn, interest will lag. If the game is too easy, or too difficult, interest will lag.

A skillful counselor will speed up a game by providing more than one runner, or chaser, or "It"; by turning one large circle into two smaller, concentric circles; by using more than one ball or other object; by increasing or decreasing the distances to be run, or thrown, or covered in any way; by changing the size or weight of a ball or other object used.

Active games usually are made up of one or more types of body action—running, chasing, hiding, throwing, catching, dodging. They may be varied by changing the emphasis, by adding or subtracting an action.

Changing the *focus* is one of the best ways of adapting a game. This can be done sometimes by changing the *name*—making the game become part of a dramatic situation, by appealing to the child's imagination. This is often accomplished by using a *theme*. For example, the Treasure Hunt on Pirate's Day can become the Gold Rush on Western Day. A young pirate may "walk the plank"; a young circus performer may be a "tightrope walker." Both will do the same thing—try to walk a chalk line while looking through the wrong end of binoculars or opera glasses, or walk along the side-strip of a ladder lying flat on the ground. The drama is different—and so the same game becomes something new.

Sometimes outdoor games are changed into indoor games by modifying or reducing the movement and equipment. Table tennis is a classic example, along with table shuffleboard, dart baseball, and box hockey. The *movement* in dart baseball is only the throwing of the dart, but the imagination turns the dart thrower into a man at bat hoping for a home run.

An indoor table game like checkers can be transferred into an outdoor game by marking off a checkerboard on the ground, and using big blocks for checkers. They may be moved by pushing with a pole. (Shuffleboard equipment can be used, too.) If an even larger checkerboard is marked off, *Human Checkers*, using boys and girls for the "men," moving when directed by their captain, makes a game that is fun to watch as well as to play.

A game should always be dynamic, never static. It should be played to the hilt, not lackadaisically. It should *require* something from the player—endurance, quick wit, agility, observation, daring, perseverance, fair play, dexterity.

To the child, a game must be fun. To the counselor, it will be fun with a purpose.

## Choosing "It"

Choosing "It" is a serious matter in childhood. Sometimes "It" is the coveted role; sometimes "It" is the victim. His selection provides an integral, and often dra-  matic, part of many informal games suitable for day camp.

Many methods can be, and should be, used to add to the delicious suspense. Drawing straws is an old favorite—the one drawing the shortest is "It." Flipping a coin or guessing the number of fingers held behind one's back are old standbys.

Sometimes Fate, in the form of a blindfolded child, points to a victim from inside a circle of youngsters. Sometimes a race to touch a given tree lets the first—or the last—become "It."

Sometimes the leader asks "Who wants to be 'It'?", pointing to a child on each word. After the last word, each child names a letter of the alphabet starting with A. The one to say the letter I becomes "It."

Counting out rhymes are the most fun, the most traditional, and the fairest. Many of them have come down to us through the centuries, based originally on magic incantations, or the selection of victims for religious rites. The gibberish used in some can be traced to numbers used in other languages.

Many have been changed or revised by youngsters in different sections of the country. Many become adapted to local news or conditions. Every youngster will know some and be eager to use them. Every youngster will enjoy hearing new ones. Here are a few out of the hundreds chanted by youngsters all over the world. In using counting-out rhymes, point with each beat, not necessarily with each word. It's the rhythm that counts.

- My mother told me to take Y-O-U.
  (An old, simple favorite often used at the very end of other counting-out rhymes, just to delay the action and increase the suspense. The leader points to a different child with each beat.)

- Engine, engine, Number Nine
  Running on Chicago time
  If it's polished, it will shine
  Engine, engine, Number Nine

- Eeny, meeny, miney, mo
  Catch a monkey by the toe
  If he hollers let him go
  Eeny, meeny, miney, mo
  (This has many, many variations.)

- Crickety, crackety, cranery crow
  I went to the spring to wash my toe
  High or low, out you go
  Crickety, crackety, cranery crow.

- Onery, twoery, threesy, four
  Fivery, sixery, seventy more
  Eightery, ninery, tenery score
  One, two, three says out.

- Ibbety, bibbity, sibbety, saw
  Cannery, tannery, clippety claw
  Zum, zam, zibbity zee
  Out go you, One, two, three.

- A-E-I-O-U
  Y-E-S spells yes
  And out goes you.

- One a penny, two a penny
  Three a penny, four
  Five a penny, six a penny
  Seven a penny more
  Eight a penny, nine a penny
  Twenty makes a score
  O-U-T spells out.

- Riminy, siminy, sibbety sue
  Lom, tom, rim, rue

Teacher, teacher, ring the bell
Ding, dong, ding, dong
One, two, you're through
O-U-T spells Y-O-U.

Sometimes "It" is chosen by using counting-out rhymes to eliminate everyone else, leaving the last person to be "It." This delicious, suspenseful manner is a favorite of children in Trinidad. Here are three examples. Two are full-length, ritualistic rhymes, the other a "quickie," to be used when the recess bell is about to ring, and only a fast game can be played.

- I went up a higgy, higgy mountain
  And I saw some higgy, higgy people
  Some were red and some were blue
  Which color do you love the best?
  (If answer is "red") *

  R-E-D stands for red
  So you must come out of this
  higgy, higgy game at once.
  Take him in and put him *out*.

- My father and your father
  Live across the sea
  Every night they have a fight
  And this is what they say
  Accra, baccra, soda cracker
  If your father
  Out goes he.
  Take him in and put him out.

- Pig snout walk out.

---

* Likewise, if answer is "blue," the line to follow is "B-L-U-E stands for blue."

## INFORMAL GROUP GAMES

The *democracy* of the informal group games of childhood is their main attribute, and their most important characteristic. The leader, or "It," is chosen by chance or by group selection. Every youngster can play, regardless of his individual skill. There's a range of action in most of these games that serves as a leveler: one child may be a better runner, but another may be more daring, or more careful; and his contribution to the game will be just as useful. These games have an ebb and flow in them that maintains interest. They can be molded by the child; the child does not have to fit into the rigid framework of rules and techniques required by a team sport. Most of them, except for some of the challenges, can be played by boys, by girls, or by mixed groups. Most require very little if any special equipment.

Someone has said that the hardest thing an adult can require of a child is to do nothing. Growth means action. The day camp game program must provide all sorts of action, through a wide variety of running, line, and circle games, plus the competition provided by relays and challenges.

During the years of childhood, boys and girls need open space in which they can run, shout, laugh, and feel the earth under them. City streets, apartment house living, and even many playgrounds cannot offer this space for the really active games that develop physical endurance, stamina, strong muscles, and quick physical reactions.

The chief physical characteristic of a day camp—the thing that separates it from other also valuable facilities such as the back yard, the school or agency gymnasium, the basketball and tennis courts, baseball diamonds, and other play areas available to children in a community—is its *setting*—a large, outdoor, natu-ralistic area, where the program will not depend upon game courts and play apparatus, but upon the innate, naturalistic characteris-tics of the area.

In this section will be found many of the old, traditional games of childhood that are the birthright of children. As the age levels in many team sports sink lower and lower, many youngsters have been, and are being, deprived of this birthright. "Little League" or its equivalent is not a substitute for the daring, initi-ative, suspense, and action in games like Run, Sheep, Run! and Stealing Sticks.

## Group Games in Alphabetical Listing

The games in this section fall into many classifications, and can be used in many different situations. For that reason, they are alphabetized here and listed in the Index, along with other games included under other activity headings.

### BIG LANTERN, LITTLE LANTERN *(O-ke cho-chin, chi-chai cho-chin,* Japan)

*Formation:* Children sit in a circle.

*Equipment:* None.

*Action:* One player is "It." He turns to his neighbor on either right or left, and says "Big lantern" (O-ke cho-chin). At the same time he makes the shape of a big lantern with his hands. The person addressed then turns to his right or left neighbor and says "Little lantern" (chi-chai, cho-chin), making the shape of a little lantern.

The play goes on, to the right or to the left. The size of the lantern described with the hands must correspond with the words. Go slow at first, until a rhythm is established, then speed it up.

*Variation:* Use like Simon Says. Leader faces group, and calls out the Japanese words, trying by his gestures to get a youngster to make the wrong shape of the lantern.

Or develop as a *rhythmic* game, going around the circle, each player passing along either the big or the little lantern, as he pleases, without breaking the rhythm.

*Note:* This is very much like Simon Says.

### CATCH THE CONE

*Formation:* Informal. Players may compete as teams, or as individuals. They stand behind a line.

*Equipment:* Two straight sticks, about 15 inches long.

*Action:* One player "launches a missile" by throwing a stick as far as he can. The second player (rescue team) tries to throw his stick so that it will hit the missile. If he succeeds, no points are scored. If he misses, the rescuer loses a point for every jump he can take between the two sticks.

Players then change roles—the launcher becoming the rescuer. Player or team with lowest score wins.

### CHINESE HOP

*Formation:* Players in single line, behind starting line. Ten sticks are placed in a row in easy hopping distance in front of each player.

*Equipment:* Ten sticks for each player. Substitute spools, blocks, rocks, clothespins, or other small articles if necessary.

*Action:* Each player takes his position about a yard in front of his row of sticks. At the signal, he hops on one foot down the row and over each. He may change feet, but may not touch a stick in hopping over it. When he gets over the last one, he turns (still on one foot), picks it up, and hops back over the others to the starting line. Dropping the stick, he starts back, again picking up the last stick, and so on until he has retrieved all of the sticks. The first to finish without a mistake, is the winner.

*Variation:* Play as a team relay, with the same number of sticks as there are players for each team. First player hops over the sticks, brings back the last one, and goes to end of line. Second player follows, and so on, until each player has taken part and is back in starting position.

CROWS AND CRANES

*Formation:* Players line up in two teams, facing each other in the middle of the play area, and standing three or four feet apart. Each team has a safety area marked off about 30 feet behind it.

*Equipment:* None.

*Action:* The two teams, the crows and the cranes, face each other, each ready to whirl around and dash for its safety line. The leader stands where all can see and hear him, but not in the line of action. If he calls "Crows," all the crows race for their safety line and the Cranes try to tag as many as possible. Those tagged join the Cranes.

If the leader calls "Cranes," they race for safety to avoid capture by the Crows. The team that has the greatest number of players at the end of a given time wins.

The leader keeps suspense high by rolling his r's, so that neither team can be sure which will be called.

*Variations:* Modify the distance to the safety line to suit the age of the players, the temperature of the day, or other factor. Vary the names, too, like Soldiers and Sailors, Saints and Sinners, Friend and Foe, Bread and Butter.

DOWN AND AROUND

*Formation:* Two or more teams, each team sitting down in a compact group, backs together and legs extended.

*Equipment:* None.

*Action:* At a signal, the first player on each team gets up, runs around his team, and sits down in his place. As soon as he is down, the next player must jump up, run around his team, and return. The first team to be all seated after all have run, is the winner.

THE EAGLE AND THE CHICKEN (*El Gavilan y lo Pollitos*—Latin America)

*Formation:* Informal.

*Equipment:* None.

*Action:* One child is chosen to be the Eagle, and another the Mother Hen. All the other children are chicks, and line up behind the Mother Hen, their arms around each other's waists. The Eagle must stay in front of Mother Hen. She holds out her arms to protect the chicks from the Eagle, who tries to touch one. The line of chicks moves back and forth as Mother Hen tries to protect it. If a chick is touched, he goes behind the Eagle. The last chick to be touched becomes the Eagle in the next game.

### FACE IT!

*Formation:* A circle, or line, or informal grouping.

*Equipment:* Nothing but a good memory and a straight face.

*Action:* The first player says, "I have a face." The player on his right asks, "What kind of face?" Player No. 1 answers with any adjective starting with an A, such as "An angry face," or "An awful face," or "An attractive face," and so on. Player No. 2 then turns to the person on his right and says, "I have a face." Question, "What kind of face?" "An average face," and so on until every player has had a chance to describe his face with an A. Then they go on to B, and so on through the alphabet.

*Variation:* For older youngsters, or to make the game more difficult, each player must repeat in order all the adjectives that have been given, in answer to the question "What kind of face?"

Try changing "Face" to "Nose," or "Voice."

Try requiring that each player keep from smiling. A good variation for that day when everybody seems to be in a bad humor!

### FIND THAT MAN!

*Formation:* Informal. Youngsters choose up sides, making two teams.

*Equipment:* None.

*Action:* This is a team version of Hide and Seek. Those on one side all hide their eyes while their captain counts to a hundred by fives. The other youngsters all hide.

As each "man" is found, he is brought back to a designated station. Game continues until each person has been found. Then teams change places—hunting team becomes the hiders.

*Note:* When necessary, designate limits and set rules, such as "no hiding in a building," or "no hiding beyond the road."

FORTY WAYS TO GET THERE

*Formation:* Players stand in line at one end of a playing field, facing a goal line 30 feet away.

*Equipment:* None.

*Action:* At a signal, one player at a time crosses the area to the goal line, using any method he wishes—run, skip, hop, walk backward, somersault, roll, or whatever. *But*—no two persons may use the same method. The second player starts when the first has reached the line. The game gets pretty difficult for the last players in line, so use with not too large a group.

*Variation:* As a team relay race, the leader can call out a method, such as "Run," and the first player on each team races by that method to the goal line. First to reach it, scores a point for his team. Leader then calls out a second method, such as "Hop on right foot," and so on. Appoint a scorekeeper at goal line, or require each player to go to goal line and *back*, taking his place at the end of his team. Teams can keep their own scores.

KICKOVER

*Formation:* Teams sit on ground, facing each other, feet almost touching. They may support themselves by putting their hands on the ground behind them.

*Equipment:* A basketball or volleyball.

*Action:* The basketball is thrown down the line of feet by the leader. Each team tries to kick it over the heads of the opposing team. The ball may not be touched by the hands, but may be blocked by the shoulders. If the ball goes out between players or at the ends, it does not count.

Every time a team gets the ball over the heads of the opponents, it scores a point. (If a player knocks it over his own team, the other side gets the point.) Game is 21 points.

*Variation:* This makes a good, strenuous indoor game for rainy or cold weather, if space permits. Or play with a balloon, using only the *hands*, feet placed against feet of opponent.

THE OCEAN IS STORMY

*Formation:* All the players except two stand in pairs, holding hands. Each pair draws a 3-foot circle around themselves.

*Equipment:* None.

*Action:* Each pair, in its own little circle, secretly selects the name of a fish. The two extra players are the sharks. They walk hand in hand around the area, calling out names of fish. When their name is called, each pair must fall in behind the sharks and walk with them.

When the sharks have called all the fish they can think of, they yell "The ocean is stormy!" All the fish dash to get back to their circles. If the sharks reach a circle first, the pair that is left out becomes the shark.

Encourage daring. Encourage the sharks to make the game full of suspense and mounting excitement by hesitating, and other pantomime as they go past the various couples.

*Variation:* This is an old, old game. It can be played as Fox and Chickens, or Wolf and Sheep, or Hawks and Sparrows, or any other name to suit an occasion. Instead of waiting to be called by name, each pair must leave its circle as the Fox, or Wolves, or Hawks pass them.

### PEBBLE TOSS

*Formation:* Players stand behind a throwing line ten feet away from a target two feet in diameter. The target should be divided into three circles, an outer, a middle, and a center. The target may be cut from cloth or cardboard, or marked on the ground.

*Equipment:* Each player has five pebbles.

*Action:* Players take turns in tossing a pebble at a time into the target. Scores are counted after each "round." First to reach 100 points wins. Score as follows:

> outside circle—3 points
> middle circle—5 points
> inner circle—10 points

*Variations:* Change distances to suit ages of group. Use as indoor game by using milk bottle tops instead of pebbles. Keep individual scores and use as a self-testing device—player tries each day to better his own record.

PEPPER BALL

*Formation:* Six players per team, numbered and in position on volleyball court as in sketch. Extra players in waiting line on each side of net. Net is volleyball height.

*Equipment:* Volleyball.

*Action:* The volleyball is caught and thrown back and forth. It cannot be batted. If the volleyball hits the ground on the opponents' side, or if a foul is committed, the other side scores a point. Batting the ball is a foul.

One team starts the play. At any time the leader may call "ROTATE!" This means that while the game continues, each team moves one space clockwise. The first player in each waiting line steps quickly into the space left by player No. 1. Player No. 6 leaves the court and goes to the end of his team's waiting line.

The game is 15 points.

This is a fast, strenuous game, popular wherever it is used. It keeps players moving in and out of the game, so that larger numbers can play. It develops catching and throwing skills, and players must stay very alert.

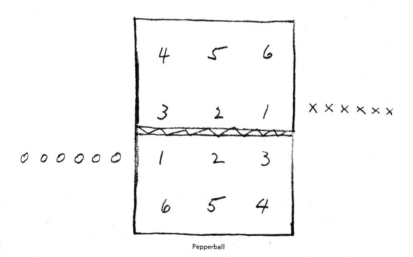

Pepperball

PETER PAN TAG

*Formation:* Informal.

*Equipment:* None.

*Action:* Count out to get the first "It." He then chases the others and tries to tag one by stepping on his shadow. If even one foot touches the shadow, the new "It" becomes the chaser. Players protect their shadows by dodging and by running.

*Variation:* Players are safe when they reach a shady spot.

POM, POM, PULL AWAY

*Formation:* All the players except one ("It") stand behind one of two safety lines that are 30 to 40 feet apart. (Trees, posts, fence, or other type of safety goal may be used.)

*Equipment:* None.

*Action:* "It" stands in the middle of the danger zone and chants,

> "Pom, pom, pull away!
> If you don't come
> I'll pull you away!"

All the players must leave the safety line and dash across the open area to the other safety line. "It" tags as many as he can. Those tagged must stay and help "It," but only "It" can do the calling.

The game proceeds, the players being called to go from one safety line to the other, until all have been caught. Then the game starts all over, the last player caught (or the first player) being the new "It."

*Variation:* This game is sometimes called *Red Rover.* In it, "It" stands in the middle of the danger zone and calls,

> "Red Rover, Red Rover
> If Bill (naming any player) won't come
> I'll pull him over."

Bill has to run across, trying to avoid being tagged. Anyone tagged joins "It" in trying to tag the others, but may not do any calling.

### PRISONER'S BASE

*Formation:* Two teams, each with its own goal (often a tree or post) and its own prison area about 4 feet square, the same distance away from the opponents' goal.

*Equipment:* None.

*Action:* Each team tries to capture the players of the other team by tagging them. The territory between the two goals is neutral, and players come away from the safety of their goal to "dare" the others. Who can capture whom depends on which player most recently touched his goal.

When a player is captured, he must go into the opponent's prison. He may be rescued by any team mate who can get to him to touch him without being tagged. He and the rescuer can go back safely to their goal by holding hands while they run.

The team capturing all the others, or the team with the most players still free when time is called, is the winner.

*Variation:* See Stealing Sticks.

Prisoner's Base can be a "serial" game, played for a half hour every day, players taking off where they left off the day before. There are many different variations of this game—a sign of its popularity.

### THE PUMPKIN PLANTER *(Il Cucuzzaro—Italy)*

*Formation:* One player is *Il Cucuzzaro,* the Pumpkin Planter. He stands in the middle of a seated circle made by the other players who are Pumpkins. "It" gives each player a number. Then "It" says, "In my garden there are five (any number) pumpkins." Pumpkin No. 5 says, "Why five pumpkins" "It" answers, "If not five, how many?", and No. 5 says, "Twelve" (or any other number). No. 12 must be alert and answer promptly, "Why 12 pumpkins?" to which "It" replies, "If not 12, how many?" The game goes on, questions and answers; and, if a player forgets his number, or fails to answer promptly, or gets mixed up, he may be given a simple penalty to perform.

*Note:* This game is very much like The Prince of Paris Has Lost His Hat.

RIDE UP HIGH, O UNCLE! (Lebanon)

*Formation:* Informal. One player is chosen to be "It."

*Equipment:* None.

*Action:* Players scatter, and "It" tries to catch one. Any player about to be caught can save himself if he can *step up* on something—a rock, a stair, a doorsill, a tree root—any place that's higher than the playing area. Any player caught before he can step up becomes "It,"

*Note:* This is another tag game, like others using safety devices, such as Squat Tag.

RUN, SHEEP, RUN!

*Formation:* Two teams, each with a captain. A goal, which can be a tree, post, fence, or other object.

*Equipment:* None.

*Action:* One team stays at the goal, with eyes shut, or in a place where they can't look. The other team goes out with its captain, and finds a hiding place. Everyone but the captain hides, after agreeing on a set of signals.

The captain comes back and tells the other captain that he's ready. The opposing team then goes out hunting. The captain of the hidden team calls out warnings or directions, such as these:

"Red"—meaning danger
"Yellow"—getting close
"Blue"—move to the right
"Black"—move to the left
"Green"—all clear, get ready to run

If he thinks that any member of his team has a chance to get to the goal first, he yells, "Run, sheep, run!", and both teams race to the goal. The player reaching the goal first* wins that round for his team, and his team becomes the hiders.

If, however, any member of the hunting team sees a player on the hiding team, he reports it to his captain, and *that* captain calls "Run, sheep, run!" Only the captains may make that call.

This game involves plotting, following directions, suspense, and swift action. It is especially effective in an area with lots of hiding places, and with five to ten players on a team.

*Variations:* The signal system may be varied, the name changed; but this is such an old favorite that it'll still be Run, Sheep, Run!

SIMON SAYS

*Formation:* Informal, or in lines.

*Equipment:* None.

*Action:* Players must watch and listen to the leader carefully. When he says "Simon says—arms up!" everyone must lift his arms. If he says "Arms up!" no one must move. The leader makes the movement he gives, and varies both the movement and the words. A player who follows a direction *not* preceded by "Simon says," drops out of the game. The last player becomes the new Simon.

*Variation:* For an indoor game around a table, Simon can demand "Thumbs up!" "Thumbs down!", rather than any more active movement.

This game has another version called Horse Feathers, in which the leader flaps his arms as he says "Birds fly," "Horses fly," and so on. The players must flap *their* arms whenever the leader mentions anything with wings, but remain still at other times. Those making a mistake and flapping at the wrong time drop out, and the best player becomes "It" for a new round.

SNAKE IN THE GRASS

*Formation:* All players stand in a large circle, facing "It" in the middle.

*Equipment:* A long rope, with a bean bag, old shoe, or other soft object tied to the end.

*Action:* "It" swings the rope around in a circle not more than six inches above the ground. Each player must jump over it as it goes past him. Anyone not succeeding in jumping over it is eliminated. The last player left is winner.

SQUAT TAG

*Formation:* Informal.

*Equipment:* None.

*Action:* Count out to get the first "It." Players may escape being tagged by squatting quickly—but no one can squat more than three times. When those times are used up, the player must run to escape the tagger.

*Variation:* Players must stand on one leg to avoid being tagged, but can do this only three times. Or substitute other body movements. Or substitute wood, or metal, or circles, or other safety spots that may be touched to save being tagged.

STAMMER JAMMER

*Formation:* Circle or any informal grouping around leader.

*Equipment:* Nothing but a quick tongue.

*Action:* Leaders calls out a letter of the alphabet (omit Q, X, Z). He points to a player, who must start naming, as fast as he can, all the words he can think of that begin with that letter. Time limit is 30 seconds, or until leader counts slowly up to ten. Somebody keeps score.

*Variations:* For nature group, leader can call out "Birds," "Animals," "Snakes," "Stars," or any other category. Or use geography, such as "Rivers," "Cities," "Nations," "States." Or mix them all up!

STEALING STICKS

*Formation:* A line down the middle divides the play area into two sides. Players on each team spread out over their playing area. Each playing area has a goal about 4 feet square at the center back, and in it are five or more sticks.

*Equipment:* Five or more sticks per team.

*Action:* The object of the game is to steal all the sticks from the other team's goal. Only one stick may be stolen by a player at one time, and if he gets to the goal pile without being tagged he cannot be tagged as he brings a stick back to his team's goal pile.

If he is tagged, however, he must go into the opponent's goal, and his team cannot steal a stick until he is rescued. He is rescued by a teammate getting to him and touching him without being tagged. When so rescued, he and his teammate may return to his side without being tagged.

The team that gets all the other team's sticks, and has no player needing rescue, wins the game.

*Variation:* Sometimes the "prison" is in a corner of a team's area, and is not the same area that holds the sticks.

## THIS IS MY NOSE

*Formation:* Informal.

*Equipment:* None.

*Action:* The leader, or "It," faces one of the players, points to one part of his body but calls it another. The person facing him must point to the part of his own body that was mentioned, but call it the part to which "It" pointed. For example, "It" points to his ear and says, "This is my foot." The other person must quickly point to his foot and say, "This is my ear" before "It" can count to ten. If he succeeds, "It" moves on to another player. If "It" counts to ten before a player gives the right answer and gesture, that player becomes "It."

## TOSS BALL

*Formation:* Two teams of equal number standing side by side facing each other across a center line, far enough away to toss a ball back and forth.

*Equipment:* A volleyball. (Use a bean bag for small children.)

*Action:* At starting signal, players toss the ball back and forth across the line. It must be fairly thrown. If a player on a team misses the catch, or drops the ball, the other side scores a point, and gets the chance to put the ball in play again.

Set the game at 10 or 15 points. The first team to make that score wins. Play two out of three games.

*Variations:* This simple game can be made more difficult for older or skilled players by using a smaller ball, by using more than one ball, and by increasing the distance between the teams. It can also be given a time limit, rather than a point limit.

It is an excellent game for developing throwing and catching skills.

## TWO SYLLABLES (Greece)

*Formation:* Players sit in a circle.

*Equipment:* A man's handkerchief tied into a soft knot, or a stuffed sock, or bean bag.

*Action:* One player is chosen to be "It." He begins by giving the first syllable of any two-syllable word, such as "flash," and at the same time he tosses the ball to some other player. This player must instantly add the second syllable, as "light" (making the word flashlight). If he fails, he gives some article of clothing to "It," to be redeemed later by paying a forfeit, and drops out of the game.

If he does *not* fail, he gives the first syllable of another word and throws the ball to another player. The last player left in the game is the winner. He holds up each forfeit, one at a time, and the owner must redeem it by performing some stunt.

WHO WAS IT? (Iran)

*Formation:* All the youngsters except one stand behind a safety line. They are the Mice. One, chosen to be the Cat, sits down a short distance away, hangs her head, and shuts her eyes.

*Equipment:* Informal. A stone, block, or other small object is placed between the Cat and the Mice. The Mice have a small stone, or stick, or something that will make a noise when it hits the Cat's stone.

*Action:* While the Cat's eyes are closed, one of the Mice runs out from the line, taps the large stone with the little one, while the others chant, "Little Mouse, Little Mouse, beware! The Cat may get you!"

The Mouse runs back to the line, and the others chant, "Who was it? Who was it? It wasn't I." The Cat must guess the name of the one who tapped the stone. If correct, that Mouse takes the place of the Cat. If not, the Cat tries again.

## Relays

Relay races are important games. They offer a chance for intensive competition, but as a *group*, rather than individuals, and against *time* rather than against team.

Co-operation between teammates is essential in a relay. There can be no stars, and no player is penalized. Each player, skillful or not, has the same chance and the same importance to the team.

In some relays, speed is important, as in Up and Over, and Forest Fire. In some, speed plus accuracy is needed, as in Run and Roll. Still others depend upon individual accuracy to score a team point, as in Kick the Bag, and Bean Bag Target. Some, like Indian Pass, require manual dexterity and have a high dramatic quality. Some, like Living Obstacles, with its rapid variations, require mental concentration and self-discipline.

A few general suggestions for relays follow:

- The teams and players should be evenly matched.
- The more players, the more teams. Too many players on a team slow the action. From five to fifteen players per team are usually used.
- Vary distances to suit the skills and abilities of the players. Use large balls for smaller children.
- When relays are fast, and over quickly, run the best two out of three, or three out of five.
- Avoid relays requiring running with any pointed object, or running backward.
- Use substitute equipment when necessary. Pebbles, boxes, blocks, bean bags, broomsticks, hoops, rope, paper plates, all are useful substitutes.

### BEAN BAG TARGET

*Formation:* Two or more teams of equal number of players, in file formation, lined up behind a starting line. Draw a 3-foot circle about 15 feet ahead of each team.

*Equipment:* A bean bag or substitute for each team.

*Action:* At the starting signal, the first player of each team starts passing the bean bag back over his head down the line to the last player. When this player gets it, he runs to the head of the line and tosses the bean bag into the circle. If it lands in the circle, it scores one point for his team.

The player then runs up, recovers the bean bag, and returns to the head of his line. He does not start passing it over his head until the starting signal is given. The game continues until each player has had his turn and is back in his original position. The team with the most points is the winner. Accuracy is more important than speed in this game.

### FOREST FIRE

*Formation:* Two or more teams in single file behind a starting line, facing a goal line about 30 feet away.

*Equipment:* None.

*Action:* At signal, player No. 1 on each team races to the goal line, races back, and takes player No. 2 by the hand. They race back to the goal line. No. 1 stays there, but No. 2 dashes back to rescue No. 3. Then No. 2 stays behind the goal line and No. 3 goes back to the fire. Play continues until one team has all its players safe behind the goal line.

*Variation:* This is another old, old game, known under many names, and easy to adapt to new situations.

### KICK THE BAG

*Formation:* Two or more teams of equal number of players, in file formation, standing behind a starting line. Mark a goal line about 20 feet in front of the starting line.

*Equipment:* Bean bag or its substitute for each team. A light block of wood, or a strong box, will do.

*Action:* At the starting signal, the first player in each line kicks the bean bag hard enough to send it over the goal line. He then runs down, picks it up, and runs back across the starting line. The first player back scores a point for his team. After kicking, running, and returning, each player goes to the end of his line.

The second player does not start until the signal is given. This relay is thus a contest for each point, and does not require continuous running.

The game continues until each player has had his turn and is back in his original place in his line. Team with the highest score wins.

### KICK THE STICK

*Formation:* Teams in file formation behind a starting line. Goal line about 30 feet away.

*Equipment:* A crooked stick about 12 inches long in front of each team.

*Action:* At the signal, the first player kicks the stick (pushing it, not lifting it into the air) to the goal line and back, leaving it in front of player No. 2, who does the same. The team finishing first wins.

*Variation:* For indoor use, and for a laugh-maker, use milk bottles and sticks with which to push them. Sometimes called Driving the Pigs to Market.

### LIVING OBSTACLES

*Formation:* Teams lined up behind starting line. Five players from each team make up the "obstacles" for their team. The first boy stands erect, the second stoops in leapfrog position, the third stands with his legs apart, and the fourth and fifth join hands to make a "bridge."

*Equipment:* None.

*Action:* At signal, the first player from each team must run forward, go *around* the first obstacle, jump over the second, crawl under the third, and go between the fourth and fifth and then around the "bridge." He then runs back, tags the next in line, and goes to the end of the line. First team to finish wins.

*Variations:* Depending upon the number of players on each team, add or subtract "obstacles."

### MAN—MONKEY—CRAB

*Formation:* Three players per team, each team in file position at starting line. As many teams as necessary. A goal line about 25 feet away.

*Equipment:* None.

*Action:* The first player of each team is the man; player No. 2 is the monkey; player No. 3 is the crab. At the signal, the "man" runs to the goal line and back. He slaps the hand of No. 2, the monkey, who must race on all fours to the goal line and back. The monkey then starts player No. 3, the crab, who races on all fours but *face up,* and back. The first crab in the line of teams to get back to the starting line, wins for his team.

*Variations:* Different methods of racing to the goal line can be used—rolling a hoop, taking two steps forward, one step back, and so on. Encourage the youngsters to make up their own variations.

### RUN AND ROLL

*Formation:* Two or more teams of equal number of players, in file formation, standing behind a starting line. Mark a goal line 20 feet in front.

*Equipment:* A ball per team. The younger the children, the larger the ball.

*Action:* At the starting signal, the first player in each team runs with the ball to the goal line, turns and rolls the ball to the second player on his team. The second player must pick up the ball after it crosses the starting line. The first player then steps aside and stands just behind the goal line.

The second player, after getting the ball, runs forward, turns, rolls the ball to player No. 3, and steps back of No. 1.

The game proceeds until all the players are behind the goal line. As the last player runs to it with the ball, he hands the ball to player No. 1. No. 1 runs to the starting line, rolls the ball back to No. 2, and so on. The first team to complete the entire action and get back into original formation, wins.

### SEVEN-LEGGED CATERPILLAR

*Formation:* Groups of two boys, kneeling, one facing one way, one the other. One ankle of one boy tied to ankle of other boy.

*Equipment:* None.

*Action:* At signal, the caterpillars race to the finish line. When the boy in front touches the finish line with his fingertips, he yells "Back," and his partner becomes the caterpillar's head. They race back to the starting line, and the first "caterpillar" over the line is the winner.

*Variation:* Tie both ankles of both boys. Also, for a large number, use game as a relay, each "caterpillar" touching off the next in his line. Or play against time.

TUNNEL RACE

*Formation:* Teams stand in files. Each player stands with legs apart.

*Equipment:* None.

*Action:* At the signal, the *last* player in each file begins to crawl through the tunnel made by the legs of the others. As soon as he passes through, each player follows him. The first team in which the first player is back at the head of his team after crawling through the tunnel, wins.

UP AND OVER

*Formation:* Teams line up in single file facing a starting point.

*Equipment:* A wooden or metal hoop, or piece of rope tied into a small circle, for each team.

*Action:* At a signal, each player at the head of the line puts the hoop over his head, then steps out of it and hands it to the player behind him. That player steps *into* the hoop, raises it over his head, and hands it to the third player, who brings it down over his body. When the last player has finished, he runs to the head of the line and holds the hoop high. First team to get the hoop back up front, wins. Try two out of three, or three out of five.

## Mystery and Magic Games

Everyone loves to try to guess and solve a mystery. Everyone likes to try to baffle others. Children enjoy being an accomplice and mystifying the others.

Mystery and magic games offer a chance to match wits, to try to outguess, to observe accurately, to solve a problem. They are

excellent links with home and family, too. A youngster can play Prisoner's Base only with a good-size group of his peers, but he can take a match trick, or a magic game, or a mathematical trick home and try it on his parents and friends.

These games fit nicely into special situations, such as bus trips or rest periods, council ring ceremonies or during lunch hour. They are excellent ways to provide a change of pace.

Some require learning a formula, like the way to tell a prisoner's age (youngsters love to spring this on their elders!). Others require an accomplice. Still others require keen observation, or making a correct deduction. Many can be varied after one solution has been guessed. Many, in fact, are the same game, but with minor variations as to the "key" to solve it.

Since they require a quiet setting, and almost no action, only a few very typical ones are given here. Others will be found in various chapters.

### BLACK MAGIC

This is an old favorite. "It" requires an accomplice who hides his face or leaves the room while the group selects some object to be guessed. "It" boasts of his partner's remarkable mind-reading ability. When the object has been chosen, the accomplice comes in. "It" points to various objects, and asks "Is it this?", "Is it that?", and so on. The accomplice says "No" until "It" points to something black. The next object pointed to will be the right one.

This can be played as "White Magic," "Blue Magic," or any other color if "It" and the accomplice agree on it ahead of time.

### I LIKE COFFEE

An old favorite with many variations. The leader or "It" starts off by saying to another player, "I like coffee but I don't like tea." The others ask him any questions, like "Do you like water?" "No, but I like root beer." "Do you like salt?" "No, but I like pepper." Finally somebody gets the clue and asks "Do you like yellow but not red?" Or "Do you like eggs, but not bacon?" If the leader thinks the guesser has solved it, he can make sure by asking, "What else do you like?"

The trick is that the leader likes only those things that have double letters in them.

The game can be varied by saying, "I like tea but I don't like coffee"—"toast but not bread," "tangerines but not oranges"—in other words, anything with a *t* in it.

Work it out with other letters: "I'm wise (*y*'s) but not bright." "I like yams, but not potatoes." "Days but not nights," and so on.

"I like seas (*c*'s) but not lakes." "Cities but not states," and so on.

"I like peas (*p*'s) but not beans." "Pumpkins but not squash," and so on.

### LEGS AND NO LEGS

Another favorite, quite mystifying. The accomplice leaves the room or hides his eyes while the group selects some object to be guessed. When he returns, "It" asks questions or points to the objects until his partner guesses the correct one. The trick is in the first question or the first object pointed to. If it has legs, the partner knows that nothing else with legs will be pointed to until the right object. If the object has no legs, then "It" will point first to something with no legs, then point only to objects with legs until he points to the right object.

This type of "magic" can be varied by using metal, or wood, or china, as the key. It is a good mealtime magic.

### MYSTERY CITY

This is a mystery word game. "It" and his partner boast that they can read each other's mind. To prove it, the partner leaves the room, or covers his ears, while the group selects the name of some city. The partner then returns, and "It" questions him, naming city by city until finally the partner guesses the correct one.

The trick is simple. Ahead of time, "It" and his partner have agreed that the correct city will be the first one *after* a city that has an animal name, like *Buffalo,* New York, *Deer*field, Massachusetts, *Elk*ton, Maryland, and the like.

The clue can be changed by making it any city of one syllable, like *York,* Pennsylvania, *Ames,* Iowa. The game can be played using any geographical objects—mountains, rivers, or lakes, as well as cities.

## Challenges

Challenges fill a great need in children to test their personal strength, skill, and stamina, and to test themselves against their peers. Often they have a real dramatic quality, especially in those in which the movements imitate birds or animals, such as Quack-Quack and Crab Walk.

Those contests involving two players, called dual contests, are excellent outlets for aggression. They offer a sort of formalized, acceptable fight setting, or miniature warfare, done in good humor, without anger, but definitely aggressive. Socially acceptable opportunities to push, pull, and slap are sometimes denied youngsters, with the result that wrestling and fights can get out of hand.

Challenges are useful, but should be used with care. Many are suitable only for boys. All should be conducted under strict rules, and should give a chance, to the loser, to try again. Players in dual contests should be evenly matched as to height and weight.

Challenges are excellent ceremonial activities for the council ring. These following will illustrate the major types—single, dual, and group.

### CEMENT MIXER

Keeping one arm on ground, arm stiff, body stretched out straight, head back, walk around in a circle using the arm as a pivot.

### CRAB WALK

From squat position, reach backward and put hands flat on

ground without sitting down. Then walk in the direction of the feet, keeping body and head in straight line.

### DITCH PULL

Players are divided into two teams, standing on two parallel lines, facing each other. At signal, each player reaches across the "ditch" and tries to pull his opponent over it. At the end of three minutes, a count is taken and the team with the most players on its side wins.

*Variation:* Play as a dual contest for council ring or rainy day activity.

### HAND PUSH

Two players stand toe-to-toe, facing each other, with feet spread about twenty inches. Each raises his hands and places them against the palms of his opponent, level with the shoulder.

At a signal, each pushes against the hands of the other, trying to make him step back. No other body contact. First to step back loses the bout. Try three out of five.

### HEEL CLICK

Stand with feet apart. Jump into the air and click heels. Land with feet apart. Try to increase number of clicks. Click at least twice.

### HERON HOLD

Put hands on hips. Raise one leg and place foot against the inside of the other knee. Bend the raised knee outward and hold position for a count of ten.

### HUMAN ROCKING CHAIR

Lie face downward, grasp ankles, rock body back and forth, keeping chest and abdomen stiffly curved.

### KING OF THE RING

Players stand in a compact group, arms folded and held close to body. A circle is then drawn around the group.

At a signal, each player tries to push his neighbor out of the circle. If any player unfolds his arms, falls down, or gets both feet outside the circle, he must go back to the "council ring." The last player to remain is King.

*Variation:* Often played as a dual contest called Rooster Fight.

### KNEE DEEP

Stand on one foot. Grasp the other foot behind the back, with the opposite hand. Try to touch the bent knee to the ground and return to standing position without losing the balance. Use the free arm for balance.

### KNEE SLAP

Two players face each other about five feet apart. At a signal, each tries to slap a knee of his opponent with one of his hands. They use sparring, feinting, blocking, and side-stepping tactics but may not clinch or hold each other. The first contestant to slap the other's knee, wins the round.

### MEASURING WORM

Support the body on hands and feet with legs extended backward. Keeping hands in place and knees stiff, walk on toes with short steps, until feet are as near hands as possible. Then keeping the feet in place, walk forward by taking short steps with hands until the stretch position is reached. Continue designated number of times, or designated distance.

### QUACK-QUACK!

Squat down, place hands behind back, palms together, fingers pointing back to indicate a duck tail. Walk a given distance, quacking all the way.

### SIT AND STAND

Cross arms and legs while standing. Sit down and stand up without uncrossing. (Try to keep back straight.)

SLIP SLAP

One player extends his arms with hands palm up. Second player extends his arms with hands palm down on opponent's hands. The one with hands underneath tries to withdraw his hands quickly and slap the backs of the opponent's hands. Players alternate. Score two points for striking both hands; one point for striking one.

*Note:* This is a good game to use to settle an argument or stop a possible fight. It allows aggression but not injury.

THREAD THE NEEDLE

Clasp hands in front, step through with one foot, then the other. Reverse with hands at back.

WOODEN SOLDIER

Fold hands on chest. Lie flat on back. Rise to standing position without using elbows or unfolding arms.

CHAPTER **17:**

# SPORTS AND
# PHYSICAL FITNESS

Previous chapters, particularly those in Section I, have emphasized the importance of indigenous environmental activities in day camp programs. Challenging programs that stretch the mind *and* the muscles of campers and that are at the same time particularly camp-oriented, are numerous. Day camp need not duplicate playground and school gymnasium programs in order to provide the opportunities that produce physical fitness.

The term "youth fitness" is often substituted by counselors, teachers, and leaders concerned not only with physical growth and stamina, agility, and strength, but concerned also with other qualities important to the "whole child." Every counselor should be deeply concerned with each child's personal development—his mental growth; the development of emotional stability and social adjustment; his growth toward responsible citizenship and ethics, and his spiritual response to his environment, shaping his awareness of beauty and his appreciation of the world around him. Every activity should be selected and conducted in such a way that it will have a positive effect upon one or more of these ultimate objectives in child development.

There is no doubt, however, that day camping, like camping, is highly salutary. It is (or should be) in a natural outdoor setting that stimulates physical activity. Hills and mountains are to climb; lakes and oceans are to swim, water ski, canoe, sail, and explore underwater; trails are to hike; fields and meadows are to run and romp in; woods are to explore. The need for physical exertion that is in all children finds healthy, exciting, and challenging outlets in a good camp or day camp program.

For small children, consideration of a sports program is purely academic. Their play periods should be active but informal. Included in them, however, should be many opportunities for those movements that involve the big muscles—running, jumping, pushing, pulling, throwing. Co-ordination comes slowly and should not be pushed.

Day campers from around eight to nine and up are ready to learn skills involved in many sports. These skills can be taught in the active games program.

## Sports Appropriate for Day Camps

Sports best suited for day camps are the ones that develop individual skills at the child's own rate of progress, and which he can enjoy alone, or with a very small group. They are the ones which, on future camping or outdoor trips, when the child is an adult, he can continue to enjoy by himself, or with his small group of friends and family. (Team sports so important during the high school and college years become spectator sports in later adult life.) Opportunities to participate in team sports are readily available on playgrounds, in school athletic programs, and in the sports programs offered by youth-serving agencies. The day camp program should not duplicate these opportunities if it has areas and facilities that can be used for more camp-oriented sports.

Highly suitable for day camp use are sports such as the following:

| | | |
|---|---|---|
| Archery | Canoeing | Casting |
| Hiking | Sailing | Bicycling |
| Swimming | Boating | Horseback Riding |
| Diving | Fishing | Water Skiing |
| | | Skittles |

Certain track and field activities can be adapted to day camp use. For example, a natural obstacle course can be developed that will provide climbing, vaulting, jumping, running, crawling, and balancing—and that fits into not only the terrain but the theme of the program. For example, an Indian theme can require certain initiation

tests, such as crossing a pool or brook on a narrow log, or jumping across its banks. The theme provides physical skills through self-testing rather than competition with others.

Instructions in the sports listed above should be based upon official rules, but *modified and adapted* to the ages and skill level of the youngsters. The development of skills should be stressed. Learning *how* is important to future enjoyment.

In conducting sports, the degree to which they will contribute to physical fitness will depend upon the *way* they are played. Any sport worth playing is worth playing *hard*.

*Warm-Ups* that are really intensive calisthenics can be introduced easily and accepted by youngsters who know that star athletes always warm up before playing. Include such exercises as these:

| | |
|---|---|
| Running in place | Hopping and skipping in place |
| Arms raised and lowered | Rope jumping |
| Deep breathing | Body bending |

*Hoops* laid out on the ground about a foot apart provide good exercise. Youngsters line up and take turns

- jumping from one hoop to the other
- hopping from hoop to hoop
- running, each foot going inside a different hoop

*Crossed Stakes* set up about six feet apart are useful, easy-to-use equipment. Youngsters crawl through them, and frog-hop through them.

Stretch a ¾-inch steel cable 18 inches above the ground. Youngsters can walk it, like a tightrope performer at a circus, or jump it, or hop over it.

The Boys Clubs of America are trying out a theme-motivated program called Space Men of the Future. "Crew training" includes not only science projects, and health education, but also physical exercises and sports.

## Sportsmanship

Sportsmanship can be taught—and caught. It should be stressed in every activity, not just sports. A good sport

- Does his best to the very end
- Thinks of his team or partner, not just himself
- Applauds others when they succeed
- Obeys the rules even when no one is looking
- Does not delay the game
- Does not brag, boast, or "rub it in"
- Accepts defeat *and* winning gracefully

Sportsmanship applies to other activities:

- Sharing tools, equipment, and supplies
- Helping others
- Saying "Please," "Thank you," "I'm sorry."
- Taking turns
- Playing fair
- Accepting blame when justified
- Thinking of other people's feelings

Just knowing about conduct and manners is not enough. Youngsters need opportunities that create an atmosphere conducive to putting such knowledge into actual practice. The counselor who is courteous, kindly, fair, and understanding of how others feel will very likely bring out similar qualities in the campers. Taking time to chat, to work along with the child, to listen, to suggest, and to help when needed are ways of establishing this empathy.

## Competition

Competition is a controversial subject. Some camps minimize it; others employ it in almost every activity. Like team sports, it should be used with discretion.

Most youngsters past the preschool age have already been caught up in the pressure of competition. It is, in various degrees, part of the American way of life. For that very reason, it is often wise to minimize competition in the summer day camp program.

Children get a great deal of it at home and in school. Day camp can provide a relaxed, informal program.

Many—in fact, most—games have some element of competition in them. Competition in many, however, is *group*, rather than individual, so that each youngster plays a part, but only a part, against the other team. Also, the very informality of most low-organized games emphasizes the play rather than the competitive elements. It doesn't much matter *who* wins the relay race. The fun of it is in playing, not in winning.

Competition, especially in those activities that are planned specifically for physical fitness, should focus on self-improvement. The whole purpose should be to become *personally* stronger, better co-ordinated, more agile, not to be better than someone else. Self-testing activities are therefore more important than peer competition. To be able to swim the length of a pool, for a child who started out afraid of the water, is as great if not a greater achievement than twice that distance might be to another child.

Too much emphasis on winning has caused many youngsters to lose interest in team sports. If the best players get all the attention, those who need the experience the most will be left out. Somebody has to win, of course; but there are many levels of skills, not just the top level. Everyone needs the experience of playing and the possibility of winning.

The importance, selection, and various types of games suitable for a wide range of day campers, have been included in Chapter 16, "Games." Others, for specific purposes such as bus trips, or rainy days, will be found in Section IV. Sources of official rules for high-organized games and sports are available from the Athletic Institute, Room 805, Merchandise Mart, Chicago 54, Illinois. Sources of physical fitness tests are listed in "Selected Resource References" at the end of this book.

## Awards

Awards are another controversial problem. Some camps provide elaborate cups or sporting equipment; some provide letters

or special T-shirts; some provide medals or
certificates; some provide only verbal recognition. The degree of problem concerning awards will be in direct ratio to the degree of emphasis on competition.

Certain activities have their own "built-
in" awards—and these are the best kind. Before learning to sail,
a camper must know how to swim. Before he can go around the
island, he must be able to handle the sailboat safely. A certain
system of checks and balances like these encourage a progression
in skill development. Learning each new skill leads on to new
and challenging adventures, available *only* to the camper who
has earned them, and is ready for them.

With the exception of the formal learn-to-swim, and the life-
saving courses which require specific tests and bring specific certificate awards from the American Red Cross, the day camp program, if possible, should try to avoid formal awards based on
highly competitive events.

In general, awards that make for the happiest, most relaxed
campers are based on one or more of the following types:

- Amusing, make-believe awards, such as pie-plate size badge
  covered with aluminum foil, with "CHAMP" painted across
  it.
- Special group treats—a sleep-over or a watermelon feed.
- Formal recognition at a council ring ceremony.
- Special privilege, such as an extra swim period or raising
  the flag.
- Award-in-kind—a privilege permitted only after demonstrat-
  ing ability to perform or use the privilege safely, such as an
  "overnight," when campcraft skills have been demonstrated,
  a long sail after swimming and sailing skills have been demonstrated.
- Awards based on degree of self-improvement, not necessarily
  on outstanding achievement.

In general, the sports program of a day camp should not duplicate playground and gymnasium programs. It should offer new

sports experiences typical of the out-of-doors, and suitable for the age levels of the campers. It should provide also a wide variety of games, carefully selected to provide a physical outlet while developing individual skills. The atmosphere of any game and sport program at day camp should be one of informality and co-operation, rather than that of serious competition.

In planning day camp policies involving competitive sport, fitness programs, and awards, the decisions should be based solely on the effects of the program upon the individual development of each camper. Limitations of space, facilities, and leadership may have to be considered, but in every phase of day camping— as in every other good recreation program—the child's welfare through creative recreation experiences comes first.

*Every child should have mud pies, grasshoppers, waterbugs, tadpoles, frogs, mud turtles, elderberries, wild strawberries, acorns, chestnuts, trees to climb, animals to pet, hay fields, pine cones, rocks to roll, sand, snakes, huckleberries, and hornets— and any child who has been deprived of these has been deprived of the best part of his education.*

LUTHER BURBANK

CHAPTER **18:**

# WATER PLAY

No activity in a day camp (or other summer program) is more popular than water play. This expression, rather than "swimming," or "water sports," is used purposely, because programs involving water can be made much richer than they usually are.

In many camps and day camps, the waterfront schedule is the most highly organized and the "tightest" in terms of time, of any of the camp activities. This may be necessary in a concentrated learn-to-swim program. The camper's day, however, can include many more relaxed, creative activities involving or dependent upon some sort of water supply.

These can range from the simplest fun of pouring water from one receptacle into another, and running in and out of water from a hose, to blowing toy boats across a washtub or plastic wading pool, blowing bubbles, making and sailing toy boats, wading in a brook, rowing a boat, paddling a canoe, sailing, and swimming—dependent only upon providing time for them in the schedule, and upon the ages and skills of the day campers.

Learn-to-swim programs and the teaching of boating and sailing skills require qualified, specialized leadership. The water play activities in this chapter are designed to precede and to supplement such specific instruction, and to provide other activities that involve the use of that wonderful element, water.

### The Brook

Any day camp with a running brook on its site is highly blessed. Wading in a brook, building a dam, walling or planting the banks, looking for colored, smooth pebbles, watching minnows and dragonflies, finding the tracks that deer or other animals made in the night—these are all magic, time-consuming parts of water play. Following a brook in and out of thickets, through pools and shallows, over rocks and sand, is one of the most engrossing activities any child can do.

Such simple, informal activities *free* a child. He finds it easy and inevitable to dramatize his play. He can be Robinson Crusoe, Huck Finn, Henry Hudson, even Columbus, as he and his crew explore the new world of a brook.

Plant and animal life along and in the brook provide informal nature education. The importance of water, the work of erosion, the usefulness of plants all show up in ways that make conservation a reality and not just a name.

With the fun of splashing and wading, building dams and dikes, floating leaves, and sailing toy boats and ships down the brook go all sorts of *intangibles*—the feel of the sun, the cold swish of the water, and the grit of sand under the feet, the glitter of wet pebbles, the golden shimmers of the water, the dark shadows of rocks and pools, the blue of the sky through the leaves. Brooks make their own magic in water play. Counselors need only be ready to suggest questions and answers if and when the occasions arise.

## Sand and Water

Sand and water, separately or mixed, are a wonderful combination. Day camps with beaches are as fortunate as day camps with brooks. Sandboxes or sand piles, however, can be provided at any site. They should vary in size according to youngsters' ages. Most sandboxes are too small for any but very young children, below the age of even the youngest day camper. A big sand area, without the "kid-stuff" look, will provide hours of creative play activities for day campers in a wide age range.

The sand should be clean and should be kept moist. Dry sand is a temptation to throw—there's not much else to do with it! But *wet* sand can be pushed, and patted into pies and cakes for the little girl playing house or store; or into an Elizabethan castle by her older sister who has read Ivanhoe, or seen such castles in the movie or on TV. It can be made into whole villages, into statues of heroes, into launching pads for new space ships. Youngsters can model sand together in groups—or alone as individual artists. Very little equipment is needed. A pointed stick, a board, a tin cup, and a spoon will be helpful; but the youngsters will find what they need.

There is something very *engrossing* about sand modeling. Youngsters usually work in it very amicably. It is a real, creative outlet for hands and imagination.

A few safety rules should be observed:

- Animal pets should not be allowed in the sand area.
- Sand should be kept moist enough to be adhesive, but not soppy.
- There should be no eating of food in the sand area.
- Permit no glass bottles, cups, or other glass articles in the sand area. Broken glass is dangerous.
- No throwing of sand should be permitted.
- Sand should be raked daily to remove any debris. Sand area should be in the sun.

## Toy Boats

Sailing a toy boat is a childhood delight. It can be a walnut shell with a pebble for a passenger. It can be a leaf, a flower, a piece of cork, a block of wood. It can be an improvised raft, a paper canoe, a tiny sailboat with a matchstick mast. Given a  body of water from the size of a wash basin, wash tub, or plastic wading pool to a pond or swimming pool, plus a few odds and ends, children will devise small water craft, and ways to use them.

Youngsters old enough to use simple tools will enjoy making

different kinds of watercraft—and taking part in activities that use them, like toy regattas, boat parades, and boat races.

Some youngsters have model boats, or toy boats, or ships at home. Encourage them to bring their craft to day camp, but set up *classes* for different types, so that the child with a simple, handmade craft will not have to compete with an expensive boat model.

*For toy sailboat races,* the owners line the boats up on a starting line. At a signal, the boats are allowed to take wind. The first, second, and third boats to cross the finish line win first, second, and third place.

For any type of toy watercraft, *a string race* is fun. Each boat has a small tack in its bow, to which a string is attached. The other end of the string is tied around a one-inch dowel stick or other small object. The string must be long enough to reach from the starting to the finish line. Each owner's boat is lined up on the starting line by his pal, or other volunteer. The owner holds the dowel behind the finish line. At a signal, the helpers let go of the boats, and the owners reel them in by winding the string around the dowel. The string cannot be pulled and then wound. It must be reeled in by turning the dowel.

A *guide race* can be held by giving each contestant a stick, spoon, or other small object not more than six inches long and two inches wide. Each child must *push* his boat with this stick. His boat cannot be touched with his hands except to right it if it capsizes. No sailboats in this race.

*Wind races* are fun for toy sailboats. All the sailboats are placed in the middle of the pool, and the wind does the rest. The first sailboat to reach the side of the pool is the winner.

(See Chapter 13, "Arts and Crafts," for instructions for making several simple kinds of watercraft.)

### Soap Bubbles

What is more fun on a hot summer day than gathering around with friends and blowing bubbles? A bubble-blowing can make a pleasant change or a surprise. Make up a formula ahead of time, so that it will be available on just the right day. The following recipe will make extra-strong and very bright bubbles:

⅔ pint of very hot water
¾ tablespoon soap flakes
½ tablespoon of sugar
1 heaping tablespoon glycerine (olive oil or vegetable oil may be substituted
Several drops of vegetable coloring, if desired

*Directions:* Pour the water into a pint jar and add the soap flakes. Let them dissolve, then add the sugar, glycerine, and coloring. Shake until everything is dissolved, strain through a cloth, and let it cool. Don't use until all the bubbles are gone. When the time comes, pour the mixture into a shallow pan so that the youngsters can get to it more easily, and there'll be less waste. It takes just a tiny bit on the end of the blower.

The Association of American Soap and Glycerine Producers provides a formula for even stronger, stretchier bubbles:

1 cup of distilled water
⅛ cup of soap flakes
½ cup of glycerine
Food coloring as desired

Mix water and soap flakes in a bowl until soap is dissolved. Add glycerine and coloring, and mix well. Let it stand for an hour, then skim off any bubbles with a spoon or edge of paper towel. If ingredients for the fancy bubbles aren't available, or there isn't time to prepare the mixture, the old formula of soap mixed with water, about one part soap to eight parts water, makes perfectly satisfactory bubbles, although not so strong or so large.

Experiment with different sizes and shapes of blowers. Use a drinking straw. Split one end in four places, spread out the cut pieces, dip *this* end into the solution, and blow through the other. Spools make fine blowers. Cut off the tip of a cone-shaped paper cup, dip the *wide* end in the solution, blow through the pointed end. A funnel makes a big, beautiful bubble, but takes a long, steady breath. These glycerine bubbles are tough. If a finger is dipped into the solution, it can be poked into the bubble without popping the bubble.

Try fanning the bubbles, trying to keep them in the air. Look at the delicate colors, the reflections. What *makes* a bubble? Will it float on water? Try and see.

### Reed and Raffia Work in the Water

If basketry using reed and raffia is one of the craft skills of a counselor, it will have twice the appeal if it permits self-immersion! Reed and raffia must be kept wet while being woven. On a hot day, take it to the wading or swimming pool, the lake or the pond—and weave while sitting in the water *with* it! It'll be a very popular craft.

### Water Games

Playing games in the water is a well-known technique for overcoming fear of the water. Such games have many other values, however, besides creating self-confidence. They have *novelty*, for one thing. Every youngster has played games in a yard, playground, or around a table. Many have never played them in water, where the slow-down of movement, the splashes, the sudden spills lend excitement.

Some of the following games are played in shallow water. Some require swimming. Some may use both shallow and deeper water. The counselor should select them with the skills of the group in mind. Even the simplest games, however, acquire new magic when played in water. Many land games can be adapted easily to water play. Circle games are particularly good to use with beginners because of the security that holding hands gives the youngsters.

#### BIG BLOW

Players try to be first to blow Ping-pong balls across the pool. *Variation:* Get them across by splashing the water behind them. Play with balloons, too.

#### BOW-WOWS

Players race across pool using dog paddle. When they reach the side they must stop, bark three times, and race back. Good for water show—and for laughs.

*Variation:* Quack three times after coming across with arms extended in front, propelled only by foot movements.

### CORKERS

Leader scatters thirty or forty corks on the water. At a signal, players dive in and bring back the corks *one by one.*

*Variation:* Paint corks several different colors, and give each color a different value—but *don't* tell the players:

> White—5 points
> Red —3 points
> Blue —1 point

Provide scorekeepers to keep count.

### DUCK DECOY

Players form a circle, holding hands in shallow or deep water. Inside the circle is a toy duck or other floating object. At a signal, the players all push and pull each other, keeping hands joined, trying to make somebody in the circle touch the duck. When this happens, that player leaves the circle. Last one in the game wins the duck.

### FOLLOW THE LEADER

Very good for beginners, or for shallow water. Everyone gets in line and follows the leader, doing everything he does. He may jump with both feet, hop, stoop, splash with his hands, pour water over his head, or duck his head under. Keep actions simple until youngsters have confidence. For good swimmers, all sorts of water and swimming stunts can be used.

### HOOPLA

Leader throws out a number of barrel or hula hoops. At a signal, players dive in, and each tries to come up *inside* one of the hoops. Reduce number of hoops, eliminating players, until only one hoop is left.

### KING (OR QUEEN) OF THE WAVES

Each player is given a gold paper crown that fits loosely on his head. At signal, players race across the pool. Crowns must not fall off or get wet.

*Variations:* The familiar one of holding an open newspaper and, for older groups, the lighted candle race both belong to this type.

### POLARIS RACE

Swimmers lie on their backs in the water, holding one leg up like a periscope. They race across pool using any stroke. Periscope must never go under water.

*Variations:* Require other sorts of physical restrictions such as one arm up or arms crossed on chest. Also, can be combined with Follow the Leader.

### QUACK-QUACK

Leader is the duck, who dashes back and forth in shallow water calling "Quack-quack" and trying to tag the others. To avoid being tagged, player must duck under water. Good for beginners who are scared to put heads under.

### SINK THE SHIP

Leader scatters toy boats or wooden blocks over the pool. Players line up on the shore or side of pool. Each throws an old tennis or other soft, floatable ball, trying to hit a ship. As a ship is hit, it is removed, and the successful thrower does not get another try until everyone has had a turn.

### TUG OF WAR

Teams fairly equal in number and weight. Play it

- in 6 *inches* of water for small, nonswimmers
- in 3 feet of water for beginners
- in 4 feet of water for intermediates
- in 6 feet of water for good swimmers

### WATER HIP

Good active game. Can be played in shallow water by nonswimmers, or in deeper water by swimmers. Players all group around the leader. Leader throws a soft water ball in any direction and calls out the name of a swimmer. This player must swim to the ball, get it, throw it, and try to hit any other player. If he succeeds, that player joins him by grabbing the ball and trying to hit another player. If the first player *fails* to hit any-one, he must swim to the ball and try again.

### WATER WRITERS

Each swimmer takes a pencil, and a 3 x 5 file card thumb-tacked to a piece of wood. While treading water he must write his name and address on the card, then get back to shore—with-out getting the card wet.

*Variation:* Write a four-line jingle on the card while swim-ming on the back and bring it to the other side of the pool with-out getting the card wet.

These two stunts can be used in a water show or carnival.

### WHALE

One player is chosen to be the whale, and floats on his back. The others splash around in the shallow water or swim around in the deeper water. Without warning, the whale yells, "Thar she blows!" and starts to chase the players. The shore or sides of the pool are safe. The one caught becomes the new whale, or in a large area of water, may join the first whale to become a "school" of whales, continuing until all fish have been caught.

## Water Safety Suggestions

*Never* leave small children in or near even shallow water. A child can drown in a few inches of water. This applies to tubs as well as pools!

*Never* frighten a child by splashing him, duck-ing him, or pushing him in, even if you are there to hold him up.

*Never* coax a child to come into the water, or to take part in any water game or activity. Adopt a take-it-for-granted manner that the child is coming in, and will enjoy it. If this *doesn't* work, let the child stay on shore or pool-side. If possible, *involve* him in something that will keep his at-tention on his peers—like holding a floating toy, or giving a sig-nal. If and when he *does* come in, make no comment—just ac-cept him as part of the group.

*Never* scold, nag, or coerce a child in any sort of water play.

*Watch* for signs of chilling, of sunburn, and of fatigue.

*Initiate and use* some sort of buddy system, and *accept no fooling* in it.

*Never* allow floating equipment like a rubber ring, big rubber animals, or floats outside an enclosed area on a beach. A breeze will carry them—and the children—right out into deep water.

*Never* allow youngsters who cannot swim to use such equipment in deep water. They are too easy to fall off of, or to be upset.

*Never* allow young children to use snorkles or fins. They can cause serious accidents.

*Be sure* that the swimming instructor is fully qualified by the American Red Cross or other authoritative source.

*Be sure* he has been taught the new mouth-to-mouth method of resuscitation.

*Allow no* nonswimmer in a boat unless he wears a life preserver.

Provide program *motivations* for learning to swim well—such as an all-day canoe trip, boating privileges, a part in a water carnival or circus, permission to learn sailing.

*Change procedures and routines*, even in a pool. Use different sides, go in in different ways, vary distances, swim at different times of the day. Adaptability in water aids safety. Youngsters used to a specific routine may react badly if this routine is changed. They must learn to be at home in the water *anywhere*, at any time. Let them swim with different groups, too—or for special treats.

*Never* leave a group alone in the water, and never leave the water before making sure every child is out.

*Never* allow any horseplay in the water. Provide some active games like Water Hip for a group full of energy.

*Don't* allow nondivers in the diving area—and teach youngsters to get out of the area quickly after their dives.

*Do* provide an all-out signal, giving a few minutes leeway.

*Do* provide an *emergency* signal which must be obeyed *instantly*.

# Composite Programs

To me every hour of the light
and dark is a miracle.
Every cubic inch of space is a
miracle.

—WALT WHITMAN
*Miracles*

CHAPTER **19:**

# THE BUS
# PROGRAM

The trip to and from the day camp site, whether by family car, station wagon, or bus may take anywhere from a few minutes to an hour or more, with an average of around half an hour. It cannot be dismissed as immaterial to the activity program.

The material in this section will deal with those trips to and from the day camp site on which the campers are accompanied by day camp leaders or counselors. Such material, of course, can be used for any period of time or in any place where freedom of movement is specifically limited.

## Rules and Regulations for Going and Coming

Certain travel rules must be set for the sake of health and safety. They should be kept as few and as simple as possible, and should be discussed and thoroughly understood by the youngsters, their parents, and the leaders. The following are examples:

- *Every child must have a seat, and stay in it.* The only persons allowed to move around should be counselors, and then only when the activity demands it.
- *Allow no eating on the bus.* This is to help prevent car sickness, indigestion, and the danger of having something like a lollipop stick in the mouth in case of a sudden jolt or stop.
- *Nothing must hang out the windows.* This applies to heads, arms, toys, hats, or whatever. A safety measure.
- *Nothing must be dropped out of a window.* Provide litterbags and encourage their use.
- *No matter what the weather, some windows must be open at least partially.* A health and safety measure to prevent car sickness and carbon dioxide poisoning.

285

- Follow airplane procedure. *One counselor should be in the bus to receive the campers; another counselor should be on the ground, helping campers in, and keeping count.* The second counselor should be the last person in the bus and the first person off.

- *A First Aid Kit and disposable refrigerator bags* (in case of car sickness) *should be readily available on the bus.*

- *In case of car sickness, the bus should pull over to the side of the road and stop as soon as it can with safety.* One counselor should take the child out. The other counselor should explain what has happened in a matter-of-fact way, then start a game or song to distract the others. When the sick child returns, he should sit up front, by an open window.

- *No campers under ten years old should cross a street or intersection before getting on the bus or after getting off the bus,* unless accompanied by a counselor or other adult.

- *In case of unforeseen delay or in case of a bus accident or breakdown, have a plan for notifying parents. Give them full and frank information.*

### Play Props for Bus Trips

When the bus trip is fairly long, or when the activity plans require them, a few props can be very helpful. Often they can gain the attention of the youngsters, act as a surprise, teach a lesson through play, or quiet a noisy crowd.

One of the most useful is a hand puppet. It can become a sort of mascot. It speaks to each child as he enters the bus: "Hi, Bill!" "Where's Sue? Oh, there you are!" "*Look* at that new dress!" "Jim, where's your lunch bag?"

It can tell a story. It can scold. It can praise. It can "sit by" the child whose best friend didn't come, or who is new or shy. A change in hat, or scarf—and it can become a different character. It can "live" in the bus, and act as host, guide, friend, magician—whatever is needed.

A musical instrument can be a great asset. The leader

who can strum a ukulele or guitar, or play an accordion or harmonica will have a singing bus, and music is likely to run through the entire day camp. Simple rhythm band instruments can be played by the youngsters, too. One day, everyone can make and decorate a drum and beat this on the bus trips as they sing. A bit of tissue paper over a pocket comb makes sounds for varying the bus songs. Half can sing, the other half hum. Ocarinas are inexpensive and fun. Rattles, especially if made and decorated at camp, make singing more fun.

Sometimes a special poster, or a sailor's cap, or stuffed animal, a rope, a balloon, or a brown paper bag can be just enough "prop" to set a mood and motivate the bus program. Counselors should be on the alert for such simple "props," and encourage the youngsters to devise their own.

## Going and Coming Songs

Youngsters like to sing while traveling. It passes the time. It gets attention from other people in cars or on foot. There's a fine feeling of freedom, of anonymity, of being away from the homes they have left, but not yet in the camp to which they are going.

One of the counselors should start and lead the singing. He can hold the attention by moving up and down the aisle of the bus, or turning so that he can see the youngsters if they're in a car or station wagon.

Songs that require motion are excellent outlets for early morning, precamp exuberance. So are the highly repetitive ones that youngsters never seem to tire of—like "Old McDonald Had a Farm."

Coming home, the youngsters will be tired. Some will fall asleep. Others will talk quietly to their seat mates. Singing on the return trip may be desultory. The songs should be quieter ones, with smooth rhythm. Folk songs, cowboy songs, ballads, and rounds are good choices.

The element of surprise is important. The bus music program should be well planned. Cowboy songs might be used one day. Another day everybody tries to think of songs that have a color in their title, or a girl's name. Another day might bring sea chanteys.

The selection of songs can go along with bus decoration, if the bus is privately owned and operated. For a cowboy theme, branding iron signs can be put on windows. Youngsters can wear cowboy bandannas around their necks. The bus can be given a name "Rancho Del Toros," or "The Flying M," or what not. Pirates, Robin Hood, Circus, Space, Pioneers, Huck Finn, Zoo—could all be developed for themes, if the length of travel time warrants it.

The following songs are only a few of the many action and endless verse songs dear to the hearts of all campers. They are not great music—but they are great fun. They fit the sense of the ridiculous so strong in the five to twelves. They are easy to learn and to sing—but demand remembering words and action. Best of all, they are good-humored, simple, and have the sort of chant that runs through counting-out games, singing games, and jump-rope rhymes. They seem to answer some rhythmic need. Purists may shudder, but the children keep on singing!

LITTLE PIG (sing up the scale and down)

> *Words*

> I had a little pig, he had a curly tail
> He became very fat, so I took him to a sale.
> But now that he is gone, I'm feeling quite forlorn
> I sold him to the butcher man
> And now he's breakfast bacon.
>
> Oink, oink, oink, oink, oink, oink, oink, oink! PORK CHOP!

*Action:* Place thumbs and fingers together to form a circle on the words "little pig." Move right forefinger in a spiral upward on the word "curly tail." Use hands to indicate large circle on words "very fat." Place hands on knees on the word "sale." Raise hands in exclamation on word "gone." Wring hands on word "forlorn." Point right forefinger and shake in admonition on words "butcher man." Cover eyes with hands on words "breakfast bacon." Snap fingers on each "oink" and clap hands loudly on "Pork Chop."

LITTLE PETER RABBIT

(sung or chanted to the tune of John Brown's Body)

*Words*

> Little Peter Rabbit had a fly upon his nose
> Little Peter Rabbit had a fly upon his nose
> Little Peter Rabbit had a fly upon his nose
> And he flipped it until it flew away.

*Action*

- Sing through once.
- Sing through, leave out word "Rabbit," and substitute hands waving over ears.
- Sing through, leave out "Rabbit," waving hands over ears, and also omitting "fly," waving fingers in the air instead.
- Sing through, leave out word "nose," pointing to nose instead; omit all words previously omitted.
- Sing through, leave out word "flipped," fanning past nose; omit all words previously omitted.
- Sing through, leave out word "flew," flapping arms; omit all words previously omitted.

THERE'S A HOLE IN THE BOTTOM OF THE SEA

(sung to the tune of "In the Sweet By and By")

*Words:* Verse

> 1. There's a hole in the bottom of the sea
> There's a hole in the bottom of the sea
> There's a hole in the bottom of the sea
> There's a hole in the bottom of the sea

Chorus

> There's a hole. There's a hole
> There's a hole in the bottom of the sea
> There's a hole. There's a hole
> There's a hole in the bottom of the sea

> 2. There's a rock in the hole in the bottom of the sea, etc.
> Chorus—There's a rock, etc.

3. There's a frog on the rock in the hole in the bottom of the sea, etc.
4. There's a wart on the frog on the rock in the hole, etc.
5. There's a hair on the wart on the frog, etc.
6. There's a flea on the hair on the wart, etc.

(If the youngsters get this far, and still aren't ready to stop—and if *you* can stand it!—start them back down the verses: from 6 to 5 to 4, et cetera.)

## Going and Coming Games

Games that can be played in a car or bus, and are not too involved or difficult for the youngest of the group, are not always easy to find. A travel game has specific qualifications:

- It usually involves observation.
- It often involves simple arithmetic for score keeping.
- It is capable of continuing for some time.
- It must not require leaving the seat.
- It requires a degree of concentration and quick reaction.

The seating arrangement of the campers should be noted, because it has a specific influence on how the game must be played or adapted, who keeps score, who takes turn, and so on. For example, a bus with seats going lengthwise, so that youngsters face each other in rows, will make certain travel games impossible. A large bus with seats for two along the aisle makes a game like Buzz very difficult—or any game where it is important to see all the players. Kneeling, standing, and turning in the seat is not conducive to good travel manners, and games that stimulate such reaction should be avoided.

Sometimes, when youngsters are somewhat lost in big buses or large seats, it is best to concentrate on singing, or a story by the leader. As a change, paper and pencil games for two players can be taught. Tit-Tat-Toe is an example of such a game. There are many others, including some that are often classified as puzzles.

The following are games that have been used successfully in travel situations. They are only a few, but they will indicate the types that fit the rather abnormal setting, and that also contain elements of value, such as the requirements of concentration, quick reaction, score keeping, fair play, and the like. Game books contain many others.

### ALPHABET

Players choose opposite sides of the road as their own, noting the letters on the signboards they pass, on their own side. Each tries to find letters of the alphabet in order on the successive signs. The first sign might yield an A and B, the second a C, the third a D and E, et cetera. The first to complete the alphabet is winner. Both are on their honor, of course, not to "fudge."

### AUTO LICENSE GOLF

First player writes down, or calls out for leader to write down, the license number of a passing car. Next player takes the next car's license number, and so on until everyone has had his turn. Player whose license number adds up to the highest total wins. Play off ties.

For younger children, leader can do the writing and adding. For others, the child should call out the numbers. Game develops observation and quick reactions.

### DAILY LISTINGS

Players keep count of such things as number of whitewall tires, new models of cars, most of any one make, women drivers, out-of-state cars.

### EAGLE EYE

Players look out of windows and watch for specific objects decided upon in advance. For example, a list might require these for scoring:

A woman carrying a baby—5 points
A woman looking out of a house window—10 points
A redheaded girl—3 points
A brown dog—2 points
A bird on a telephone wire—2 points

A church steeple—1 point
A baldheaded man—3 points

First player who spots each item gets the points. Play for total score of 50 points for game.

### ONE HUNDRED

A simple variation of Auto License Golf. Player No. 1 notes the first and last digits of the license number of an approaching (or passing) car. He adds them, and the sum is his score on round one. Each player takes his turn.

When everyone has had his turn, player No. 1 starts the second time around, adding *that* number to his previous score. First player to reach a given score wins. For young children, 25 points can be game. For older ones, and for longer trips, 100 points can be game.

### TELEPATHY

One or more players, the more the merrier. As the bus or car passes the guard rails on curves or cliffs, each player takes a big breath and holds it until the guard rail is passed. If the breath can be held all the way, a girl (or boy) friend will think of you. The last few yards will be the hardest; the facial expressions and gestures of "hurry, hurry" to the driver usually dissolve someone in giggles.

### TEN PAIRS

Each player selects a different digit as his number. (In case of a bus load, play this with seat partners working as a team.) He watches the license plates of passing cars, and scores on any license number that has a pair or more of his number.

| | |
|---|---|
| 2 of a kind | = 1 pair |
| 3 " " " | = 2 pairs |
| 4 " " " | = 4 pairs |
| 5 " " " | = 6 pairs |
| 6 or more of a kind | = 10 pairs |

For example, if a license plate is number 25-3553, the player who chose 5 as his number would score 2 pairs; the player with 3's would score 1 pair; the player with 2's wouldn't score at all. First player to score ten pairs wins.

To make it harder, require the player to get *exactly* ten to win. For example, if a player has 9 pairs, and the next license plate has 3 of his number, counting 2 pairs, he can't use it. He must wait for a license plate with one pair of his chosen number before he can go out of the game.

## Tongue Twisters

Tongue twisters, though not really games, are excellent play activities. They require concentration. They're laugh making. They teach articulation. They are challenging. They train memory.

The counselor starts off by saying, "One old ox opening oysters." Each player must repeat this without smiling. Then the counselor adds, "Two toads totally tired, trying to trot to Troy," and each player must say this. (For older campers, they should repeat the first and say the second, adding a new twister on each round.) Here are twelve. If these become too familiar, ask each camper to make up one and try it out on the others.

- One old ox opening oysters
- Two toads totally tired, trying to trot to Troy
- Three tawny tigers tickling trout
- Four fat friars fanning and fainting
- Five fat flirts flying to France for fashion
- Six scotch salmon selling six sacks of sauerkraut
- Seven small soldiers successfully shooting snipes
- Eight elegant elephants embarking for Europe
- Nine nimble noblemen nibbling nonpareils
- Ten tipsy tailors teasing a titmouse
- Eleven early earwigs eagerly eating eggs
- Twelve twittering tom-tits on the top of a tall tree

Tongue twisters are good activities for those rainy or hot days, too. They fit nicely into a hike, or around a campfire. In fact, laugh makers are very useful. They can bridge those events or occasions when a giggle or a laugh relieves tension and saves what might be a disagreeable or unhappy situation.

## Riddles

Riddles, like tongue twisters, aren't really games, but who cares? They are the prized possessions of the underteens. Youngsters ponder over them, guess at them, hoot and chortle over them—and take them home to stump Mom and Dad.

Every counselor should have his own private fund of riddles. Once he starts them, youngsters will add their own, and then everybody's collection will swell to magnificent proportions. Encourage not only collecting, but making them up.

Here are a few as a starter:

1. Where was King Solomon's temple?
2. What's the difference between here and there?
3. Why is A like 12 o'clock?
4. What can you give away and still keep?
5. What has four legs and one foot?
6. What table hasn't a leg to stand on?
7. What has only one finger?
8. What bow cannot be tied?
9. When can you carry water in a sieve?
10. What's the difference between an old dime and a new penny?
11. What runs across the floor without legs?
12. What's the best thing to put into pies?
13. What is a pig after it's three days old?
14. What is it that speaks all languages?
15. What is the biggest jewel in the world?
16. What is the best material for kites?
17. When do you sneeze three times?
18. What word is always pronounced wrong?
19. Where does Thursday come before Wednesday?
20. What did one ghost say to the other?

*Answers:*

1. On his head
2. The letter T
3. Both are in the middle of day
4. A cold
5. A bed
6. Multiplication table
7. A mitten
8. A rainbow
9. When it's ice
10. Nine cents
11. Water
12. Your teeth
13. Four days old
14. An echo
15. A baseball diamond
16. Flypaper
17. When you can't help it
18. Wrong
19. In the dictionary
20. Do you believe in people?

## In Conclusion

The bus trip to and from day camp should be regarded as an integral part of the daily camp experience. It should set an atmosphere of relaxed, warm, friendly camaraderie, good travel manners, and compliance with health and safety regulations.

It is also an opportunity for counselors to learn a great deal about the youngsters—to discover the shy, the homesick, the too aggressive, the child who doesn't feel well. The counselor also may find that the sound-protected privacy of the bus provides many opportunities for camper-counselor talks of great value to both.

# CHAPTER 20:

# THE FLAG
# IN DAY CAMP

Most day camps, like resident camps, use the raising of the United States flag in the morning, and the lowering of it at the end of the camp day, as part of the camp activity program. The flag serves as a symbol of our nation, and of our responsibilities as citizens. It is also a reminder of our good fortune to be living in a democratic society of free men, and a reminder also that freedom should not be taken for granted. President Kennedy's simple statement is one that every child should know and can understand. "Ask not what your country can do for you. Ask rather what you can do for your country."

The United States flag is a symbol. The rules and customs pertaining to its use and display have been fixed into a Flag Code, established by Congress in 1942 as Public Law 623, and amended in the same year by Public Law 829.

Respect for the flag, based upon understanding of what it symbolizes, should run through any program requiring its use. (Saluting the flag, however, cannot be made compulsory.)

Actually, the Flag Code is very interesting, and youngsters will enjoy knowing about it. A discussion of it can be a fine activity, and will open the eyes of the campers to many customs they have seen but not thought about or understood. Sitting down as a group and talking about the flag, for example, will open the doors for new feelings of pride, and an understanding of what up to now may have been only a habit.

For example, why do visitors in Washington or in London look up at the flagpole of the White House or of Buckingham Palace? The flag will be flying if the Head of the State is in residence. Some youngsters will remember reading about castles in olden times, when the nobleman's pennant over the battlements showed whether he was at home.

296

The youngsters may not have noticed or thought about it, but nothing should be pinned or sewed to the U. S. flag. No design, or picture, or word, or mark of any sort should ever be put on it. Why? What would happen if the U. S. flag were used to advertise a candy bar, or a kind of car, or a certain brand of chewing gum? It would be cheapened. Its symbolism would be lost.

Why should the flag *never* be used to carry anything in? Or be allowed to touch the ground? Or nailed? Or left out in the rain or overnight?

Why should the flag be flown on all public buildings—the Post Office, for example. And on public schools?

Why should the flag *never* be flown upside down, except deliberately? What does it mean? It would symbolize a great disaster. A ship in distress might hoist the flag upside down so as to get help from any ship or plane that might see it.

What happens to old flags? The youngsters might make a ceremony out of proper disposal of any old flag that is torn, soiled, or worn out. The Union (the blue, starred section, symbolizing the fifty states united into one Nation) is what *makes* our flag. It should be cut carefully out. Then there's no flag, and the pieces can (and should) be burned—*never* used for anything else.

Why, when the U. S. flag is flown with flags of other nations, should they all be the same size, and flown at the same height? (The flags in front of the United Nations building are good examples of this.) Some youngsters may guess "So the other nations won't be mad at us"—which is fairly close. International usage forbids the display of one flag above that of another nation in times of peace.

The Flag Code can be found in many books, pamphlets—even in the *World Almanac*. It is impressive, to youngsters, to *see* the Code in print, and to realize that the leaders of our nation have made this Code into law. The following are important parts of the Code, important to know, discuss, and understand:

- *The flag itself.* It has thirteen horizontal stripes, seven red and six white, so that the top and bottom stripes are red. These thirteen stripes symbolize the thirteen original states. (Who can name them?) It has a "Union" or "Canton" of white stars on a blue background, a star for each state. The stars are now arranged in nine horizontal rows, five of which have six stars each and four of which have five stars. Each star has five points, and is placed with one point upward. The last two stars, of course, represent Alaska and Hawaii.

- The flag should be displayed only from sunrise to sunset, except at night on special occasions for patriotic effect. It should be displayed every day, weather permitting, and especially on national and state holidays and historic occasions. It should be displayed on or near administration buildings of every public institution, polling places on election days, and schoolhouses on schooldays.
- In a parade or procession with another flag or flags, the flag of the United States should be either on the marching right (the flag's own right, which is the observer's left) or, if there is a line of flags, the U. S. flag may be in front of the center of that line.
- When displayed with another flag against a wall from crossed staffs, the U. S. flag should always be on the right (the flag's own right) and its staff should be in front of the other's staff.
- When other flags (state or city, for example) are flown on the same halyard, the U. S. flag is always at the top. It is hoisted first and lowered last. No other flag is ever placed above or to the right of the U. S. flag. There are only two exceptions. In church services conducted by naval chaplains at sea, the church flag may be flown above the U. S. flag; and, by special legislation, the UN flag may be flown higher than the flag at UN headquarters.
- When the flag is not flown from a staff, it should be displayed *flat*, never used as drapery. When drapery is needed, bunting should be used, blue above, white in middle and red below.
- When hanging over the middle of a street, or between buildings, the flag should hang vertically with the Union to the north in an east and west street, or to the east in a north and south street.
- When used on a speaker's platform, the flag, if displayed flat, should be behind and above the speaker.
- Flags at half-mast indicate mourning. When flown half-mast, the flag should first be hoisted to the peak for an instant and then lowered to half-mast position. Before lowering the flag for the day, it should be hoisted again to the top, then lowered. (Half-mast means one-half the distance from top and bottom of staff.)

**Rules to Remember**
NEVER
- display or store the flag in any way that will soil or damage it. (When it is no longer in good condition, cut out the Union, then burn the flag.)
- let the flag touch the ground, the floor, or water.

- display the flag on a float in a parade except from a staff.
- drape the flag over the hood, top, sides, or back of a car, truck, train, or boat.
- use the flag as a part of a costume or uniform.
- use the flag in which to receive, hold, or deliver anything.
- carry the flag any way but aloft and free.
- use the flag for advertising anything, or put any advertisement or sign on a pole on which the flag is flown.
- never fly the flag with the Union upside down except in dire distress.
- never dip the flag to anybody or anything. (State, city, and other flags may be dipped as marks of honor.)

## Saluting the Flag

The U. S. Supreme Court ruled, in 1943, that State Boards of Education or local school boards cannot make the flag salute compulsory. It is customary, however, for all present to salute the flag during the ceremony of hoisting or lowering the flag, and when it passes in parade.

Girls and women should stand at attention, face the flag, and place their right hands over their hearts. Boys and men remove their hats or caps and hold them over their hearts. If bareheaded, then they place their hands over their hearts. Men in military uniform give the official salute.

PLEDGE OF ALLEGIANCE

The official pledge of allegiance is as follows:

I pledge allegiance to the Flag of the United States of America and to the Republic for which it stands; one nation under God, indivisible, with liberty and justice for all.

The Flag SHOULD be flown on:

| | |
|---|---|
| Inauguration Day ............. | January 20 |
| Lincoln's Birthday ............. | February 12 |
| Washington's Birthday ......... | February 22 |
| Easter Sunday | |
| Mother's Day ................. | Second Sunday in May |
| Armed Forces Day ............ | Third Saturday in May |
| Memorial Day ................. | May 30 |
| Flag Day .................... | June 14 |

Independence Day ............July 4
Labor Day .................First Monday in September
Constitution Day .............September 17
Columbus Day ...............October 12
Veteran's Day ...............November 11
Thanksgiving Day
Christmas Day .............December 25

Other occasions by proclamation.

## Flag Language

It's fun to know the right words for things, and our flag has its correct language.

The *length* of a flag is called its *fly*.
The *width* of a flag is its *hoist*.
The blue field and stars is the *union* or *canton*.
The stick to which the flag is attached is its *staff*.
The cord by which a flag is mounted is its *halyard*.
The edge of the flag nearest the staff is its *heading*.
The *Red* in our flag stands for Courage
The *White* for Purity
The *Blue* for Justice
The *star* is an ancient symbol of sovereignty. Stars are added on July 4 following admission to the Union. The last two were Alaska, 1959, and Hawaii, 1960.
The flag when carried by dismounted units, is a *Color*.
When carried by mounted, mechanized, or motorized units, and by Air Force groups, it's a *Standard*.
When used on ships, small boats, and planes, it is called an *Ensign*.

George Washington explained the symbolism of our flag by saying, "We take the star from heaven, the red from our mother country, separating it by white stripes, thus showing that we have separated from her, and the white stripes shall go down to posterity representing liberty."

## Flag Raising and Lowering Ceremonies

If raising the flag is the opening ceremony for day camp, make it an impressive one. The color guard (those who bring in, unfold, fasten, and hoist the flag) should be neat and clean, and should do their work with calm precision. It's not always easy to unfold, hold, attach, and hoist a flag, so it's always a good idea to practice ahead of time.

The youngsters should stand where each can see the ceremony without getting the sun in his eyes. A compact group also sings much better. The salute should be crisp, and the pledge of allegiance, if made, should be given with eyes upon the flag.

It's a good idea to use the same color guard for lowering the flag in the afternoon, or in case of rain.

Folding the flag has its own rules. The flag is held, of course, so that it does not touch the ground or floor. Fold it before detaching it completely from the halyard. The flag should be folded lengthwise in fourths. Then starting at the red and white, outside end, it should be folded back and forth diagonally until all that remains to be carried away is a triangle of blue with stars.

*Raising* the flag comes before anything else in the opening program. *Lowering* the flag is the very last thing in the closing program. It should be *raised* briskly; *lowered* slowly.

## The Flag and Other Activities

The flag of the United States has been a long time in the making, and has taken a number of different forms before it became our present flag. The story of the flag, and of its forerunners, makes an excellent theme for a pageant or festival. It fits into storytelling, into drama, into music. It has color and vitality. It can be talked about, pantomimed, painted, and sung, because all our history is there to choose from. Also, the part played by local communities and by individual states is a prideful thing for youngsters to learn and to appreciate.

Patriotism does not mean "I'm better than you," nor does it represent boastful might and wealth, military strength, scientific achievement, and so on. It is based on knowing our history, loving our homeland, and knowing that others feel the same way about their native lands. It is a counting of blessings, and a helping hand to others less fortunate. It is not fanaticism. It is knowledge, understanding, and love. It is one of the roots that strengthen childhood, and from which citizenship will grow. Opportunities for understanding should be abundant in camp, but patriotism cannot be forced. Like most virtues, it is easier caught than taught.

### Other Flags

Old Glory is not the only flag in the day camp day. State, city, church, and organization flags may have their appropriate display and place in certain programs. Flags of other nations, too, are often used in international and intercultural programs.

There are other flags, too, that have other uses besides representing sovereignty—safety flags, weather flags, signal flags, unit and tent flags, award flags, and flags and pennants designed and used for decorative purposes.

Signal and weather flags have been discussed in Section II.

Safety flags can be made and set up by the day campers. Red flags indicate danger. They should mark the archery range, the rifle range, any area when it is in use by a possibly risky activity, and any area that is precarious, or dangerous in any way, such as an unfenced cliff edge, a slippery bank. Locating and marking such areas is a good way to emphasize safety.

Similarly, an area when not in use by a hazardous activity should be marked with a green flag. A group then knows the archery range is safe to cross, the bank has been mended, a fence repaired. It is important to "spot" danger points in day camp. It is also important to correct them when possible, and to call the corrections to the campers' attention.

Award flags can be simple indications of group accomplishment. It is more in keeping with the co-operative spirit that is an objective in camping if such awards are not given in terms of competition between groups, but for acknowledgment of group success. The skill learned, the spirit shown, the obstacles overcome, all are far more important than the award itself.

Tent, unit, and group flags can be an interesting project for design and construction. The decisions about colors, the symbols to be used, and their meaning, all can have a unifying effect upon the youngsters.

CHAPTER **21:**

# COUNCIL RING PROGRAMS

The council ring is the heart of the day camp. It can provide the tradition, symbols, formality, and rites so dear to campers. If possible, it should be roughly circular, since the ring is the symbol of unity.

## The Council Ring

The term "council ring" is used here to indicate a central meeting place, large enough to seat all campers at one time, and to provide an open area that can be used for special games and stunts. Technically it can be indoors or outdoors. Hopefully, it will be outdoors, and will provide space for a symbolic fire.

This fire should be a *small* one. All too often council ring fires are so large that they take up too much room, cannot be seen over, and are too hot, especially on a summer day. A small fire, well-laid, and tended with ritualistic care, is much more suitable for a day camp.

Also, the time has come when leaders and campers, no matter how young, should be aware that our wooded areas are disappearing rapidly, and that conservation means that everyone takes care and is economical in using natural resources.

The seating need not be circular—in fact, semicircular seating is better for seeing and hearing, but the area itself should be enclosed. If possible, four open spaces or entrances should lead into it, and these should face north, south, east, and west. They should be fairly narrow, so that a camper enters as an individual, but once inside, is part of the whole camp group.

Entering and leaving should be ceremonious. There should be no pushing, or running, or giggling. Once inside, the program can, and should, vary. Some activities will be hilarious. Some will be serious. Some will be loud, some quiet. Some will be formal, some highly informal. But coming in and going out must always be done with dignity and in single file.

The council ring or other meeting place can be ready ahead of time, or it can be built by the youngsters. Seating can be stones, logs, cement blocks, benches, the ground, or the floor. It should be so arranged that everyone can see and hear.

The activities in this chapter are programs that bring all the campers together for the special purpose of creating an atmosphere of all-camp unity. Throughout the camper's day he will be with his own group, or with varying groups. He will take part in the planning, and will participate in many different kinds of activities—campcraft skills, games, water sports, art, creative dramatics, and the like.

At least once, and usually twice a day, however, he will meet with all the campers, in a special place at a special time for an all-camp get-together. The place is usually the council ring. The time is usually at the opening and the closing of the camp day.

### Traditions and the Council Ring

Daily opening and closing activities, though they are not always, or necessarily, council ring programs, are a means of providing a combination of surprise and of tradition. The surprise comes in the selection of the games, stunts, songs, or other specific activities. Traditions, so loved by children, are built into specific ceremonies, such as singing a certain song at a specific time, perhaps on the way from or to the bus, or just before departure, or upon arrival. They give the "old" camper a pleasant status, and the "new" camper a warm feeling of being accepted. "We always sing that song when we leave" or "When you hear us start singing that song it means that camp has started"—and the leader knows that *esprit de corps* has been established.

Traditions, however, do not have to last forever, or be incapable of change. In fact, each camp group can establish its own small symbols, or rites, or customs. Any tradition should be maintained only so long as it serves to unify and to give pleasure to the group. When it begins to sound "dated," or to amuse, or to seem slightly ridiculous, or when it begins to be neglected, then its usefulness is over and it should be dropped, no matter how fond adults might be of it. After all, the day camp serves the children of the current season; it is not operated for the adults who may be on the staff year after year.

Sometimes the *material*, rather than the idea, may need to be changed. For example, the singing of an opening or a closing song is a good idea. The song itself, however, may need to be changed. It may have become too well-known; it may be too hard to sing; it may no longer sound amusing, or friendly; it may no longer be appropriate.

A poem, read impressively by a leader, or chanted by the group, can be a fine tradition, but the choice of poems can change from year to year.

### TYPES OF TRADITIONS

A tradition, to a day camp owner or organizer, may mean something that goes back for years and years. To a leader, the same tradition may mean something that has been done ever since *he* came to the camp. To a child, a tradition is something that is repeated often, and is accepted as a definite part of the daily program. The concept of time is very different to a child. Camp traditions should be based on the child's, not the adult's concept. They will fall into certain types:

*Themes.* A common day camp tradition may be a theme that runs through the entire camp, and the entire summer. This may vary. One camp may operate on the ever-popular Indian theme, in which various groups become tribes, or villages within the same tribe. Such themes may be not only seasonal, but also monthly, weekly, and sometimes daily. Often used are themes such as these, but counselors and executives will think of many others that will catch the imagination.

| | | |
|---|---|---|
| Indians | Gold Rush | Cowboys |
| Pioneers | Robin Hood | Fairy tales |
| Colonial | King Arthur | Folk lore |
| Transportation | Space | World neighbors |

Such themes should be used with care—in fact, it is wise to think well before deciding to use one. No matter how good, or how easily correlated, a theme does have a certain hampering effect upon program and choice of activities. Unless used with care, a theme can become the tail that wags the dog.

*Rites.* Childhood is filled with little rites—evidence that children enjoy them. Rattling a stick across pickets in a fence, avoiding stepping on a crack, jumping to touch the edge of a certain awning, turning around three times when going back to get a forgotten object—these are all little rites, sometimes based on superstitions from the far past, sometimes invented by the individual. Making a wish and blowing out the candles on the birthday cake is a rite. So is looking at a new moon over the left shoulder, or putting a four-leaf clover in the heel of the right shoe.

A rite in a day camp may start spontaneously. Perhaps there's a big tree that must be passed every day on the way to camp site. One child touches the trunk, or pats it. His friend does the same. They repeat it the next day, and another child copies them. Or a child says, "Better go back and touch the lucky tree." And from then on, Druids couldn't be better tree touchers!

Rites can be very simple little things, or impressive, symbolic actions. Here are a few of each type:

- *Tree Touching*—mentioned above.
- *Mascot Patting*—a tree, rock, totem pole, gate, or other object must be patted on arrival and/or departure.
- *Circle Seat*—each camper walks around his seat in the council ring before sitting down.
- *Friendly Magic*—all campers join hands in council ring before sitting, or before leaving for the day.
- *Lucky Stone*—any stone of unusual color or shape. Anyone finding one brings it and passes it around the council ring to share his luck.
- *Special Handshake*—to be used in greeting and in saying goodby.

- *Rain Dance*—or Special Parade—or other special rite used specifically to bring good weather. (The Hopi chant would fit this nicely.)
- *Chant*—a simple poem or chant, given by all campers at the beginning or end of council ring program.

*Response Chant*—a very fine type, with real meaning when done with deep conviction. The leader calls out, "Are we friends?" Campers call back, "We are friends." Repeated three times, this makes a fine ending.

Another variation is a form of the Mizpah theme: "Is all well between thee and me?" and the reply, "All is well between thee and me." Such chants must be done seriously. There should be no screaming or yelling. The question and answer should be thoughtful and deliberate.

Camps in which the youngsters are all of one faith can adapt many of their religious songs or responses to this sort of program.

## Religion in Camp Programs

The strengthening of spiritual values and the placing of emphasis on ethics of conduct are certainly major objectives in any group situation with youngsters. The place of any type of specific religious instruction, however, should be determined by the sponsoring agency in advance, and its policy specifically stated. It is not a subject to be decided upon by individual leaders. In day camps supported by public tax funds through school or public recreation agencies, for example, no religious instruction is usually permitted, and no child is excluded because of his religion.

This point is made because it has an effect upon the choice of such simple activities as the grace said or sung at meals, the opening and closing songs, or the choice of poetry. Since the day camper is home-based, so to speak, and since day camps usually operate only five or less days a week, it is the responsibility of the parents to provide whatever religious training and instruction they wish.

Those day camps owned and operated by religion-based organizations for youngsters of their particular faith usually follow their own clearly established policy.

The day camp, whether public or private, which accepts youngsters of different faiths should make sure that no activity that could embarrass or offend a child of any religious affiliation is conducted, no matter how unintentionally.

## Council Ring Games

Since space is limited, and the number of campers is large, the games for playing within the council ring must be chosen with care. They may include such types as the following:

- Games in which each group is represented by one or more players. These may be challenges, or puzzles, magic games, or single or dual contests.
- Games in which each player takes part in turn.
- Games in which the players are called upon by the Big Chief, or Master, or Mayor, or whatever title is given to the Person-in-Charge.
- Games that can be taken home to try out on the family.

Council ring games should be played ceremoniously. They should be slowed down, so that everyone can see or hear. They must be presented dramatically. Like pantomime, they must be played with timing and gestures larger than life, so to speak.

If a game requires leaving the council ring, the players should be escorted to an exit. The action of the game should be in full view of the others. Whenever possible, the game should be played within the confines of the ring. Save the space-needing games for other times of the day.

The following games are typical of one or more of the groupings listed above. The methods of presentation may be changed. They are given only to show a general pattern. With this general pattern, it will be very easy to select and/or adapt games from those described in "Games," Chapter 16.

### CATCH THE RING

Each group selects two players to represent it. Partners stand about ten feet apart. One holds a plastic knife or fork or straight stick. His partner throws six rubber jar rings to him one by one, and he tries to catch as many as possible. The pair with the most catches wins for their group.

## CHIEF'S ROLL CALL

As each camper or every fifth camper (or each group, if the number is large) enters the council ring he draws a slip of paper from a box or pouch held by the Chief. On each slip is the name of a trade or a profession.

The Chief takes his place, raises his arms for silence, and says, "Each (or some) of my brothers has a secret trade that we would find out. Let each come before us and show us his work." He then calls each person (or group) in turn, one at a time, to the center. Each must act out the "trade" written on his slip and the others try to guess. All acting of course is pantomime. No word may be spoken, although sounds may be made. Some professions and trades follow (add lots of others):

| | | |
|---|---|---|
| mechanic | airplane pilot | airplane hostess |
| doctor | lawyer | preacher |
| riveter | farmer | sailor |
| soldier | teacher | policeman |
| fireman | window washer | bricklayer |
| dancer | bull fighter | nurse |

## CONTROL TOWER

Each camper gets a sheet of paper, and makes an airplane. Each player in a group tosses his in turn, trying to land his airplane on a landing field. This landing field is made of a large sheet of paper, or area marked on the ground. Each group scores the total of the number of planes landed safety on the field.

This can be given all sorts of variations. Each group can have a different-colored paper, for example. Or the game can be played by representatives rather than each member of a group.

## IZZY DIZZY

An old favorite. Out-of-circle. A representative from each group stands two or three feet apart from the other representatives. Each one bends his body so that his hands can touch the ground. Knees may be bent. In that position, he turns around in place four or five times, all starting at a signal. They then race to a given point—or perhaps "weave" would be a better description. Play for fun, not speed. Supervise for safety.

JUNIOR JAVELIN

Played outside the circle by representatives of each camp group. Hang a hoop from a tree. Players line up about twenty feet away from it. A long broomstick, or bamboo pole or dowel is the javelin.

Each player gets five chances and scores a point for his group every time the javelin goes through the hoop. Change the distance if the action is too easy or too hard. (*Safety Note:* Be sure the area behind the hoop is empty and safe. Appoint a Watchman to make sure that no one walks or runs across the danger zone.)

LAST MAN OUT

The Chief ceremoniously takes sixteen objects—stones, sticks, colored cardboard or other, large enough to be seen by all. With grave dignity he places them in a row on the ground. Raising his arms for silence, he calls out, "Send me two warriors, O my people!"

When two campers are by him, side by side, on the far side of the row, he instructs them. "You may take one, or two, or three stones (or sticks, or whatever objects) at a time, but no more. Take turns in fairness, my brothers. Try to make the other take the last one. We await the winner."

One boy wins, and, if interest has been high, the Chief might say, "Test thyself against another brother. Whom would you call?" And the game continues.

THE MAGIC STICK

The Chief appoints a Medicine Man (or Co-pilot, or Wagon Master) who has been briefed on the secret ahead of time. He announces that his helper has magic powers to read the mind. He then very ceremoniously puts down five or six sticks, stones, or other objects, in front of him, and sends the helper out of sight and hearing. He then asks the group to decide upon one of the objects, and to concentrate on it.

The helper is called back. The Chief tells him to select the stick chosen by the group. The helper stands by the Chief, look-ing intently at the sticks—but also watches the Chief's feet. The Chief points to various ones and asks, "Is it this one?" "Is it that one," and so on. The helper says "No" to each, until he sees the Chief's foot move just a bit. The next stick pointed out will be the right one. Very mystifying to campers if done well. May be repeated on other days, or campers may try out their guesses. Clue can be changed, too.

PLUS AND MINUS

This requires a two-foot square of plywood, cardboard, canvas, heavy paper, or floor or ground area suitably laid out. Divide the square into sixteen six-inch squares, and paint, crayon, or mark them in alternate colors or lines. Number each square as in dia-gram.

Make ten disks or smaller squares out of cardboard, leather, rubber, dowel stick, or other material. Paint five of these one color; five the other, to match the board.

| 14 | 13 | 16 | 15 |
| 9 | 10 | 11 | 12 |
| 6 | 5 | 8 | 7 |
| 1 | 2 | 3 | 4 |

The Chief calls for a war-rior (or noble, or such) from two groups, to uphold the prestige of their group. Each player gets five disks, and they take turns in pitching them onto the board from about six feet away. (Vary the distance de-pending upon the skill and age of the players.)

If more than half of a player's disk lands in a square of his color, he adds that number to his score. If a disk is more than half on the opponent's color, he subtracts that number from his score. When all five disks have been thrown, a "round" is over.

Play two rounds out of three, highest final score winning for his group.

*Variation:* Use five players per team, each throwing one disk.

ROPING CONTEST

Decorate a post or stick so that it resembles the head of a horse or steer. Campers take turns, as individuals or as group representatives, trying to rope it from a set distance. A practical game to use after campers have learned to tie a good loop knot.

SHOOT THE HOOP

Another out-of-circle contest. Two teams of players line up facing each other across a lane about nine feet wide. Each player has a paper dart. Use a different color for each team.

The Chief rolls a hoop down the middle of the lane. The players on one side take the first turn in trying to throw their darts through it, and score the number of successful tries. On the second roll, the other team takes its turn.

*Variations:* Players on both teams throw on the same roll. A scorekeeper for each team counts official scores.

Or players throw the darts one by one—the first players on each team, then the second, and so on.

TAKE OUT

Very similar to *Last Man Out* and developed the same way. The Chief places twelve objects in three rows, one row of five, one of four, and one of three. A player may take all, or as many as he wishes from any one row, but not from more than one row at a time. The object again is to force the opponent to take the last one.

TRY AN ANGLE

This is a wonderful take-home-and-try-on-Dad puzzle. If possible, run off a copy of this puzzle on a sheet of paper and give everybody a copy. Ask them to bring back the answer to "How many triangles here?" If the answer isn't right, say mysteriously, "No, that's not right. Take it back and try again." Keep a running list of the answers.

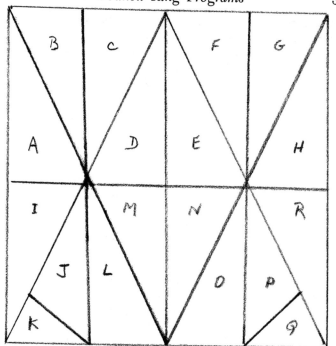

If you have to prove the answer, letter the triangles. The big ones will be combinations of letters, like HROPQ. There are 33 triangles, and if you don't believe it, count them!

### "BRING AND SHOW" PROGRAM

Nowadays families, or members of families, travel a great deal. Many have flown or driven across the United States. Many have visited Canada and Mexico. Trips to Europe and to Asia are no longer rare—in fact, many fathers have served military duty in far places. In most homes, there are interesting souvenirs or home decorations that are unusual and interesting.

A good way to start this sort of "foreign exchange" is for a counselor to bring something that will interest the youngsters. It may be a Japanese kimono with its obi. It may be a Chinese mandarin robe, heavy with embroidery. It may be a gay cock carved and painted in Portugal, or wooden shoes from Holland, or a grass skirt from Hawaii. Toys, jewelry, clothing, mats, carvings, games, crafts—the possibilities are endless.

Whatever the item, it should form the basis for spirited discussion. How does a Japanese girl have to walk in a long, tight kimono? What effect would this have on what she does all day? Do girls in Japan still wear kimonos? Talk about movies or TV programs involving Japan and its people. Let the questions, conjectures, and comments flow.

Someone in the group is sure to say, "My mother has a _____ that Dad brought her from _____!" Or "We bought _____ when we were in Mexico." And so someone promises to bring something to show the others at council ring tomorrow, and the "Bring and Show" program is rolling.

### "SEE AND TELL" PROGRAM

"See and Tell" programs are similar to "Bring and Show," in that they offer the youngsters the opportunity to share with each other—share interests and information. "Bring and Show" belongs in the opening council ring, because excitement, curiosity, and pride can't wait too long. "See and Tell" is a closing activity. It is a final sharing with the others of something odd, lovely, rare, or interesting. It may be an odd-shaped rock, or a small turtle, or an unknown beetle, fern leaf, cocoon, or shell. It may be a feather or a bone or a piece of driftwood.

Whatever it is, it is passed around so that everyone has a chance to see and touch, while the lucky finder tells his friends where and how he came to find it, and anything about it that he knows. Here again the counselor keeps the door open for questions, discussions, and arguments. Here again time is left open for finding the answers and reporting to the group. Campers are encouraged to ask about it at home, to use their books, or to visit a library. The sense of wonder and curiosity is kept alive, and given opportunities to grow.

# CHAPTER 22:

# RAINY AND HOT
# DAY ACTIVITIES

Some day camps relying primarily on outdoor areas and without adequate indoor facilities adopt a policy of not operating on rainy days. Such camps work out ways of notifying parents by radio, television, or telephone, or have a standard policy about which parents are told in advance.

Other day camps in similar circumstances have a standard policy of using rainy days for trips to educational institutions such as museums, zoos, planetariums, and the like, where pre-arrangement is not necessary.

Most day camps, however, do have indoor facilities, sometimes crowded, sometimes more than adequate. The facilities may be borrowed, rented, or owned, but a day camp program goes on, rain or not. The suggestions in this chapter are for leaders in such camps.

These activities will also be helpful for other occasions, such as very hot, humid days. Some will fit nicely into other parts of the day's program, such as the rest period, the lunch period, the council ring program, and the like. Activities in other parts of this book, especially in Section III, are suitable for or can be adapted to rainy day use.

## OUTDOORS IN THE RAIN

Taking the youngsters out of doors for activities on a rainy day involves a number of factors. First, they should be dressed suitably—either in raincoats and boots, or in bathing suits. The latter are unexpected fun when the day is warm, or when a shower has come up unexpectedly.

315

### Water Play

Running around in the rain, paddling in the brook, making a dam, sailing leaf boats, all are new experiences to many youngsters.

Fishing is a wonderful sport in the rain—if it's legal! Check local and state laws, and find out if they apply to minors. Digging for worms, collecting other types of bait, fixing up the line, and finding a place along the bank of the brook, the pond, or the beach of a lake or ocean, is extra fun in the novelty of rain.

A model boat regatta can be conducted, too, if the rain is not too heavy. The boats might be made in the morning, and the regatta scheduled in the afternoon.

See Chapter 18, "Water Play," for directions for many different kinds of water games and other activities.

Swimming in the rain is also unexpectedly pleasant. When the air is cool, the water feels warm, and raindrops on the face are exhilarating. Swim periods should be active, however, with special water games and stunts to keep everyone busy with physical exercise. They should be followed by brisk showers, rubdowns, and dry clothes. A hot drink, and an open fire to sit around for storytelling, or singing, or guessing games are good follow-ups.

### Campcraft Skills

Rainy days can be show-up days—the days that show how well campcraft skills have been learned. The youngsters learned all about tinder, kindling, and fuel, and their fires burned nicely. How well will they burn in the rain? Where can dry tinder, dry kindling be found? It didn't seem to matter yesterday when Bob forgot to cover the woodpile with a tarpaulin. Suppose that wood meant the difference between eating and not eating, being warm or being cold, being dry or being wet? Firemaking and its importance take on new meaning.

*Cooking* is different, too. The smoke hangs low and gets in the eyes. The raindrops sizzle. The pan or pot needs some sort of protection. Is the tin-can stove useful? Were the matches waterproofed? Where's the best place to sit down to eat?

*Shelter* is suddenly very important. That lean-to that went up so easily last week is not so easy to put up when it's wet. The place where it was last week is now a small pond—a lesson in choosing sites more carefully. Suppose a sleep-out was necessary. Where would be the driest place? How could the sleeping bags be kept dry?

What happens to rope when it gets wet? When it dries? How will this affect the tent? Will the stakes hold in the wet ground? The ropes, in the wind? Suppose that tent were all the shelter available? Is it dry inside?

*Weather* can be checked. What direction is the wind? What's the temperature? What sort of clouds are in the sky? What's the camp forecast for tomorrow? How much rain fell? How well did the camp weather bureau's forecast work out?

*Wildlife* is interesting to see on a rain-hike or walk. What birds are out? Can any be heard but not seen? Any animal tracks in the mud or soft earth? Are insects flying? Where do animals *go* in the rain? Was that mushroom there yesterday? See how thick the moss is—feel it! It's like a sponge!

*Conservation* becomes real. Look at the way the water is running down that steep, short cut to the pool or beach. It's cutting into the soil—and washing it away. A gully is being made right there! What should be done? All right, let's *do* it!

Look under the leafmold. How far down is it moist? Any little roots there? Any larvae, or beetles, or worms?

The Five Senses can have new experiences. *Look* at the different shades of green, brown, and other colors. They're different from what they were yesterday in the sun. That tree trunk that looked light brown, and felt warm and dry, now looks almost black and feels cool and moist. *Smell* the wet earth, bark, leaves, flowers. *Taste* a berry that is cool and wet. *Listen* to the rain on the leaves, the wind in the trees, the running of water, the chirp of a bird. *Look* at the drops of rain on a spider web, on the tip of a leaf. Hold the face up and *feel* the rain on it. They may not all be new sensations to some boy or girl, but no matter how often they are felt, they never grow old.

INDOORS ON A RAINY DAY

Indoor activities in the day camp can be a problem. Space may be limited; movement restricted. The atmosphere may be humid and depressing. Tempers may be short, and youngsters restless.

There's a difference, too, between one day of rain and a long wet spell that sometimes settles in. (Counselors should make a special point of reading long-range weather forecasts. They help in anticipating such a period, so that it can be planned for in advance.)

Recreational needs of youngsters are the same, whether it's rainy or sunny. They need *activity*—physical exercise. They need mental stimulation. They need the satisfactions of creativity, and of service to others. All these they can have, indoors, in limited space—if carefully planned. Instead of a running game that requires space the equivalent of a baseball diamond, a game that requires up and down movements, or an active folk or square dance, will give exercise to the big muscles of the body. Instead of taking easels down to the lake, painting and sketching can be done in a very small space—if planned. Instead of a bird walk, making birdhouses or bird models can be substituted. Storytelling, stunts, and creative dramatics are all naturals for rainy days.

There is one important factor, however, that must be used in selecting rainy day activities. This factor is *good humor*. A rainy day can be a great disappointment to youngsters who long to be outdoors. Activities indoors must not only provide outlets for exercise and handskills: they must also create a warm, happy atmosphere. *Surprise* can be one ingredient. *Laughter* is another. Intense *interest* is still another, as is *novelty*. Counselors should look for these qualities in rainy day activities. They should be used with care, however. Too many surprises cease to surprise. Too much novelty ceases to be new. Too much laugh making becomes silly instead of funny.

Some activities should bring everybody together. Some should be left to smaller groups. Within the framework of a general plan, individual choice should be not only permitted but encouraged. There should be an opportunity for a sense of accomplishment, also. A rainy day is not just a time for passive entertainment, like a television Western.

*Themes* often help. An indoor circus, for example, requires arts and crafts (posters, decorations, props, frames for animals, costuming, and the like). It requires music (a rhythm or kitchen band must decide upon music, and rehearse). It must have *clowns* and *performing animals* (stunts, tumbling, and other exercises). It needs pink lemonade and popcorn (food preparation and serving). In such planning, many small groups prepare for, and come together in, one big affair.

Special events of this type may include such themes as these:

| | |
|---|---|
| Indoor Circus | Indoor Treasure Hunt |
| Talent Show | Christmas in July |
| South American Fiesta | World Neighbors |
| Indoor Track Meet | Mock Television Show |
| County Fair | Trip to the Moon |
| Rodeo | Across the U.S.A. |
| Pirate Day | |

## Special Equipment for Indoor Occupation

Wise counselors keep on hand a box or shelf of special equipment not used except for rainy day programs. If such supplies are kept in a special box decorated like a treasure chest, and used *only* for such times, their use will be looked forward to with eager anticipation. Surprises are always fun.

Contents will vary, with the number, age, and sex of the youngsters, and the type of camp program. Usually included, in addition to the customary supplies, are items such as these:

>  Table games not used at other times
>  Pencils and paper, for quizzes, and pencil and paper games
>  Crayons, watercolors, tempera, and other art supplies
>  Balloons—for balloon games
>  Rhythm band instruments
>  Soap-bubble pipes
>  Ping-pong balls, playing cards, marbles
>  Paper plates, soda straws, scotch tape
>  Pipe cleaners—different colors
>  Shelf paper; newsprint; aluminum foil
>  Paint brushes of several sizes
>  Stapler, scissors, string, cardboard
>  Hoops, clothespins, toothpicks

A *costume box* is a tremendous boon to a rainy day program. It can contain old hats, skirts, dresses, shoes, coats, trousers, feather boas, beads, scarves, fans, pocketbooks—and be the inspiration for many stunts and skits.

If space is available, it's a good idea to look into the many indoor adaptations of outdoor sports and sports equipment available nowadays from manufacturers, such as the plastic bowling pins and balls; the cork, rubber, and plastic balls.

Such games as darts (rubber), shuffleboard, deck tennis, quoits, hopscotch (many varieties), jump rope, and many others are feasible for day camps in facilities that permit their use, and in programs that are not limited entirely to indigenous camp activities. Older campers enjoy them because of their familiarity, and they do provide physical outlets.

### Games for Rainy Days

The best games for rainy or very hot days—when youngsters must be indoors for sizable periods of time, are games that are simple, impromptu, and happy-making. The games used should include *lively* ones to work off steam and stretch muscles tired of sitting; *relaxed* games not too competitive; games *different* enough to arouse curiosity, and *off-beat* enough to cause laughter.

Examples of such types follow. Many of the games in Section III fit into these types. So do some of the games in Chapter 21 on "Council Ring Programs."

Excellent table games, puzzles, and other indoor activities are available from manufacturers, and from local sporting goods and department stores. New games of this sort are available each year, and many youngsters would enjoy them. They also have an added carry-over value for family play.

## Improvised Games

These can be more fun than games out of a box! They can be used as separate games, or as parts of a larger activity, like a carnival. Many of these are good small-group games, too, and can be just as easily played outdoors. Youngsters should be encouraged to improvise such games.

### ALPHABET STICKS

Players toss short sticks from a set distance, and try to make various letters like H-V-N-T-L-M. Lowest number of tries before success, is winner.

### BRIGHT EYES

Youngsters draw a funny face, minus eyes, on a piece of paper or cardboard. Then they drop buttons, pennies, bottle tops, or other small, round objects to make the eyes.

### FEED THE SPIDER

Draw a spider web on a large sheet of paper, and number the sections, highest numbers toward the center of the web. Players form two teams. Each player has a pebble, or bottle top, or cardboard marker, a different color for each team.

Players stand around the web, and, at a signal, all the players on one team toss their marker into the web. They then add up the total points scored and remove their markers. The other team then takes its turn.

The game may be scored by winning the best two out of three

tries, or by reaching a total score previously selected, such as 100 points.

### LOLLIPOP GRAB

Draw a 30-foot circle. Sprinkle lollipops in the center. Youngsters take off shoes (for safety!), face outward at the circle, and are blindfolded. Then they get on their hands and knees and, at the signal, crawl *backward* to try to find a lollipop.

### MISS THE TARGET

Put a paper plate or a pie tin in the middle of a chalk circle about 5 feet in diameter. Players stay outside the circle and roll marbles or click checkers toward the plate. The object is *not* to touch or get into the plate, but to *come as close as possible.*

### SPIN THE WORD

Make a dreydl or simple top by sticking a cardboard square through a toothpick or sharp stick. Crayon a letter on each side of the top square, the letters spelling some word like C-A-M-P or P-L-A-Y. Youngsters take turns spinning the top, and each records the letter he gets at each turn. The first to complete the chosen word wins.

*Variations:* This game is so simple that it can be played anywhere, anytime—on a hike, at a picnic, during rest period, or whenever. It can be used for nature themes by selecting trees, birds, flowers, and the like to be spelled. The top can be given more than four sides for longer words.

### UMBRELLA RACE

Cut several silhouettes of open umbrellas, minus handles (roughly semicircles, the diameter edge scalloped to indicate the spokes) out of a piece of heavy cardboard, make a hole in the top of each, and run a 12-foot length of string through it. Tie one end to the leg of a chair or other object. Divide youngsters into teams, a team for each umbrella. The first person on each team takes the free end of the string and tries to wiggle the umbrella down until it touches the other end. The second player then takes the string and tries to wiggle the umbrella *back* to him, and so on. Team finishing first wins. The umbrella and the string must never touch the floor. The game works best when the string slants very gently but not much.

### LAUGH MAKERS

These are games that are off-beat, impossible to play without giggles. Here again they are not limited to indoors, or to rainy days—but my!—they do help to keep campers happy when other activities fail.

### BOAT RACE

Active to do, fun to watch. Play as a relay, or in heats. Provide two dishpans, a starting line, and a finish line. Players sit in pans and race by propelling the pan with arms and legs.

### CHINESE FINGERNAILS

Two teams, lined up facing each other. Give the first player of each team five wooden clothespins (the straight kind). He must put the clothespins on the fingers of one hand. When they're in place, the next player must remove them one by one and put them on *his* fingers. The last player must bring the Chinese finger-nails up to the first player to remove. First team to finish wins.

### EGYPTIAN SALUTE

Two teams, single lines, lines facing. The youngster at the left end of each line uses his right hand, and touches the top of his head, his nose, and one of his feet. He then makes a complete turn and touches the top of the head of the person on his right. This continues to the end of line, and line finishing first wins.

### POOR PUSSY

This is an old game—so old that many modern youngsters have never played it—yet it is a game of dramatic skill in bringing smiles. The youngsters sit in a circle, in chairs, or on the floor. "Pussy" is chosen. Pussy goes to various members of the circle, kneels, and says "Miaow." That person must pat Pussy on the head and say *without smiling,* "Poor Pussy." Pussy may use his voice and his face in any way he likes, trying to make the other break down. If he succeeds, the smiler becomes Pussy.

### YOU'RE IT

Draw a big circle on a large sheet of paper, and divide it into segments. Write a forfeit in each segment—things like "Fly like a bird," "Spell your name backward," "Walk like an elephant." Then stick a pin in the middle of the circle, and put a paper clip over it. Youngsters take turns flicking the clip around and following the directions it gives.

### PENCIL AND PAPER GAMES

Such games can be very useful when the group is fairly homogenous in age and in school grade. Games that depend upon writing skill, and sometimes spelling, should be selected carefully —not too hard to be discouraging, and not too easy to be "kid stuff." Luckily there are all kinds of pencil-and-paper games, because such games sometimes provide opportunities for achievement for youngsters who fall behind their peers in physical skills. They also provide opportunities, sometimes, for full play of the imagination, reasoning, and humor. Like other games in this section, many can be played outdoors, and in situations besides rainy days.

### DOUBLE-YOU-ARE

Youngsters take the letter W and the letter R, and see who can write the most words beginning with W and ending with R.

### WHAT WOULD YOU DO?

Two lines of players, perhaps facing each other across a table or sitting on each side of the fireplace. Each player has a piece of paper and pencil. The players on one side all think of some object—anything animate or inanimate—and write it down. The players opposite them write down what they would do with some object, each player thinking up his own action, and writing it down.

Then the first player on the "object" line reads his object, and the player across from him reads what he would do with it. Tom, who likes sports, might have selected a baseball as his object. Bill, who is getting hungry, might have written, "Fry it in olive oil and pour tomato sauce over it."

Vary by changing sides. Vary also by one side selecting and agreeing on one object, and each member of the other side writing down what he would do with it. The different solutions are very child-funny.

### SPELL IT

Each player draws a large square on a sheet of paper, and then divides the square into 25 sections by drawing five lines across, and five lines down. Players then take turns, each calling out a letter of the alphabet, and each placing that letter anywhere he wishes, trying to make as many words as possible. Words must have at least three letters. Player with the most words wins.

### UNITED STATES

Not new, but always a challenge. Each player tries to list all the fifty states in the United States. First to do so wins. (It helps if the states are numbered as they are written.)

A follow-up is to go back and try to add the capital cities for the states.

### WORD FENCE

Any word with about six letters is chosen for the "fence." Each player writes the letters of the word down the left side of his paper, and then writes the word *backward* down the right side. The first and last letters then form a fence for closing in new words. The paper might look like this, using the word CAMPER:

|   |   |
|---|---|
| C | R |
| A | E |
| M | P |
| P | M |
| E | A |
| R | C |

Each player tries to fill in the spaces between the letters, and tries to make as long a word as possible. The first line might use C-O-U-N-T-E-R, and would count 5. The last line might be R-E-L-I-C, counting only 3. The player with the greatest number of letters added to make words wins the game.

### WORD MAKER

In a given period of time, youngsters see how many smaller words they can make out of one long word. Letters can be used any number of times. No proper nouns. Use words like CONCENTRATE, ATMOSPHERE, SATELLITE, TRAVELOGUE.

## Muscle Stretchers

No matter how interesting the rainy day activities may be, there are times when *movement* is needed. Muscles demand action. Dual and individual contests are excellent for this purpose, but other games that require limited space can also provide the necessary exercise. In addition to games in Section III, here are a few others that are particularly suited to rainy days.

### CHAIN TAG

A good tussling game for young boys. The group chooses "It," and he selects an assistant. They join hands and try to catch others. When they surround someone, he must join the chain; but the two "Its" remain at the ends of the chain and are the only ones who can do the tagging. A player may crawl under, or break the chain, if he can, providing he has not been tagged by one of the end players. When the chain is broken, it must rejoin before anyone can be tagged. The game ends when everyone has been caught. The last two players caught become the new "Its." (When girls play this, better not allow breaking the chain.)

### HOOK ON

Another rough game for letting off steam. Four boys are "It." The others line up across the room. At a signal, they all dash over and try to hook on to one of the four "Its." The "Its" try to evade the others, but cannot roughhouse. When everyone is hooked on to someone, the counselor counts the four groups, and the group with the fewest players in it wins.

#### KEEP IT UP

A good, hearty, active game, with no stars. Divide players into several groups, each in its section of the room. The counselor throws a volleyball or basketball to group No. 1, and those players bat it among themselves trying to keep it in the air. Each time the ball is tapped, the players count aloud "One, two, three," and so on, until the ball hits the ceiling, or a wall, post, or floor. The number counted is that team's score.

The counselor then tosses the ball to Group No. 2, which tries to better the score. The game goes on until each group has played, and the highest score wins.

#### KICKUP

So active that it requires a three-minute time limit. Players lie in a circle, feet toward center. Leader tosses a light ball or balloon into the foot area. Ball must be kept in the air by the feet only. Every time the ball touches the floor counts a point *against* the players. Players try to beat their own record, or compete with other groups.

#### THE NOBLE DUKE OF YORK

A fine game to play after youngsters have been seated a long time. Play vigorously.

*Words:*
 Oh, the noble Duke of York,
 He had ten thousand men.
 He led them up to the top of the hill,
 And led them down again.

Now, when they were up, they were up;
And when they were down, they were down;
And when they were only halfway up,
They neither were up nor down.

*Action:* Sing the melody through one time; then on repeat, or second verse, add the action as indicated.

"When they were up"—all stand
"When they were down"—all sit
"When they were only halfway up"—hold a half-standing position.

PING-PONG BASEBALL

Use a ruler for a bat, and lots of fielders. The Ping-pong ball is hard to catch, and even with short bases, there'll be *lots* of exercise.

PLEASE

An old favorite with many names, often used when a group has sat too long and needs to stretch. Everyone stands, and follows the words and actions of the leader or counselor.

1. Hands on lips
   Hands on knees
   Put them behind you
   If you please.

2. Touch your shoulders
   Touch your nose
   Touch your ears
   Now touch your toes.

3. Raise your hands high in
      the air
   At your side, on your hair
   Raise your hands just as
      before
   While you clap 1-2-3-4.

4. My hands upon my head I
      place
   On my shoulders, on my
      face
   Then I raise them up on
      high
   Make my fingers quickly fly
   Then I put them in front of
      me
   And gently clap them 1-2-3.

POISON SNAKE

Players join hands in a circle. Put an Indian club, milk bottle, or other easily upset object in the middle. By pushing and pulling each other, players try to make someone knock over the club. When this happens, the person touching it leaves the circle.

As players are eliminated, they should form another circle and keep playing. In this way, everyone is active until only one person is left in the original circle. He is the winner.

TOUCH!

Divide the group into two or more teams standing facing each other in the middle of the playing space. The counselor calls "Touch . . . a door!" or other object in the playing area. Instantly everybody dashes to touch a door and then rushes to get back in his line. First line in place wins that round. Leader maintains suspense by hesitating before naming the object to be touched—a door, wall, post, window, table, chair, floor, and so on. (Likely to be strenuous, so don't name anything delicate!)

## Other Rainy Day Activities

The following are only a few samples of how wide a range of interesting things can be done indoors on rainy or excessively hot days:

ALPHABET TREASURE HUNT

Each youngster goes around and looks at the indoor area, making a list of items, one for each letter of the alphabet. Longest list wins. (A—ashes; B—board; C—chair, and so on.)

DAY CAMP LOG

A group project that requires lots of planning by the youngsters. It is really a scrapbook of the day camp and that particular group of youngsters. A cover must be designed and made.

Pages must be cut, put in by sewing, binding, stapling, glueing, or looseleaf style, and decorated. Photographs must be decided upon and mounted. Brief stories of activities and trips must be prepared. Poems must be written, cartoons drawn. Each camper must have his own page to write in—what he likes best, or whatever he wants to record—and to sign. Then a ceremonious presentation.

### DOG-NAMING CONTEST

Display a live dog (or any other animal) or a stuffed toy. Youngsters think about it, and some time during the day, write a suggested name on a slip, and drop it into a box. Before leaving, names are read and listed. Take a vote for best name. (Use the stuffed animal as a mascot puppet.)

### GROUP CRAFT PROJECTS

Very good for rainy days. Projects might be a dollhouse, made and furnished; a miniature circus; a camp mural; a day camp flag; a model of the day camp site; a miniature Indian village; pioneer village; farm; rocket or satellite; puppets and stage.

Once youngsters start on a group project and get absorbed in it, they are amazingly ingenious, full of imagination, and they can expand a simple project into one of major proportions.

### MAGAZINE TREASURE HUNT

Nice for small groups. They decide upon, and each writes down, a dozen or so items, such as a flower, tree, animal, bird, river, or sea. Then each goes through old magazines to try to locate and cut out each item. First to finish wins.

### MAKE-UP BOOTH

Provide a box of make-up, and a dress-up box. After everyone has had fun, work into a fashion show, a costume parade, a play, circus, fairy story.

### MORSE CODE

A rainy day is a perfect time to teach the Morse code by tapping, *and* by flashlight. The Boy Scout Handbook has the symbols.

NEW DANCE

Practice all the folk dances learned, and add a new one. Build a dance festival around them.

NEW GAMES

Make a tradition of teaching a new table game every rainy day.

SINGING

Youngsters see how many songs about rain they can think of and sing. Then songs about sun or sunshine.

SOAP BUBBLES

For tough, beautiful, iridescent bubbles make up a mixture ahead of time and have it ready for use on some rainy or hot day. Use the recipe in Chapter 8, "Water Play."

Try all sorts of things to make bubbles: a soda straw, funnel, cone-shaped paper cup with tip cut off, empty spool.

Make up bubble games. Play bubble races.

THIS IS YOUR LIFE

Each is given one magazine, scissors, paper, and paste. He must find pictures, cut out, and paste them in order to show someone's complete life. Best collection wins.

CHRISTMAS IN JULY (or August)

Not a new idea for experienced counselors, but new to most youngsters, and they always enjoy it. In some camps, it is a tradition that on the third rainy day in a row, the camp celebrates with decorations, gifts, and a Santa Claus. This sort of all-day group project can—or should—be used only once with the same group of youngsters.

# CHAPTER 23:

# TRIPS

A trip is a special event. It is planned in advance. It is looked forward to and talked about when it's over. It's more than a hike, different from a ramble or walk. It involves leaving the day camp site, usually for a sizable length of time. Sometimes a trip is substituted for a day at camp. Sometimes a trip is the answer to a rainy day. Except for a once-in-a-while mystery trip, it should be planned specifically, in advance, by the group that is going.

Trips should have a *reason*. They usually fall into one of two patterns: trips to find out or trips to try out.

### Trips to Find Out

These are the exploratory, mind-stretching, question answerers. They are interesting in themselves, but they are most successful when they serve as highlights or culminations of daily program activities. The more youngsters know about an interesting subject, the more they want to know.

For example, if the group has learned the names of clouds, has kept a weather chart, made a sundial and a rain gauge, studied weather flags, and talked about hurricanes and storms, a visit to a local or nearby weather bureau will give real meaning to those previous experiences. If near a sea or lake coast, a visit to a Coast Guard Station, with emphasis on its rescue and emergency work, is a further revelation.

Suppose the group has learned several fire-making techniques, has been taught how to make sure the fire is out, has experimented with a magnifying glass, has operated a simple pressure pump and fire extinguisher, perhaps has seen a burned-over area. A trip to a fire tower will be a tremendous experience. A trip to a local firehouse will take on new meaning, too.

So it goes. The youngsters who have learned to recognize—and to catch—fish in the pond, lake, or sea get a great deal more out of a trip to a fish hatchery than just watching baby fish. The exhibits in an aquarium—even a big fish market—become tied in with previous projects and gain new meaning.

The group that has studied conservation, planted new trees, worked a garden, tested the soil, studied local environment and found out what grows where, will have a background of knowledge and information for a trip to a botanical garden, a large nursery, a lumber mill, a wholesale flower and vegetable market.

Trips to find out must be scheduled in advance. This means that a program geared to arouse interest must *also* be planned in advance. Though day camping is informal and relaxed, it is not haphazard.

All research builds upon what is known. Interest breeds interest. Trips should not merely transport the body from one place to another. They should satisfy the need to know, to find out.

Here are only a few of the many possible trips. Check locally, and add your own.

| | |
|---|---|
| Airplane factory | Historical museum |
| Airport (control room) | Ice plant |
| Botanical garden | Indian village |
| Caves and caverns | Lumber mill |
| Children's museum | Military base |
| Coast Guard station | Museum of natural history |
| Cotton or woolen mill | Nature museum |
| Dairy farm | Planetarium |
| Dam | Power plant |
| Fire department | Tree and flower nursery |
| Fire tower | Vegetable or grain farm |
| Fish cannery | Vegetable market |
| Fish hatchery | Weather bureau |
| Fish market | Wild life sanctuary |
| Flower market | Zoo |
| Fruit packing plant | |

**Trips to Try Out**

This type is similar to the former, but it has one major difference. On these trips, the youngsters try out, under different circumstances and in a different environment, the skills they have learned and practiced at day camp. It is, therefore, an extension of the day camp activity program. It is really more, though, because it implies a tribute, an acknowledgment of skill —in fact, sometimes a reward—for what has been learned.

An example might be a fishing trip. Such a trip depends upon individual skills. No one goes, for example, who cannot swim, or who does not know how to row, or sail. The meal depends upon the skill in catching fish, preparing them, cooking them— and that depends on firemaking, collecting wood, and other skills.

Trail hiking means that the youngster who goes has learned how to act on a hike. He has learned outdoor manners. He has learned trail signs, how to carry a pack, what to wear, what to cook, how to use an axe and a knife, what plants to avoid, and the like. The trip is a chance to tie all those skills together into one exciting experience.

A trip to a beach, after learning to swim in a pool, gives a new dimension to swimming. There are no sides to cling to. The salt stings the eyes. The waves pull the sand from under the feet. And the immensity of sky and sea is a great discovery and adventure.

**Pointers for Planning Trips**

- Decide what type of trip, and where to go. Then talk about it, work toward it, plan for it.
- Know what type of transportation will be needed—bus, car, train, bike, truck, or legs. Arrange for it as far in advance as possible. Have a specific pick-up and discharging point.
- Decide what to do on the trip, and how long it will take. Have a definite time schedule and hold to it.
- Decide what will be needed in the way of equipment, supplies, tools. Who will bring what?

- Make sure parents know and give their permission. Notify them, too, if the youngsters are to bring lunch, or need extra money for entrance fees, or should bring bathing suits, towels, or other gear.
- Special appointments are necessary before taking any group to busy factories, farms, offices, or agencies. Often, if museums, zoos, aquariums, or other institutions know that a group is coming, they will provide a special guide and sometimes special privileges. Always give the number and age levels of the youngsters.
- Keep a careful list of all youngsters, and make a check so that no one is forgotten. Use a "buddy" system. Have a leader for at least every eight youngsters—more leaders for children under six.
- Keep a card file on places visited, with any hints or suggestions for next time, like "Don't get there at noon—far too crowded," or "Take plenty of time here. Youngsters are fascinated."
- *Use* the trip to motivate activities afterwards—improve skills that weren't up to par, serve as discussion leads, themes for drama, poetry, art, or clay work.
- Don't push information, science, or culture too hard. Provide the opportunity and the encouragement, but let the need come from within the child, not superimposed by you. As Joseph Lee used to say, "Don't tie on the flowers. Water the plant."

For what to do while traveling, see "Bus Activities," Chapter 19.

> *If I were to name the three most precious resources of life, I should say books, friends and nature; and the greatest of these, at least the most constant and always at hand, is nature.*
> **JOHN BURROUGHS**

# CHAPTER 24:

## SPECIAL
## THEME
## PROGRAMS

The selection, planning, and conducting of special programs that for one reason or another bring all the day campers together in a co-operative and correlated program will vary widely from camp to camp. Factors influencing such programs are these:

Size of day camp and facilities available
Number of campers and age groupings
Length of stay at day camp
Availability of transportation of families
Number of leaders, both paid and volunteer
Activity emphasis (Day camps that are highly specialized in some one activity will need a different type of demonstration or exhibit program.)

Trips, cook-outs, council ring ceremonies, story dramatizations, and other activities involving several areas of program are all special events. The material in this chapter is designed to give a counselor a few specific suggestions for developing an activity program around a central theme.

### Special Days

The suggestions have been developed as special "days." They might just as well have been called "weeks," or "hours."

Such events, developed through a central theme, have certain specific values:

- They offer every youngster a chance to participate, thus giving him an integral place in his peer group.
- They give an opportunity for democratic and co-operative planning, so that each camper feels the program is *his*.

- They provide an opportunity to improvise and to create; to use physical, mental, and creative skills in developing the theme.
- They stimulate the imagination and create a dramatic atmosphere that is conducive to self-expression.
- They do not rob the child of precious camp time, since the activities involved are camp activities, not superimposed, or requiring special rehearsal. Time spent in planning them is part of the camper's creative camp experience and of the activity program of the camp.
- They offer simple and interesting activities that demonstrate to parents, without formality, what their children have acquired in the way of social, physical, and creative skills.

There are all sorts of special events ranging from simple, spontaneous "surprises" to all-day, all-week, or all-session theme programs. The ones used here are only a few of the usual types. They are not developed in full. They are designed to be merely suggestive. Details, adaptations, and changes should be made by the day campers and counselors working together. Co-operative planning is the biggest single factor for success, and provides the most valuable opportunities for the social integration of the day camper.

Readers may note that no outline or suggestion for an international program is included. This is omitted purposely, for several reasons. First, such programs, to be really effective, should be authentic, and this requires considerable research and study. Summer days are few, and day campers' lengths of stay vary widely, making such study and research difficult.

Second, programs *not* authentic can give a false impression. The costume, for example, of most European youngsters today is not the folk costume of years past.

The finest way to create interest in and understanding of people from other lands is by *meeting* them—talking, laughing, learning, and playing together. The day camp that provides such opportunities by including children and leaders from other cultures will not need artificial international-theme events.

ALASKA DAY

This event is to honor our 49th State—and it offers a cool theme for a summer program.

*Games and Sports*
Sled race—mock or real
Kayak race—mock or real
Spearing seals—balloons and darts
Treasure hunt—gold foil or pebbles
Snowshoe race—u s i n g boxes for shoes

Alaskan yo-yo*

---

* Eskimos use small balls made of sealskin. Day campers can substitute horse chestnuts, carved bone, or wood. Use two "balls," attaching one to each end of a string 18 inches long. Hold the string between thumb and forefinger, off center, so that one end is slightly lower than the other. This is to keep the two balls from hitting as they swing past each other. Start by swinging one end in a circle. Then try to swing the other end in the *opposite* direction. Then by moving the hand up and down slightly, keep the two objects swinging in opposite directions. It takes practice, but it's fun.

*Crafts*
Snow glasses, like sun glasses, but with small slits to look through
Dog sleds—out of cardboard, wagons, etc.
Kayaks—whittled from wood, or carved
Igloos—picture, boxes, etc.
Village—miniature or play-size-picture
Ivory carving (soap)
Totem pole (balsa wood or made of cardboard boxes of various sizes)

*Vocabulary*
Cheechako—newcomer, just arrived
Sourdough—an old-timer
"Mush"—a command to a sled dog, "Hurry up!"
Husky—sled dog

Igloo—Eskimo house of ice or sod
Kayak—skin boat for one person
Muckamucka—food
Dust—gold dust
Poke-bag—for gold dust
Potlatch—a community feast
Skookum house—jail

## HAWAIIAN DAY

This event is, of course, to honor our 50th State.

*Games*

Plan this around pool or beach activities if possible. Use all sorts of *water* games and stunts. Coconuts for relay races.

*Crafts*

Hula skirts
Big, full moons for deco-
rations
Palm tree cuts-outs for
decorations
Boat paddles decorated
Grass huts
Flower leis—tissue paper garlands for neck
Fishes and other sea life—mobiles, murals

*Special Activities*

Feature moon songs—Blue Moon, Harvest Moon, and others.
Hawaiian songs—use long-playing records.
Outdoor luau (cook-out)
Pineapple juice for refreshment
Ukulele playing

## WAGONS TO WINGS

Here is a centennial theme used in Salina, Kansas. The idea is broad enough for almost any type of program. A good theme to show *contrasts* in activities is activities from pioneer to the atomic age.

*Games and Activities*

Use types in Frontier Day, plus races, archery contests,

parade, floats, dual contests. Devise appropriate names for activities. Painting and drawing exhibition, famous scenes from history.

*Crafts*

Costumes or symbols of costumes from pioneer to modern days.

Shoebox or wagon floats, illustrating various eras.

Examples of log cabins, tepees, colonial mansion, ranch-type modern home, skyscraper. Murals or box construction.

Airplanes—from early models to jets

Automobiles—from early models to latest sports cars

Boats, canoes, sailboats, steamships, warships

Space ships, satellites, rockets, Echo, Telestar

Space men, creatures from outer space

Skyscope, planets, stars

CARNIVAL DAY

*Games*

Freckle contest

Big Feet contest

Peanut relays

Animal games—Cat and Rat, Bull in the Ring, and others

Balloon games

Carnival booth games

*Crafts*

Make carnival booths for games and shows.

Paint clown faces on balloons.

Make costumes for "carnivals," clowns, acrobats, ringmaster, fortune teller.

Decorate any apparatus.

Make puppets for Punch & Judy show.

Make posters, tickets.

*Special Activities*

Clown acts

Circus acts

Guessing contests—seeds in watermelon, beans in a jar, number of kernels on an ear of corn

Pink lemonade           Trained "seals"
Circus parade           Trained "dogs"

This type of theme can be included in a Big Top, or Circus theme, using these as midway events.

### TREASURE ISLAND DAY

*Games*

Dual contests, between various pirates—
Deadeye Dick, Long John Silver, Teach,
Blackbeard, etc.
Rope Climbing
Pirates Brawl—Dodge Ball
Pirate Pull—Tug-of-War
Mutiny on Board—Bull in the Ring
Walk the Plank—Balance Beam contest

*Crafts*

Pirate costumes           Wooden swords
Eye patches               Skull & Crossbone flag
Mustaches                 Pirate hats and sashes
Earrings                  Pirate ship
Treasure chests

*Special Activities*

Tattoo with water colors.     Hunt for buried treasure.
Dance Sailors' Hornpipe.      Sing pirate songs.
Dramatize a scene from Treasure Island.

### FRONTIER DAY

*Games*

*Round Up the Dogies*—candy hunt
*Driving the Cattle to Market*—balloon and
fan, or stick and pop bottle.
*Find Your Boats*—shoe scramble
*Pie Tin Toss*

*Crafts*

Decorate "stores" or "Main Street" with
wheels, saddles, signs, streamers.
Make toy guns, bandannas, cowboy hats, full
skirts and sunbonnets for girls.
Construct a corral. Plan a group mural.

Construct a chow wagon—wheelbarrow or wagon.

*Special Activities*
    Rope spinning
    Lassoing
    Indian dancing
    Indian wrestling
    Square dancing

MOTHER GOOSE FESTIVAL

This makes a good theme to demonstrate songs, dances, and games on Parents Day. This sort of theme is best suited to the younger day campers.

*Games*
    Looby Loo                    Farmer in the Dell
    Roman Soldiers               London Bridge
*Crafts*
    Improvising costumes and "props" for Mother Goose and nursery rhyme characters
*Music*
    Singing games and nursery rhymes
    Rhythm band
*Dances*
    Simple little folk dances
*General Outline*
    • Mother Goose characters introduce this festival. *Old Woman Who Lived in a Shoe* opens it, and youngsters pour out.

- *Humpty Dumpty* comes along and finds a place to sit on a wall.
- Children sing, dance, or play a game. Humpty Dumpty laughs so hard he falls off the wall and has to be carried away.
- *Little Miss Muffet* comes along, sits on a pillow, and eats her cereal. *Spider* comes in and tries to sit by her. She runs away.
- *Old King Cole* comes in and calls for entertainment. The rhythm band plays for him, and children sing and dance.
- *The Cat and the Fiddle* come in, and the *Cow* jumps over the *Moon*.
- *Simple Simon* meets the pie man, and all the other children. They play games, sing, and dance until the Old Woman rings a big bell. Then they all return to the *Shoe*, and the festival is over. (Other characters and acts can be added as needed.)

WATER CARNIVAL

For a big splash on a hot day. (See Chapter 18 on "Water Play" for many other activities.)

*Games and Activities*

*Davy Jones' Locker*—Place simple prizes in coffee tins, seal with scotch tape, and scatter over bottom of pool. Swimmers dive and search for them.

*Sunken Treasure*—Use metal tags, plastic red and blue poker chips, or rocks. Scatter over bottom of pool (shallow end for small children.) On signal, each person tries to find as many as possible.

*Canoe Tilting*—For youngsters who can handle a canoe *and* are good swimmers. Two campers in each of two canoes. One paddles. Other has a paddle well-padded with burlap. He tries to dislodge his opponent in the other canoe.

*Two Men in a Tub*—Comedy act. Two get into a wooden tub, paddle around in circles, pantomime dismay, puzzlement, and so on, until tub upsets.

*Broncho Riding*—Requires a watertight steel drum. Each "cowboy" gets on it, in turn, and is pushed away from the sides. Keep a time record. Swimmer who stays on the longest is the champ.

### Crafts

Make toy boats of various kinds for races and regattas.

Make costumes for special swim acts, such as a water dragon, mermaid, Neptune.

Decorate paddles, oars, boats, sails.

Make posters and awards.

Make cork necklaces or bracelets. Paint to indicate different age groups.

Make "sets" for water pageant. Throne for Neptune, and so on.

### Special Activities

Swimming to music. Simple synchronized swimming formations if possible.

Diving and swimming races performed for Neptune, at his orders.

Comedy diving and swimming acts.

## DAY CAMP OLYMPICS

### Contests

Softball throw for distance
Chinning—number of times
Push-ups—number of times
Standing broad jump—distance
High jumping—height
Pole vaulting—height
Running broad jump—distance
Races

### Divisions

Midgets—under 4′ 10″
Juniors—under 5′ 5″
Intermediates—over 5′ 5″

Groups draw for countries they'll represent.

*Crafts*—items to be made
  Olympic rings
  Olympic flag
  Flags of other nations
  Posters
  Scorecards
  Torches for opening relay
  Markers—medals

*Special Activities*
  Folk dances of other lands
  Folk songs of other lands

The Olympic theme also can be used for Indoor or Mock Olympics.

### SPACE DAY

*Games*
  Space Men relays
  Space Animal races
  Planet relay or obstacle race
  Balloon games

*Crafts*
  Robots or puppets out of boxes, and various odds and ends
  Space monsters and space men out of vegetables, or painted, or made out of boxes, foil, or pans
  Space helmets
  Goggles
  Flying saucers, satellites, rocket ships

*Other Activities*
  Improvise new words for old tunes and games, such as "Old McDonald Had a Farm," "Deep in the Heart of Texas," "She'll Be Coming Round the Mountain."

  Write a dramatic skit about landing on the moon or on Mars.

STORYBOOK LAND

Each group at day camp selects a favorite character, story-book, or event in a story. They then make sets, costumes, necessary equipment to act out, or "play like" the roles they have chosen.

Each group, after a given time (depending on whether this is a day or week event) demonstrates its choice to the other groups.

Characters may include:

- King Arthur and his Knights of the Round Table
- Tom Sawyer and Huck Finn

Alice in Wonderland and her friends, the Red Queen, the Cheshire Cat, the White Rabbit, the Mad Hatter, and others.

TOPSY TURVY DAY

Everything *backward*. Campers dress and talk backward. Try to draw by looking in a mirror. Eat dessert first. Sing chorus before the verse of a song.

(Don't use this theme too long. Make it a short "special.")

PEANUT PARTY (or picnic)

Everyone gets a bag of peanuts to use like pennies, for special contests of skill or fun.

Peanut Trail—One group tracks another.
Peanut Hunt—Treasure hunt type
Peanut Games—rolling, blowing, tossing, or passing peanuts
Peanut People and Animals—Make a menagerie, using odds and ends.
Peanut Fortunes—Write, insert in peanut shells, glue or tape the halves together. Paint. (Use these for instructions for forfeits, too.)

SURPRISE CONTESTS

These are on-the-spot, unexpected surprises as far as the day camper is concerned (the counselor knows better, of course).

Such events should not be used too often, because their charm lies in their novelty and unexpectedness.

The following have been used successfully:

*Freckle Count.* The boy or girl with the most freckles wins an extra cool drink or ice cream cone.

*Watermelon Seed Contest.* A bit vulgar, but fun out of doors. Who can spit a seed the farthest? Clean up afterward, of course.

*What's in Your Pocket?* Youngsters empty their pockets and place contents in a straight line. Child with longest line wins.

*Big Toe Show.* Silly but funny. Each child paints or decorates a big toe. Then judging—for funniest, prettiest, craziest.

*Soap Bubble Blow*—See Chapter 18 on "Water Play."

*Make-Up Models.* Bring a make-up kit. Youngsters choose partners and make up their faces. Judging afterward.

*FBI File.* Bring ink pad and index cards. Let youngsters register and compare their finger prints. Follow with print-making, using all sorts of objects and working out original designs.

*Diamond Hunt.* Scatter glass marbles in a specific area. (Know how many are hidden.) Then have a Diamond Hunt. Finders keepers. Count, so that hunt can stop at proper time.

*Magic Color Day.* After the youngsters have arrived, announce that today is a Magic Color Day. Whoever is wearing anything in that color gets a lollipop, a special privilege, a big star, or something. Don't use too often, and always change colors.

# In Conclusion

I announce a life that
should be copious, vehement,
spiritual, bold . . .

—WALT  WHITMAN
*So Long!*

# CHAPTER 25:

## DAY CAMPING AND THE FUTURE

Modern living has become so complicated that no one group or agency can provide for all the needs of childhood. The home, the school, the church, the local, state, and federal government, and a host of civic, social, and youth-serving agencies all have contributions to make to the child at his various age levels. Among such agencies the day camp plays a unique role.

Today's child grows up under many pressures. Growing up in itself brings many emotional pressures. To them are added the pressures that result from increasing emphasis on sports and social programs at earlier age levels (preadolescent team sports and early adolescent "dating" are outstanding examples), so that the child is pushed too rapidly into maturity; the pressures resulting from overexposure to mass communication media that encourage conformity and a dependence upon shallow, surface entertainment; the pressure of increased affluence that provides too much too soon; the growing pressure in some educational programs resulting from intensive emphasis on the sciences with a reduction of opportunities to enjoy the hand and the performing arts.

The day camp program is uniquely qualified to offset and to relieve such pressures. It is relaxed, informal, noncompetitive, yet stimulating and adventurous. It fosters the development of a normal, natural, curious, creative childhood. It bridges the gap between home and the resident camp. It provides a change of pace and place. It opens up a new world, different from everyday. It provides activities that encourage laughter, and curiosity, imagination, and co-operation. It provides adventure and self-testing within a framework of safety. It encourages initiative. It creates an interest in and a respect for all living things.

It is the function of day camping to provide the setting, facilities, leadership, and program best suited for child development. It is the function of the day camp program to provide a framework of activities in which each child can participate at his own rate, without pressure; in which each child has an opportunity to explore the wonders of the out-of-doors; to learn to use and to enjoy. his five senses; to learn to express his feelings and emotions through language and movement.

It is the function of the day camp to provide *leadership* for its activity program—leaders who are intuitive enough to sense the right moment to ask a question—or to suggest an answer; leaders who have curiosity, enthusiasm, and energy; leaders who not only like children but respect them; leaders who are present when needed, but who are unobtrusive when children are developing their own projects; leaders who stand ready to open a new door of interest when the child is ready; leaders who enjoy learning along with the children; most of all, leaders who know that the *child,* not the activity, is the important thing.

Not every day camp provides a camp site suitable for an effective day camp program. Not every day camp provides adequate equipment and supplies for a progressive, ongoing activity program. Not every day camp makes full use of existing community and local resources to strengthen and enlarge its program. Not every day camp provides adequate leadership, gives its leaders adequate precamp and in-service training and supplies them with professional literature and resource material. Not every day camp plans a child-centered, child-motivated day camp program, and makes sure that emphasis is placed on outdoor camping skills.

Not every day camp meets accepted standards, but every year more and more of them do. More and more realize their unique opportunity to provide a *different* program; a new, fascinating, stimulating program that does not need to duplicate the playground, the play school, or any other type of summer program, no matter how good it might be.

Much needs to be done. Accurate records and statistics need to be compiled. Leadership techniques need to be analyzed, taught, and made available. Professional literature needs to be written. Research needs to be made. Standards need constant study and re-evaluation.

All these needs are proof that day camping is alive, vital, and growing. Growing pains, though uncomfortable, are a sure sign of growth.

Day camping does not have to cling to the coattails of resident camping, or the apron strings of the playground. It has its own unique contributions to make to home and community, to education and conservation—but most of all to Childhood.

Back in the twelfth century Saint Bernard made a statement containing such a ring of truth that it has echoed down the years. The good saint's statement is not only wise but simple: *"You will find something far greater in the woods than you will find in books. Stones and trees will teach you that which you will never learn from masters."*

# DAY CAMP STANDARDS

The following material is used by special permission of the American Camping Association. Day camp leaders are urged to study all of it, but to pay special attention to Section II—*Program*, Section VII—*Safety*, and Section VIII—*Transportation*.

## AMERICAN CAMPING ASSOCIATION, INC.
## DAY CAMP STANDARDS

**DEFINITION:** *Organized Day Camping* is an experience in group living in a natural environment. It is sustained experience carried on during the daytime under the supervision of trained leadership.

Camping provides a creative educational experience in co-operative group living in the out-of-doors. It utilizes the resources of the natural surroundings to contribute significantly to mental, physical, social, and spiritual growth.

✿   ✿   ✿   ✿   ✿

In order to assure this type of experience for every camper, the day camp should be guided by the following standards:

### I. PERSONNEL

A. The camp staff should be adequate for the maintenance of the camp; for the care, protection, and education of the campers; and for business administration.

There should be a ratio of at least one counselor to every 10 children eight years of age and over; and one to every eight of those younger than eight years of age. (This ratio is exclusive of administrative staff, junior counselors, or counselors-in-training. Administrative staff is defined as those staff members whose main responsibility involves other than direct program relationships with campers, i.e., director, office staff, maintenance staff, cooks, dietitian, nurse.)

B. All members of the program staff should possess the following minimum qualifications:

1. Emotional maturity.
2. Good health and vitality.
3. Enjoyment of outdoor living.
4. Liking for children and the ability to understand the needs of the campers, placing the needs of the campers and the camp ahead of personal desires.
5. Ability to work as a member of a group.
6. Interest in contributing to the achievement of the objectives of the camp.
7. Good moral character and integrity.
8. Particular skills and abilities for the specific responsibilities they are to carry.
9. At least 18 years of age. The average age should be considerably higher.*
10. Two years of college or the equivalent in experience significant for camping.*

---

* Items 9 and 10 do not apply to junior counselors and counselors-in-training.

C. The camp director should have, in addition to the qualifications under "B," the following qualifications:

1. Education and experience
   a. At least two years' staff leadership experience in organized camping.
   b. Experience in administration and working with groups.
   c. Graduation from a college or university, or equivalent background.
2. Personal qualifications
   a. Twenty-five years of age or over.
   b. Maturity of judgment.
   c. Skill in supervision of staff and knowledge of the group process.

> d. Initiative, resourcefulness, and sense of responsibility.
> e. Ability to work co-operatively with staff and campers.
> f. Ability to administer the camp effectively in accordance with the standards of the American Camping Association.

D. The camp should have carefully prepared written job descriptions for all types of positions, to be used in hiring and supervising staff.

E. The camp should utilize the best known techniques for the selection of staff members, such as application blanks, personal interviews, and references.

F. Staff training
  1. There should be a precamp training program for a minimum of three days or 15 hours. It is recommended that two days or 10 hours of this time should be spent on the camp site.
  2. There should be in-service training throughout the season, such as staff meetings, conferences, etc.

G. The camp should have written personnel policies covering such matters as remuneration, time off, illness, job descriptions, relationships, evaluations, conditions for re-employment, personal conduct, etc.

H. All staff members who receive salaries or wages should receive a letter or written contract stating specifically the conditions of their employment.

I. There should be sufficient continuity in the total staff from year to year to give stability and cohesion.

J. There should be procedures through which staff members may readily express themselves on matters of camp policies and regulations, including those which affect themselves.

## II. PROGRAM

The camp program should afford an opportunity for the campers to participate in a creative outdoor group experience in a democratic setting, and should provide for the development of each individual.

A. The camp should develop objectives in the following areas:
1. Outdoor living.
2. Fun and adventure.
3. Social adjustment—for example, the development of independence and reliability, ability to get along with others, and values in group living.
4. An understanding of individuals and groups of varied backgrounds.
5. Improvement of health.
6. Skills and appreciation, particularly as related to the out-of-doors.
7. Spiritual values.

B. The program should be so planned, administered, and supervised as to lead to the achievement of the general objectives of camping and the special objectives of the particular camp. It is recommended that these objectives be stated in writing. Essentially, the program should be related to the central theme of living together in a natural environment and learning to enjoy the out-of-doors.

C. Within the general framework of the program there should be opportunity for co-operative planning of activities by campers and camp staff and an opportunity for some choice of activities by individual campers.

D. Program activities should be geared to the ages, abilities, and interests of the campers.

E. The program should provide opportunity for individual activity, for rest and quiet, for small-group activity, and for occasions involving the whole camp.

F. The pace, pressure, and intensity of the program should be regulated so that campers will have time for leisure and can participate in activities of their own will and at their own tempo.

G. The program should include occasional parent participation activities and/or other techniques to strengthen family relationships and parent understanding of program objectives.

H. Camps designed to offer a general program in camping should include a variety of situations in which the camper will have an opportunity:

 1. To acquire a feeling of competence and to enjoy himself in the natural outdoor setting through camp skills and other activities common in camp life.
 2. To participate in group projects, special events and ceremonies, and social activities.
 3. To share in the care of and improvement of the camp.
 4. To increase his knowledge and appreciation of the world in which he lives.
 5. To learn his relationship to his environment through such media as nature crafts, using native materials, etc.
 6. To participate in the preparation of meals whenever and wherever conditions permit.
 7. For spiritual responses to camping experiences.

I. There should be continuity in this camp experience over a period of not less than two weeks. Camp should be operated at least three days a week, preferably five, during the camp period.

J. When overnight camping is a part of the program, it should be an outgrowth of daytime activities.

## III. CAMP SITE, FACILITIES, AND EQUIPMENT

A. The camp site should provide a maximum of privacy and wherever possible be located away from densely populated areas and undesirable resorts. It should be free from unnecessary hazards and be properly drained. It should be located within a reasonable distance from the campers' homes depending upon the transportation available.

B. The site should provide natural resources that will make possible an outdoor living experience.

C. Buildings or other structures should be constructed safely and in accordance with any building code applicable to a given locality, and maintained in safe condition.

D. There should be sufficient equipment and facilities, kept in safe operating condition, to carry out stated objectives and program.

E. Adequate provision should be made for shelter of campers during inclement weather.

F. If a site other than the day camp site is used for overnights, it should meet all standards as described above in A, B, C, D, and E.

## IV. ADMINISTRATION

Administration should include planning, supervision, and management as it affects the total camp operation.

A. All published statements such as brochures, publicity, etc., should be accurate and complete.

B. The camp should have the following records:

1. Budget, financial statement, food records, and inventories.
2. All permits required by local and state authorities.
3. Written consent of parents for camper's attendance and participation in activities.
4. Registration card for each camper providing the important information.
5. Record of health examination and a statement by the camper's parent indicating the child's good health and including the disclosure of any limitations which would affect activities. These records should be kept on the camp site.
6. Record of first aid and medical treatment of campers, staff, or other persons.
7. Written agreements with all camp staff receiving salaries or wages.
8. Statement of insurance coverage. Provision should be made for all legally required insurance.

9. Other records of the individual camper during the camp season or period, as deemed desirable by the camp administration.

## V. HEALTH

A. A physical examination by a licensed physician and a medical history shall be required for all staff and campers within a month before they go to camp.

> Use of the Health Examination Forms developed and approved by the American Academy of Pediatrics and the American Camping Association is recommended.

B. Preventive inoculations required or recommended by public health authorities should be similarly required or recommended by the camp before opening.

NOTE: With reference to A and B above. Unless contrary to the laws of the state, province, or local municipality in which the camp is located, children whose parents or guardians object to physical examinations, immunization or medical treatment on the ground of religious convictions may be admitted upon written request of the parent or guardian. This request should be accompanied by the following:

1. Statement by parent or guardian that the child is and has been in normal and good health.

2. Statement by parent or guardian assuming responsibility for the child while in camp with the understanding that either be notified immediately should anything unforeseen occur. This statement to further include a provision that should the camp be unable to locate the persons designated to be notified in case of an emergency, that the camp authorities may take such temporary measures as they deem appropriate.

C. There should be a written statement from the parent as to the camper's health, including assurance that the camper has not been exposed to contagious diseases before coming to camp.

D. Food service staff should have certificates required to comply with local and state public health requirements.

E. In menu planning nutrition standards should be observed.

F. There should be a definite system of health supervision of the campers, including such times when campers are away from camp on out-of-camp activities.

G. A registered nurse, licensed physician, or a person holding a current American Red Cross certificate in advanced first aid should be on the camp staff. Arrangements should be made with a nearby licensed physician to serve the camp on call if one is not in residence.

H. The camp should follow the "Suggested Policies and Standing Orders for Camp Nursing Services" reprinted by the American Camping Association.

I. A nurse, licensed physician, or a person holding a current American Red Cross certificate in advanced first aid should accompany overnight camping groups; and first aid equipment as recommended by the American Red Cross should be available.

J. All staff members should have fundamental knowledge of health emergency procedures.

K. There should be a first aid area and a quiet resting place set apart from the group.

L. Transportation should be available at all times for use in case of emergency.

M. The camp should have ready access to a telephone.

## VI. SANITATION

A. All camps should comply with state, county, and local sanitation laws.

B. If the camp does not operate under a permit which includes approval of the water supply, a special written approval of the water supply should be obtained each year. The water supply should be of adequate volume and safe, sanitary quality, and should be tested regularly during the camp season.

C. Swimming pools and waterfront areas should be located, constructed, equipped, and operated in compliance with any applicable laws. In the absence of such laws, the standards of a national organization considered acceptable by the American Camping Association should be observed.

D. Milk should be pasteurized or certified according to state regulations and provided by an accredited source. Dried, evaporated, or condensed milk may be substituted.

E. Refrigeration equipment should be available with provisions for preserving milk and perishable foods in a temperature of not over 50° F.

F. All food storage, preparation and service space and equipment should be maintained clean and free from dust and insects.

G. Dishwashing procedures and care of equipment should comply with state, local, and county sanitation laws. In the absence of such laws effective sterilization methods should be used.

H. Liquid wastes should be disposed of by facilities constructed and operated as required by and at locations approved by the supervising health official.

I. Privy pits should be flyproof. One toilet or privy seat should be available for every 20 occupants of the camp. In camps or units of camps occupied solely by males and where urinals are used, one toilet or privy seat and one urinal should be provided for every 30 occupants.

J. Adequate handwashing facilities should be provided in proximity to toilets, privies, and urinals.

K. Garbage and rubbish cans should be watertight, flyproof, emptied and cleaned at least every two days. Garbage and rubbish should be hauled away from the camp for disposal. If disposal is within the camp (site) it should be by complete incineration or by burial under six inches of well tamped dirt. The surrounding of stored garbage and rubbish containers should be maintained clean and dry.

L. There should be a plan for control of insects, rodents, and poisonous weeds.

## VII. SAFETY

Safety factors are fundamental considerations in the conduct of any camp and should be considered in all preceding topics.

Natural hazards to safety, such as cliffs, swamps, mine shafts, dead trees, etc., should be structurally eliminated or reduced to a minimum before the camp is occupied. Every day camp should carry on a continuous program of safety education for its campers and staff.

A. The person actively in charge of the waterfront should be at least 21 years of age and should have a current water safety instructor's certificate from the American Red Cross or an organization having equivalent standards.

B. Practices and equipment for waterfront should comply with American Red Cross standards or those of other organizations with equivalent standards. Swimming pools should be protected by a fence, and its entrance gate kept locked except during periods when the swimming director is on duty.

C. Practices and equipment for boating, canoeing, sailing, and other watercraft should comply with American Red Cross standards or those of another organization having equivalent standards.

D. Where riflery and archery are included in the camp program, firearms and archery equipment should be used and stored under qualified supervision. (Standards for riflery and archery may be obtained from the American Camping Association.)

E. Two or more counselors should accompany groups leaving the immediate camp site. A ratio of one counselor to eight campers should be maintained. These same standards apply to overnight camping groups.

F. Safety rules governing the use of tools and power tools should be studied and observed. Such tools should be used only under qualified supervision.

G. Fire Protection—The Director of the camp should be responsible for the regular inspection of all fire protection facilities and equipment.

   1. Containers for gasoline, kerosene, explosives, and flammable materials should be plainly marked and stored

in a locked building not occupied by campers or staff and at a safe distance from program buildings.

The above materials should be used only under qualified supervision.

2. All camps should provide adequate lengths of hose for fire fighting, if water under pressure is available.

3. Fire extinguishers and other suitable fire fighting equipment should be placed at strategic and easily accessible points.

4. Fireplaces and chimneys should be properly built and inspected annually, prior to the opening of camp.

5. Before camp opens, arrangements should be made with the nearest public officials for protection in case of fire. Any permits required for operation of incinerators or for open fires should be secured.

6. All electric wiring and light fixtures should be installed in accordance with the local building code or the National Electric Code and maintained in good repair.

7. Emergency procedures for fire drills, civil defense drills, or any natural disaster should be planned and practiced.

## VIII. TRANSPORTATION

Where transportation is used in connection with a day camp, the following standards should be observed:

A. All transportation equipment should be maintained in safe operating condition and should meet all safety tests required by the laws of the state and the ordinances of the municipality in which the day camp operates. Every day camp should carry on a continuous program of transportation safety education for its staff and campers.

Day camp operators should realize that they carry a responsibility to their campers over and above the technical requirements of state laws or municipal ordinances. Every day camp should train its own drivers in all needed safety precautions.

B. Drivers.

1. Each driver of a camp vehicle should meet the driving requirements of the state concerning the specific vehicle which he operates.
2. Each driver should be selected for dependability, good habits, and unquestionable good character.
3. Each driver should be free from communicable disease, strong enough to handle the transportation unit he drives, have normal use of his body, both hands, both feet, both eyes, and both ears.
4. Each driver should be at least twenty-one years of age and have at least one year's experience as a driver.

C. A day camp operating its own transportation unit should carry liability insurance as follows:

1. For a unit carrying not more than eighteen campers: Minimum limits of fifty thousand dollars for injury to any one person, one hundred thousand dollars in any one accident.
2. For a unit carrying more than eighteen campers: Minimum limits of one hundred thousand dollars for injury to any one person, three hundred thousand dollars in any one accident.

D. The number of campers in transportation units should not exceed the seating capacity of such units.

E. Each transportation unit should carry adequate first aid equipment.

F. The camp should provide adequate supervision in transportation units. In a vehicle which carries more than ten campers, there should be at least one adult in addition to the driver.

G. Where a day camp charters transportation units, the owners of such vehicles should be required to produce evidence that they meet the transportation standards herein required of day camps.

APPENDIX **B**:

# HEALTH AND SAFETY CHECK LIST
# FOR DAY CAMPS

The following material is used by special permission of the New York City Department of Health. Although this list is not concerned specifically with the activity program, it is included here because safe and sanitary conditions are essential to the program.

NEW YORK CITY DEPARTMENT OF HEALTH
BUREAU OF CHILD HEALTH—DAY CAMP UNIT    BUREAU OF
SANITARY INSPECTIONS—SCHOOL UNIT

## INDOOR PLAY SPACE

*Yes   No*

1. Are windows and skylights in good working condition to assure maximum ventilation?
2. If mechanical ventilation is used in any room, is the apparatus in good repair?
3. Are windows and skylights clean to assure the maximum influx of natural light?
4. Are window shades and/or blinds in good repair to allow proper adjustment for protection against glare?
5. Are lighting fixtures in good working order?
6. Are lighting fixtures supplied with light bulbs?
7. Are light bulbs of size sufficient to furnish adequate and standard lighting for the fixture they are located in?
8. Is there an extra supply of light bulbs on hand for replacements?
9. Are light bulbs shielded from glare?
10. Are passageways, stairways, and hallways adequately lighted?

11. Are gas appliances properly shut off in rooms where children may enter?
12. Have coatrooms, cubbies, lockers been provided, or other provisions been made for the keeping of the children's garments, swim suits, sneakers, towels, etc.?
13. Are the play equipment and furnishings of safe construction and in good repair?
14. Is all sleeping and resting equipment clean and in good condition?
15. Have heavy draperies, upholstered furniture, carpets, or other articles that hold dust been removed?
16. Are walls, floors, and ceilings safe and in good repair?
17. Are adequate and proper cleaning equipment and materials provided?
18. Is there available a complete first aid outfit accessible to adults only?
19. Have all chemicals, poisons, drugs, and other hazardous substances been removed from the reach of children?
20. Have all potential fire hazards been removed such as accumulation of flammable materials, locked exit doors, inflammable chemicals, paints stored near stoves, matches in reach of children?

## TOILET AND WASHING FACILITIES

*Yes   No*

1. Is running water available for hand washing?
2. Is there an adequate supply of soap, paper or individual towels, and toilet tissue on hand?
3. Are washbasins and waterclosets in good repair?
4. Is there sufficient water pressure at the washbasins and at the waterclosets?
5. Are shower facilities in good working order?
6. Does the shower floor drain properly?

7. Are locker-room and shower-room floors in good repair, free from splinters, and safe from slipping and other hazards?

## DRINKING FACILITIES

*Yes   No*

1. Are drinking fountains of sanitary design and construction, and in good working order?
2. Is the water pressure at the drinking fountains adequate?
3. If paper cups are used is there an adequate supply of them on hand?
4. Has some provisions been made to dispense the paper cups in a sanitary manner?

## OUTDOOR PLAY SPACE

*Yes   No*

1. Is the play equipment safe and in good repair?
2. Is the outdoor play area safe—free from tripping and slipping hazards, free from holes, open pits, and sudden drops?
3. Have stumps, stones, and coarse stubble been removed?
4. Is the area properly drained and free from stagnant water?
5. Is the area free from ragweed and poison ivy?
6. Is there a vacuum breaker for the hose connection to the wading pool?
7. If your wading pool is not supplied with a continuous flow of water—e.g., a shower head and ground drain—is there a supply of chlorine on hand for chlorinating the water?
   (Chlorine in the form of household bleach 0.6 ppm or 3 ounces per 500 gallons of water.)
8. Is there some responsible person always available for the proper use of chlorine in the wading pool?

FOOD AREA

*Yes No*

1. If dishwashing is a hand operation, are there facilities for proper dishwashing, a good supply of hot water, vessels in which to adequately wash and rinse the eating utensils, and an adequate supply of soap or detergent?

   Are there facilities for proper sterilization—a supply of hot water of 180° F. to 212° F. (boiling), vessels in which to immerse the utensils (2 minutes at 180° F. and 1 minute at 212° F.) and long-handled wire baskets in which to stack the utensils for immersion in the hot water?

   Is there a thermometer to measure the temperature of the sterilization water?

2. If an automatic dishwasher is provided, is it clean and in good working order?

3. Is a thermometer provided on the dishwashing machine to measure the temperature (180° F.) of the sterilizing rinse cycle water?

4. Is the refrigerator working properly?

5. Is there sufficient refrigerator space for all perishable foods?

6. Is there an adequate supply of wrapped straws for the milk?

7. Are the equipment and utensils clean and of sanitary construction with the surfaces free of pitting, rusting, chipping, and roughness?

8. Are the eating and drinking utensils free of chips and cracks?

9. Is the stove clean and free from grease?

10. Is the stove in good working order? Do all gas burners burn with an even blue flame?

11. Is the kitchen well ventilated and the products of combustion properly vented to the outer air?

12. Are all gas appliances in good operating order, properly vented where required?

13. Is the silverware stored in such a way as to prevent contamination or handling of the eating surfaces?

14. Is food stored in rodent and insect-proof containers?

15. Is there an adequate supply of garbage cans with tight fitting covers?

16. Are custodial and cleaning supplies kept away from the food areas?

17. Are the kitchen and dining area windows and doors screened to keep out flies?

18. Are all windows, doors, and openings to outside areas protected against entry of rodents?

19. Are all parts of the food preparation, food service, and food storage areas clean and in good repair?

20. Is there hot and cold running water provided at the washbasins used by the foodhandlers?

21. Is there a supply of soap and paper towels for the foodhandlers?

22. Is there a "Wash Hands" reminder sign posted in the toilet room used by the foodhandlers?

23. Have the foodhandlers been instructed in proper foodhandling practices?

# SELECTED RESOURCE REFERENCES

The books and other resources in this section represent only a small portion of useful material readily available. Such a listing is, of necessity, subjective, based upon personal familiarity with the material or recommendations by specialists.

Few camps, camp directors, or camp counselors can afford such an extensive library. However, this list has been made long deliberately, so as to give more opportunities for using public and school libraries. Counselors are urged to use children's libraries, too, because many of the best new books on nature and science are being written for young readers.

For convenience, this list has been alphabetized, and broken down under the four main sections of this book.

Addresses of publishers and distributors will be found at the end of this list.

## Basics for Counselors

*Camp Program Book.* Catherine T. Hammett and Virginia Musselman. Association Press, 1958. Much of the program material in this book is adaptable for day camp use.

*Church Day Camp, The.* La Donna Bogardus. National Council of the Churches of Christ in the U.S.A., 1955.

*Day Camping for the Mentally Retarded.* David Gingland and Kay Gould. National Association for Retarded Children, 1962. Includes forms, budget, bibliography, and other useful material.

*Fundamentals of Day Camping.* Grace Mitchell. Association Press, 1961.

## Environmental Activities

*Art of Knotting and Splicing.* Cyrus Lawrence Day. U. S. Naval Institute. Comprehensive instructions.

*Bird Houses and Feeders.* National Audubon Society Circular No. 29. Directions for making.

*Boy Scout Manual.* Boy Scouts of America. Excellent resource for many campcraft skills.

*Campcraft Skills Flip Charts.* Girl Scouts of the U.S.A. Lashing, Tents, and Single Shelters, Fire Building, Compass and Maps, Toolcraft. These are large, 12″ x 15″ visual aids, each sold separately, or in sets of three.

*Camping Skills for Trail Living.* John Ledlie. Association Press, 1962. Units of experience in various camping skills are particularly helpful.

*City of the Bees.* A. I. Root Co. A short but interesting folder.

*Collection and Preservation of Insects.* Miscellaneous Publication No. 601. U. S. Department of Agriculture. U. S. Government Printing Office. One of many interesting and inexpensive pamphlets available from the government.

*Frontiers—Fun with Science for Camp Fire Girls.* Camp Fire Girls, Inc., 1953. Simple science projects.

*Fun with the Sun.* D. S. Halacy, Jr. The Macmillan Company, 1959. Simple experiments.

*Garden Spider.* Mary Adrian. Holiday, 1951. Child's book, well written.

*Golden Book of Camping and Camp Crafts.* Gordon Lynn. Golden Press, Inc., 1958. Attractively illustrated, covering many phases of camping.

*Grassroot Jungle.* Edwin Way Teale. Dodd, Mead and Co., 1944. A classic on everyday wonders.

*Hammond's Illustrated Atlas for Young America.* C. S. Hammond & Co., Inc.

*Honeybees.* Mary Adrian. Holiday Publishing Co., 1952. Life cycle of bees in simple language.

*How and Why Wonder Book of Weather.* George Bonsall. Grossett & Dunlap, Inc., 1960. Written in language youngsters will understand.

*Junior Book of Insects.* Edwin Way Teale. E. P. Dutton & Co., 1953. Useful, informative, and attractive.

*Leaflets, etc.* Department of Insects and Spiders, American Museum of Natural History. Free leaflets on nets, collecting, rearing insects, and the like.

*Living Like Indians.* Allan A. MacFarlan. Association Press, 1961. Includes nature, conservation, trail and camp skills, exploring, stalking, and the like.

*101 Camping Out Ideas and Activities.* Bruno Knobel. Sterling Publishing Co., Inc., 1961. Includes firemaking, trail signs, stars, codes, and other phases of camp activities.

*Safety Education Data Sheets.* National Safety Council. Camping, Counselors and Helpers for Summer Camps, Poisonous Reptiles, Poisonous Plants, Hiking and Climbing, Horseback Riding, Safety in Archery.

*Safety Films*

> *Water Rescue*—12 mm., color and B. & W. Health Research, Inc., 666 Elm St., Buffalo, New York.

> *Safety Everywhere*—14 mm., color. Office of Commissioner, U. S. Fish and Wildlife Service, Department of Interior, Washington 25, D. C.

> *Boys on the Cliff, The.* 3½ mm., B. & W. The Readers Digest Association, Inc., Pleasantville, New York.

*Science in Your Own Back Yard.* Elizabeth K. Cooper. Harcourt, Brace and Co., 1958. Excellent, interesting material.

*Story of Butterflies and Other Insects, The.* Peter Farb. Harvey House, Publishers, 1959. Well-written for young people.

*Story of Shells, The.* Curtis Martin. Harvey House, Publishers, 1956. The how and why in simple language.

*Your Own Book of Campcraft.* Catherine T. Hammett. Pocket Book special No. 893, 1950.

## Related Program Activities

*American Folk Tales and Legends.* Marie Leach. World Publishing Co., 1958. Collection for telling or dramatizing.

*Book of American Indian Games.* Allan A. MacFarlan. Association Press, 1958. 150 games requiring little or no equipment.

*Book of Indian Life Crafts.* Oscar E. Norbeck. Association Press, 1958. Almost 200 projects based on home and village life of many tribes.

*Burl Ives Song Book.* Ballantine Books, Inc. 115 American songs with piano arrangement and guitar chords, in paperback edition—1953.

*Children's Games from Many Lands.* Nina Miller. Friendship Press, 1943.

*Creative Crafts for Campers.* Catherine T. Hammett and Carol M. Horrocks. Association Press, 1957. About 200 projects, all correlated with outdoor activities.

*Favorite Stories Old and New.* Sidonie Gruenberg. Doubleday, 1955. Excellent collection for telling and dramatizing.

*Folk Dancing.* Richard G. Kraus. The Macmillan Company, 1962.

*Indian Sign Language.* Robert Hofsinde. Morrow Publishing Co., 1957. Over 500 words and how to form them.

*Junior Library Series.* Grossett & Dunlap, Inc. *Merry Adventures of Robin Hood, The; Robinson Crusoe; Treasure Island; Jungle Book; King Arthur and His Knights of the Round Table; Aesop's Fables.* These favorites plus many others are all available in this series.

*Let's Read Aloud.* Ruth Gagliardio. J. B. Lippincott, 1962. Stories and poems, well-chosen for child appeal.

*Physical Fitness Tests.* American Association for Health, Physical Education and Recreation. *Physical Fitness Tests.* Amateur Athletic University.

*Records for Dancing.* (See "Addresses of Publishers" below). *Berliner Music Shop, Educational Dance Recordings, Inc., Folkcraft Records, Inc., Folk Dance House, Folk Shop, The.*

*Records for Singing. Music of the American Indians,* R.C.A. Victor, *American Folk Songs,* Cowboy, *Animal Folk Songs, American Play Party Songs, Call and Response Songs, Folk Songs for Camp, Songs of Camp, Songs to Grow On.* All collections from Folkways Records and Service Corporation.

*Singing Games and Dances.* David S. McIntosh. Association Press, 1957. 56 group games and dances, with words and music.

*Song in America.* Burl Ives. Duell, Sloan and Pierce, 1962. A beautiful collection, illustrated, from colonial days on. Includes work songs, cowboy songs, news songs, patriotic songs, etc.

*Sources of Official Rules.* Athletic Institute. 4-page free listing.

*Spotlight on Drama in Camp.* Barbara Winslow. American Camping Association, 1962. Bradford Woods, Martinsville, Indiana. Types, facilities, and equipment, plus an excellent classified listing of one- and three-act plays.

*Treasury of American Indian Tales.* Theodore Whitson Ressler. Association Press, 1957. Forty-four stories from 27 American tribes.

*Wind in the Willows, The.* Kenneth Grahame. Heritage Press, Dial Publishing Co. A lovely edition of an old favorite.

*Wind in the Willows, The.* Vol. I and Vol. II. Nos. 1022 and 1026, 12″ records. Pathways of Sound, Inc., 102 Mt. Auburn St., Cambridge 38, Mass.

*Yankee Doodle's Cousins.* Anne Malcolmson. Houghton Mifflin Co., 1941. Delightful collection of stories from American folklore.

## Composite Activities

*All in Play.* Rowena M. Shoemaker. Play Schools Association, 1958. The *how* and *why* of play, indoor and outdoor, in booklet form.

*American Citizens Handbook.* Joy Elmer Morgan. Cooperative Extension Service, National 4-H Club Foundation, 1960. Information about flag etiquette, history of each State, patriotic songs and poems.

*Complete Book of Campfire Programs, The.* La Rue A. Thurston. Association Press, 1958. Ceremonies, songs, games, plus sample programs.

*Fun and Festival Series.* Friendship Press. Attractive booklets, each on a difficult section of the world.

*Hi Neighbor Series.* U. S. Committee for UNICEF, United Nations, New York. A series of 5 booklets, and 5 long-playing records, each giving songs, games, stories, and crafts of five nations. Books and records sold separately.

*Program Activities for Camp.* Jean Berger. Burgess Publishing Co., 1961.

*Program Planning for Bus Trips.* Bernard Warach and Rowena Shoemaker. Play Schools Association, 1954. From first-aid kits to songs and games.

*Resource Handbook.* American Association for the United Nations. A bibliography of books, games, and programs for developing world understanding.

*So You're Gonna Ride a Bus.* Jerry Wilkowsky and Mort Schrag. Jewish Center Division of the National Jewish Welfare Board, 1956.

*UN Flag Sets.* In chart or miniature forms. American Association for the United Nations, Inc.

*You and Your Flag.* Channing L. Bete Co., Inc., 1960. Clever scriptographic booklet.

## Addresses of Publishers and Distributors

Abingdon Press, 201 Eighth Avenue, South, Nashville 2, Tennessee.

Amateur Athletic Union, 233 Broadway, New York 7, New York.

American Association for Health, Physical Education and Recreation, 1201 Sixteenth Street, N.W., Washington 6, D. C.

American Association for the UN, Inc., 345 East 46th Street, New York 17, N. Y.

American Camping Association, Bradford Woods, Martinsville, Indiana.

American Museum of Natural History, New York 24, New York.

Association Press, 291 Broadway, New York 7, New York.

Athletic Institute, Room 805, Merchandise Mart, Chicago 54, Illinois.

Audubon Society, 1130 Fifth Avenue, New York 28, New York.

Ballantine Books, Inc., 101 Fifth Avenue, New York 3, New York.

Berliner Music Shop, 154 Fourth Avenue, New York 3, New York.

Bete, Channing L., Co., Inc., Greenfield, Massachusetts.

Boy Scouts of America, New Brunswick, New Jersey.

Burgess Publishing Co., 426 South 6th Street, Minneapolis 15, Minnesota.

Camp Fire Girls, 65 Worth Street, New York 13, New York.

Dodd, Mead & Co., 432 Park Avenue, South, New York 16, New York.

Doubleday Publishing Co., Garden City, New York.

Duell, Sloan and Pierce, Inc., 124 East 30th Street, New York 16, New York.

Dutton, E. P. & Co., 300 Park Avenue, South, New York 10, New York.

Educational Dance Recordings, Inc., P. O. Box 6062, Bridgeport, Connecticut.

Folkcraft Records, 1159 Broad Street, Newark 2, New Jersey.

Folk Dance House, 108 West 16th Street, New York 11, New York.

Folk Shop, The, 161 Turk Street, San Francisco 2, California.

Folkways Records and Service Corp., 121 West 47th Street, New York 36, New York.

Friendship Press, 475 Riverside Drive, New York 27, New York.

Girl Scouts of the U.S.A., 830 Third Avenue, New York 22, New York.

Golden Press, Inc., 630 Fifth Avenue, New York 21, New York.

Grossett & Dunlap, Inc., 1107 Broadway, New York 10, New York.

Hammond, C. S. and Co., Maplewood, New Jersey.

Harcourt, Brace and Co., 750 Third Avenue, New York 15, New York.

Heritage Press-Dial, 461 Park Avenue, South, New York 16, New York.

Holiday House, 8 West 13th Street, New York 11, New York.

Houghton Mifflin Co., 2 Park Street, Boston 7, Massachusetts.

Lippincott, J. B., Co., East Washington Square, Philadelphia 5, Pennsylvania.

Macmillan Company, The, 60 Fifth Avenue, New York 11, New York.

Morrow, William and Co., 425 Park Avenue, South, New York 16, New York.

National Association for Retarded Children, 386 Park Avenue, South, New York 16, New York.

National Council of the Churches of Christ in the U.S.A., 79 East

Adams Street, Chicago 3, Illinois, or 475 Riverside Drive, New York 27, New York.

National 4-H Club Foundation, 7100 Connecticut Avenue, Washington 15, D. C.

National Jewish Welfare Board, 145 East 32nd Street, New York 16, New York.

National Safety Council, 425 North Michigan Avenue, Chicago 11, Illinois.

Play Schools Association, 120 West 57th Street, New York 19, New York.

Pocket Books, Inc., Rockefeller Center, New York 20, New York.

RCA Victor, Camden, New Jersey.

Root, A. I., Co., Medina, Ohio.

Scribner's Sons, Charles, 597 Fifth Avenue, New York 17, New York.

Sterling Publishing Co., Inc., 419 Park Avenue, South, New York 16, New York.

U. S. Committee for UNICEF, United Nations, New York.

U. S. Government Printing Office, Washington 25, D. C.

U. S. Naval Institute, Annapolis, Maryland.

World Publishing Co., 2231 West 110 Street, Cleveland 2, Ohio.

---

## THE NATIONAL RECREATION ASSOCIATION

8 West Eighth Street, New York 11, New York, has a special list of inexpensive pamphlets and booklets on various phases of program activities. It is free upon request.

---

# INDEX

Classification of *games* are abbreviated in parentheses as follows:

challenge (ch.g.)     laugh maker (l.m.g.)     pencil and paper (p.p.g.)
council ring (c.r.g.)    magic (mag.g)          rainy day (r.d.g.)
dramatic (dr.g.)       muscle stretcher (m.s.g.) singing (sing.g.)
group (gr.g.)           mystery (mys.g.)      water (wat.g.)